ARLAND

Aligning Business
and IT with Metadata

b1130750X

Aligning Business and IT with Metadata

The Financial Services Way

Hans Wegener

1807
WILEY
2007

John Wiley & Sons, Ltd

Other Wiley Editorial Offices

John Wiley & Sons Inc., 111 River Street, Hoboken, NJ 07030, USA

Jossey-Bass, 989 Market Street, San Francisco, CA 94103-1741, USA

Wiley-VCH Verlag GmbH, Boschstr. 12, D-69469 Weinheim, Germany

John Wiley & Sons Australia Ltd, 42 McDougall Street, Milton, Queensland 4064, Australia

John Wiley & Sons (Asia) Pte Ltd, 2 Clementi Loop #02-01, Jin Xing Distripark, Singapore 129809

John Wiley & Sons Canada Ltd, 6045 Freemont Blvd, Mississauga, Ontario, L5R 4J3, Canada

Wiley also publishes its books in a variety of electronic formats. Some content that appears
in print may not be available in electronic books.

Anniversary Logo Design: Richard J. Pacifico

Library of Congress Cataloging-in-Publication Data

Wegener, Hans.
  Aligning business and IT with metadata : the financial services way /
Hans Wegener.
      p. cm.
  ISBN 978-0-470-03031-8
  1. Database management. 2. Metadata. 3. Business – Data processing. I.
Title.
  QA76.9.D3W435 2007
  005.74 – dc22
                                                 2007008055

British Library Cataloguing in Publication Data

A catalogue record for this book is available from the British Library

ISBN-13: 978-0-470-03031-8 (PB)

Typeset in 11/13 Goudy by Laserwords Private Limited, Chennai, India
Printed and bound in Great Britain by Antony Rowe Ltd, Chippenham, Wiltshire
This book is printed on acid-free paper responsibly manufactured from sustainable forestry
in which at least two trees are planted for each one used for paper production.

To the goddess, *felis silvestris catus*

Experience is always one's own experience. Vocabularies permit one to participate in discourse even with limited experience. Like in the succession to Christ, also in this [a] vocabulary made its way – that which is fit for church, for orthodoxy, is fit for the central committee. Language does not make such a claim, it does not lean towards becoming universalistic. Any vocabulary depends on being right. No language makes that claim. Would it make that claim, it became vocabulary. Vocabularies want to, must avoid to be misunderstood. Language can be experienced, vocabulary can be understood. Language addresses beings of existence, vocabulary addresses beings of knowledge. Language does not require being right, vocabulary is right.

Martin Walser

Contents

Foreword

In the mid-1990s, I was asked to lead a project to upgrade a global risk reporting system for a large European bank. At first, the project seemed straightforward enough – replace an aging legacy system that aggregated risk assessments from different geographic regions on a quarterly basis and generated consolidated risk position reports for top management. There were no major issues about the existing system's core functionality. However, because of a number of non-functional problems – for example, it depended on some out-dated database software – it was mandated for a 'simple upgrade'.

However, early on in our project a very strange thing happened. All of a sudden, it seemed, the old system – which had seemingly been running reliably for years – started to produce results that simply didn't match up with those of the bank's main accounting system. This was not an operational breakdown – the old system performed its task of integrating the regional data just as before – but somehow the resulting data consolidations were seriously out-of-line.

This was both baffling and very worrisome to the bank. Regulatory compliance dictated that the bank's figures should cross-check. In the worst case, the bank would have to provision against the most pessimistic risk values that the old system was now producing, and this would of course come directly off the bank's bottom line. Not surprisingly, the priority of our 'simple upgrade' project immediately went through the roof.

Fortunately, we were far enough along analyzing the data flows of the old system to suspect already what might be the problem. In short, the old system worked by directly aggregating custom data feeds of risk information from the various regional systems. But it turned out that the various regional systems had very different – and largely undocumented – ways of collecting, processing, and organizing that risk data. By the time that data reached the old global system, seemingly similar data elements from different systems might not really be that similar at all. Obviously, aggregating those elements directly could never produce reliably meaningful results.

Of course, the bank's unsuspecting risk managers had trusted implicitly the consolidated reports they had been receiving for years, and they no doubt acted accordingly. But the sad fact was that some of the 'global data' that the old system was cranking out was now seriously suspect. The only reason that this had never caused any apparent problems before was that the aggregate set of the bank's risk positions had hitherto always been below a certain threshold where they generated only minor discrepancies that everyone could simply – and safely – overlook.

But in the previous year, a major upheaval in one financial market had left certain regions of the bank holding positions that were a lot more risky then any held previously. The bank was certainly aware of this fact, but what it couldn't have known was how this was ultimately going to affect the output of the old system. Unfortunately, having now crossed some unknown and unpredictable threshold, the data associated with these elevated risk positions cascaded through to the old system in an even more unpredictable way to cause some very disturbing discrepancies that could not be overlooked.

In fact, the problem turned out to be so serious that we ultimately ended up building a whole new global risk management system to collect that information at its source, independently of the regional systems. In this way – and only in this way – could we ensure that the risk-related data elements collected in every region were truly comparable and could be meaningfully consolidated. Not surprisingly, the discrepancies between the risk data we collected and the bank's core accounting data immediately vanished.

That's an intriguing story, you might respond, but what does that have to do with this book? The problem our bank faced – whether it knew it or not – was fundamentally one of metadata management. The metadata of the various data elements associated with risk management had never been formally described or managed in any of the regional systems, much less reconciled across those systems. As a result, both the bank's business and IT managers had simply assumed that apparently similar data coming out of each system could be directly consolidated, which is exactly how the old system operated.

However, our own project's analysis of the system in question quickly showed how wrong that assumption was. Seemingly minor differences in the metadata associated with those risk-related data elements eventually added up, and reached the point where aggregating that data produced meaningless – or even worse, misleading – results. This problem was not solved until the metadata behind those elements was accurately described and reconciled. Once again, this was not a mere house-keeping exercise. Our new understanding of the metadata issues involved in globally aggregating risk information caused us to change our fundamental approach to designing a new system.

In this very informative book, Hans Wegener makes clear exactly why this sort of thing happens all too often, and, even more importantly, how it can be avoided with a rigorous approach to metadata management. In our case, the bank was lucky, as our project was already looking into this problem and was able to solve it before it caused any real damage. But those of you who take the very practical advice in this book to heart can do even better – you can take methodical, forward-looking steps to ensure that this sort of situation never again happens to you or the financial institution you work for.

Had our bank's business and IT managers been able to read a book like this one, we would also probably have had a far easier time explaining to them why a system that had seemingly 'worked' for years could suddenly fail catastrophically, but without any obvious operational breakdown. It also would have been much easier to convince them why it was necessary for us to take a whole new approach to managing their risk data, instead of simply providing a facelift to a system that had always 'worked' before. As it was, they ultimately agreed, but only after the resulting problems had become quite serious.

Metadata management problems similar to my story are so prevalent in all industries that Hans could have been excused if he had decided to write a completely generic book on this subject. However, what I think makes this book even better is that he resisted that urge, and chose instead to focus it solely on the financial services industry.

The fact is that very few people are effective generalists, and the vast majority of practitioners today respond best to material that is presented in the vernacular of their particular commercial domain. So, although metadata management may be just as big a problem in, say, manufacturing or telecommunications, few financial services managers are likely to be interested in hearing about that. What they want and need are practical examples in their own line of business, and, in this book, they get these in very good measure.

Moreover, readers of this book will get the advantage of hearing about Hans' very specific and instructive personal experiences – both successes and failures – in solving metadata management problems in the financial services industry. Somehow, Hans has managed to write about these experiences in a candid, lively, and engaging style not generally associated with such an arcane and specialized subject matter.

Finally, this book could not be more timely. Of course, as my own story clearly illustrates, the problems that Hans describes have been around for years, and Hans' ideas on how to solve them are essentially timeless. However, until recently, the idea of attacking these problems using the formalism of 'metadata management' would have sounded strange and daunting to most practitioners. In my own experience, merely using the terms 'metadata' or 'metamodel' in a presentation has in the past often sent eyes rolling and minds wandering in all but the most techno-savvy audiences.

But the times they are a-changing, at least in this respect. As Hans himself highlights, globalization of corporate data, particularly in the financial services sector, is a growing phenomenon. Coupled with the burgeoning arena of regulatory compliance, the resulting impacts can be ignored only at one's peril, as my own example also illustrates. The problems of data management must now be attacked systematically, and a strong set of formalisms based on sound metadata management principles is needed to make sense out of this otherwise overwhelming endeavor.

Also, the last few years have been marked by an increasing awareness and appreciation of the benefits of formally modeling both business and IT problems. Modeling standards such as the Unified Modeling Language (UML), the Business Process Modeling Notation (BPMN), the Meta Object Facility (MOF) and the XML Metadata Interchange (XMI) are fueling this awareness, and spawning a whole new generation of model-driven tooling and methods. A whole new discipline – model-driven architecture (MDA) – reflects and amplifies this new way of thinking about modeling and meta-modeling.

As the popularity of model-driven approaches grows, many modeling devotees are now becoming aware of the potential power of rigorous metadata modeling and management. But even today, those who are 'true believers' in metadata management are still in the minority. They are relative evangelists, and, as we all know, every evangelist needs a bible. The good news is that, with the publication of Hans' book, such a bible is now readily available, specifically tailored to the financial services industry. Finally, the book we needed more than a decade ago is now here, and it has arrived none too soon to help solve the even more complex problems we face today.

Michael Guttman
CTO, The Voyant Group
West Chester, PA USA
December, 2006

Preface

'When I use a word,' Humpty Dumpty said in rather a scornful tone, 'it means just what I choose it to mean – neither more nor less.' 'The question is,' said Alice, 'whether you can make words mean so many different things.' 'The question is,' said Humpty Dumpty, 'which is to be master – that's all.'

Lewis Carroll in *Through the Looking-Glass*

The decision to write this book came in early 2005. After years of considering whether to get into such an adventure and, even more importantly, what exactly to say, I realized that it was right in front of me. What I was doing at the time was what I think many IT professionals and finance, risk, and compliance managers in many companies were doing as well. My colleagues in other companies told me that risk and compliance had begun to occupy them – a lot. I was driving the adoption of a data architecture standard at Swiss Re, and the biggest challenge was the integration of business and IT processes under the umbrella of a unified framework. Although the origins of that standard were in the area of data quality management, it was soon dominated by the topic of architectural compliance. That had a lot to do with what was happening outside Swiss Re, for example the Sarbanes-Oxley Act in the United States, or Solvency II in the European Union. Swiss Re is based in Zurich and subject to the local law, yet events elsewhere in the world strongly, not just fleetingly, dominated its agenda.

This story is not an exception. Many financial service companies around the world are struggling with the effects of globalization. They are reorganizing the way they manage risk and compliance, and events from around the world have an increasing effect on their mode of operation. At the same time, the pressure to industrialize processes, innovate products and services, and increase the ability to react to customer demands continues. In this context, calls for an increased use of IT are understandable, because it holds the promise of more accurate and efficient execution of processes and integration of data. IT is moving closer to business than it has ever done before.

More and more, however, banks and insurance companies realize that this goal is only achieved at a hidden cost unimagined when decisions were taken. First, integration is accomplished with great pain, because colleagues in many other locations and business lines have a very different idea of how processes and data should be integrated. Then, changing the concoction turns out to be more difficult as well, because the number of stakeholders is much higher, causing frictions along the line. Yet grudgingly, and with some disappointment, business treads along. The key word is *integration*: tighter integration brings more dependencies, and that means more friction – unless you do something about it.

Metadata management is a way of doing something about it, but it must be thoroughly understood because there is a cost to it as well. Metadata management exploits leverage mechanisms, and it is crucial to bring them to bear in the right places. This raises the question of value creation – where these places are to be found. I have found over time that the answer cannot be given in a generic way, but requires that the domain be taken into account. This is why the specific problems of the financial service industry are given so much room in this book.

When you use metadata management successfully, you give yourself and the company you work for a language to speak about the data and processes ingrained in IT. Reification, which is the main mechanism of metadata management, creates that language, giving meaning to words to be used in systematic change management. The true challenge that anyone setting out on such a course must master is to choose the meaning of words wisely, bringing about the topic of *alignment*: ensuring that business and IT mean the same when they talk about the same is an age-old challenge. Practice has shown that it is a bidirectional effort, taking into account the demands, constraints, and opportunities of the business and the technical viewpoint alike.

The tradeoffs and shortcomings occurring in large financial service companies, be they organizational, financial, jurisdictional, technical, or political, affect alignment activity profoundly. They are so huge in this industry that they can, in my view, not be abstracted away. I have come to believe that they must be considered part of the problem and, by extension, always be taken into account when creating a solution. That creates design challenges of its own, and this book takes them on as well.

Metadata management is an exciting way of tackling the complexity intrinsic to large, multinational financial service companies. And as you will see, if you master it successfully, you will be rewarded with insights you were unable to obtain before. To that end, I hope you enjoy reading this book.

Hans Wegener
Zurich, Switzerland
December, 2006

Acknowledgements

A writers' words [do not] have a virgin birth or an eternal life.

Malcolm Gladwell in *The New Yorker*

Many people helped make this book possible. Some knew it, some did not. I would like to thank them all and hope I do not forget to mention their contribution here.

First and foremost, my thanks go to Gunnar Auth. He was a major source of inspiration. Approaching metadata management from the process perspective is based on his idea. He has given me new insights, and thus put the whole book concept in motion.

I would like to express my gratitude for the fantastically inspiring work atmosphere at Swiss Re in Zurich and the facilities there, especially the research desk of Global Library Services. Quite a few of the arcane publications they found shed a new light on the material presented here. Further special thanks go to the former Group Information & Process Architecture team (Stefan Sieger, Robert Marti, Dora Zosso, Alberto Desiderio, Jürg Tschirren, Tim Harris) for innovative, productive, and most of all, entertaining years. A fair share of the ideas in this book were born during this time. You were fantastic, guys! In like mind, the Data Office team (Stephan Tuor, Roger Schmid, Seraina Cavelti, Uven Pillay, Uwe Raetz) deserves credit for challenging my ideas on the practicality account, and for adding their own piece of experience.

The people who have read and commented on the manuscript, or provided ideas and feedback as to the book's structure, should not go unmentioned, either. Their names are, in alphabetical order: Jürgen Ahting, Harald Bischoff, Boris Bokowski, Wolfgang Dzida, Ulrich Eisenecker, Tammo Freese, Franz Hoffer, Aaron Hoffer, Hans-Peter Hoidn, Timothy Jones, Allan Kelly, Guido Krüdenscheidt, Phillip Kutter, Carolyn Majkowski, Stefan Meissner, Florian Melchert, Frank Meyer, Pascal Miserez, Thomas Oeschger, Ruben Saar, Fredi Schmid, Michael Schürig, Paul Sevinç, Klaus Turowski, Frank Westphal, Keith Whittingham, and Christian Wilhelmi. Thanks for putting up with my schedule!

The staff at John Wiley & Sons, Ltd in Chichester, England were really supportive in bringing this project to a successful conclusion. As can be imagined, embarking on a book journey entails its own risks and uncertainties, but writing about IT *and* financial services at the same time is a thought that can be a little scary at the outset. Nevertheless, my editors Sally Tickner, Rosie Kemp, and Drew Kennerley were always very motivating and optimistic, and guided me safely through the editorial passages. Sally also earned some extra thanks for sharing so many tips for tasteless BBC comedy shows. That certainly made my life as an author easier. Lynette James drove the production process smoothly to completion, and my copy editor Andy Finch knocked the script into an appealing shape.

I would like to thank my friends, colleagues, and family who I neglected a fair bit in 2006 – for their patience and for putting up with my occasionally scatterbrained behavior. André and Andreas: sorry for not training with you as much. I promise, 2007 will be different.

Finally, I want to thank all those colleagues from around the globe who were willing to share their own metadata management experiences with me. Without them, I am convinced, this book would not be able to illustrate all the practical problems and solutions that it does. Personal preference or, in some cases, company policy prevent them being named here. As such, let me thank all of you, even though you remain anonymous.

I

Introduction

You cannot expect the form before the idea, for they will come into being together.

Arnold Schönberg

1.1   Why this book?

Financial services institutions such as internationally operating banks and insurance companies frequently need to adapt to changes in their environments, yet at the same time manage risk and ensure regulatory compliance. This book explains how metadata is key to managing these goals effectively.

In recent years, an array of scandals has adversely affected the trust that investors, regulators, and the general public put into reports from corporations, specifically when it comes to financial accounting. Some of these scandals can be attributed to the exploitation of legal loopholes that eventually backfired, others were caused by plain old fraud and criminal energy to cover balance sheet irregularities. And yet, there were cases where people discovered that they had made, well, an honest mistake. Whatever the reason, an increasing body of legislation puts an increasing responsibility on companies to deliver accurate and consistent reports. The need for ensuring compliance end-to-end is on the up as well, and solid, systematic corporate governance has become a necessity.

In addition, worries about the stability of the global financial system caused national and international regulators to ponder further standardization, to reduce the risks inherent to the system by increasing the comparability and transparency of risk management methods and procedures, as well as to set limits for compliance. Some of these standards are driven by a desire to increase market transparency, whereas others reinforce requirements to avoid conflicts of interest, intended to reflect the improved understanding of a specific subject, or focus on market, credit, or operational risks. Regulations and frameworks like SOX, COSO, Solvency II, MiFID, IFRS/IAS, ITIL, COBIT, or Basel II come to mind. The topic of risk management is high on the agenda. Here again, compliance with regulatory requirements and corporate governance is a prominent concern.

All these obligations have to be met by businesses operating in the financial services industry, which has been particularly affected by these developments. At the same time, this industry has also witnessed a steady increase in the complexity and sophistication of its products, services, and processes, as well as the markets within which it trades. It does not exactly help that managing such a zoo is subject to a vast lineup of regulations formulated by authorities.

These challenges can be considered to be a regular side effect of maturation and industrialization. The past has also witnessed market participants engage in risks, get their fingers burnt, learn from it, and move on. After all, an important part of financial services is about engaging in and managing risks. However, a particular concern about the current business climate is the sometimes drastic effect of misbehavior or misjudgment. Investor confidence can plunge without warning, so the worry about reputational risk has grown to extremes in some areas. It is therefore no surprise that the topic of governance and risk is a concern.

Another factor to consider is the continuing push of the financial services industry towards integration and globalization of their business. Some areas are already globalized (think of investment banking or reinsurance), and others are catching up. Mergers and acquisitions will be increasingly transnational, crossing jurisdictions and markets. This raises issues that were traditionally less of a concern. A bank operating across jurisdictions that has not done so before must deal with a much wider range of constraints and comply with a larger number of rules than a national niche player. In some regions, life has been made easier by unifying the rules under which companies can operate cross-border, for example the European Union. But that offers little comfort to the businesses that truly want to compete globally.

Complexity, variability, volatility, change, cost pressures, constraints, and risks abound in financial services. The goal conflict is evident: on the one hand, the call is for increased flexibility and agility to support the change that companies are undergoing; on the other hand, wide-ranging control over the risks run is required, and the alignment of organizations with legislation (and, not to forget, stated regulation internally) is demanded by company leaders even more strongly. What is more, besides regulatory requirements there are other sources that may require you to adapt to change, such as competition, trends, or innovation.

It would be unhealthy to expect one single solution to resolve this goal conflict completely, because it is systemic: the more risks you run, the more likely you are to witness volatility in your results. If you allow employees to act flexibly, you cannot realistically expect them to comply with all existing rules, unless you check compliance with them . . . which costs your employees parts of the very flexibility you just gave them. The more complex your products are, the less you will be able to understand the risks attached. However, as these conflicts can potentially translate into direct financial gains or losses, you will be concerned with balancing them wisely. Managing this balance well gives you the ability to put your capital to the best possible use.

What comes in handy at this point is the fact that the business processes of financial services companies depend – to a large extent crucially – on information technology (IT). This offers an opportunity to use leverage effects (digitization, automation, scalability) for the benefits of supporting change, which can be understood as a business process itself. Yet, although leverage is generally a fine idea, one should be aware of the fact that too much bureaucracy and risk (into which highly automated processes can easily degenerate) can be as much of a disaster as too little.

Dealing with the above goal conflict (flexibility and speed on the one hand and risk and compliance on the other) is thus about dealing with it in a constructive, systematic fashion, while confining undesired side effects to areas that are of lesser importance or, better still, no concern at all. This is what I want to call *systematic alignment*, which means that:

- Change is supported in a way that increases the effectiveness of moving the corporation from an existing to a desired target state.
- Effectiveness is increased by giving structure to a change and leveraging this structure, using information technology, to arrive at the target state in a controlled fashion.
- The nature of a change and its impact is used for alignment with regulations, which are formulated as constraints to check compliance with the target state. It is also used to understand the risk characteristics of the existing and target state.
- Processes are put in place at each of these stages to plan, execute, and monitor goal achievement, while ensuring the necessary flexibility to cater for the complexity arising in real-life settings.

This book is about the data to support systematic alignment, called *metadata*, and the processes to handle it, called *metadata management*. It explains how the use of metadata can help you add value by improving performance, managing risk, and ensuring compliance. It is specifically a book for the financial services industry, its peculiarities, needs, and rules. It elaborates where and why metadata helps this industry to manage change.

In a word, metadata is a choice for people who want to transform their financial institution in a controlled fashion, and yet be sure they comply with regulations and control their exposure to risk. Managing this conflict in a structured, predictable fashion can be made the centerpiece of managing change successfully, confidently, and reliably. But why, again, should that worry you in the first place?

1.2   Change, risk, and compliance

In October 2003, a US Securities and Exchange Commission official cited the following key examination and enforcement issues that the SEC worried about:

1. late trading and timing in mutual fund shares;
2. creating and marketing structured finance products;
3. risk management and internal controls;
4. accuracy and reliability of books, records, and computations.

It is probably safe to assume that much of this continues to be on the agenda. The complexity and sophistication of products and services offered by the financial services industry continues to increase. As a consequence, the change frequency will also increase, and the impact of changes will become more difficult to assess, and less easy to predict. That is, of course, unless countermeasures are taken. Of the above concerns, three out of four can – at least to a substantial degree – be attributed to complexity, rapid change, and intransparency.

The reasons for this are easily explained: products and services tend to differentiate, be packaged and configured to the needs of the customers, and structured to appeal to more complex demands – in a word, evolve. Structuring is one such typical practice: as products become commoditized, they are used for putting together other products to arrive at more powerful, yet subsequently more complex products. On the other hand, the number of dependencies to be managed increases, causing management problems of its own kind.

This combination of scale, dependency, and change is a substantial source of risk. Typically you would want to carve up this cake and opt for some form of divide and conquer. But how, where, and when? There may literally be dozens of factors you need to take into account. Not all of these factors will you be able to influence, not all of them may be worth your full attention, and not all of them lend themselves to carving up, anyway.

Think about this: the typical financial institution operating on a global basis will sport a portfolio of applications numbering in the upper hundreds, not counting different releases of these applications, desktop software, spreadsheets, and the like. You will naturally be disinclined to take on the full scale of the problem just yet. Hence, you decide to put out of scope, spreadsheets and desktop software. But there the problem begins: your risk managers use a combination of spreadsheets and the desktop installation of a risk modeling and simulation package. From the relevance viewpoint this should certainly be in scope, but from the scalability viewpoint you will not want to include all spreadsheets and desktop software packages. To mix and match at will, however, just worsens your situation once again: how are you going to draw any meaningful conclusions about a bag of seemingly incomparable things?

The answer depends, to a large extent, on your perspective. Which perspective you take, which aspects of your problem you *reify* into a model to treat in a structured fashion, has a great influence on what you will be better at, but also where you will, well, not be better. The question is, which aspects should you focus on, and what are the undesirable effects of that choice? And, should these aspects constitute different, competing views on the parts of the same problem, how can you balance them in a meaningful way?

In a word, if you want to manage risk in the face of scale, change, and dependency, you need to find a way to structure it. What you also need to consider is the rate and impact of change. What does this mean for the IT applications of a large company? What are the conditions under which the business processes of such typical companies operate? What are the origins of change? Can the risk this causes be controlled? Where? And when? How can IT support this process? It is here where the topic of systematic alignment comes up again: many business processes are run by applications (partially or completely). Hence, there is substantial leverage you can exert over the risks associated with the execution of these processes by exploiting the structure intrinsic to any software product.

Take another example, financial accounting. Traditionally a complex mix of formality and fluidity – of rigid rules and flexible interpretation – this area is complexity galore: the general ledger of any larger institution can easily contain hundreds of accounts, each of which features its own list of describing attributes. But there are also the dozens of subsidiary ledgers, based upon which the general ledger is computed, and there are its numerous variations, all of which are governed by their own set of rules (both written and unwritten) and levels of detail: report to analysts, quarterly report, annual report, and so on. Chip in different accounting standards in different countries, and then imagine migrating from US-GAAP to IFRS/IAS-based accounting. Furthermore, assume your company is listed on a US stock exchange, subjecting it to the regulations of SOX. You will be bound by those rules as well, most notably those of the (almost notorious) Section 404.

Most certainly you want to make sure all these rules are abided by, but would you know how to ensure they really are? The internal control procedures in a large organization are typically complex, often interwoven, changing, and most likely not understood by any one single person in the company at every level of detail. Therefore, you will want to get a grip on understanding, for example, which processes enact changes on accounts considered significant enough to merit control, and then subject those processes to controls. Yet, there are many different ways in which a process can be enacted, e.g. by IT only, by humans supported by IT, or by humans only. As new applications are developed, these ways change, and as new entities are acquired or merged with, the whole fabric is put under tension. Sometimes it tears and needs to be fixed.

The complexity cannot be done away with. Hence, as a measure of caution you will want to give the problem some structure so to understand it better – a framework. Today, many organizations interested in achieving SOX compliance use the COSO framework. In a stable environment, you are certainly safe with this. But the framework does not (directly) answer the question how to approach the issue of integrating a – possibly large – acquired company, or reorganizing the entire corporation, such that the proverbial fabric does not tear.

This is where systematic alignment comes in: frameworks such as COSO, COBIT, and others take specific structural decisions in order to achieve predefined goals, which can be technical, legal, financial, or something else. They do so by classifying things – be they tangible or not – in a certain way and then establishing rules on their (structural) relationships.

For example, concepts in the world of the Sarbanes-Oxley Act include accounts, risks, and processes; the relationships are 'transacts on,' 'is child of,' and 'can affect;' the rules are 'aggregate' and 'cascade.' If you want to integrate the other company, its accounts, its processes, its risks, the whole lot must be aligned with the ones you are managing in your own company. Here is where the framework, its concepts, and its structural rules, along with metadata come to your rescue: by mapping the other company's processes to your own (capturing metadata), you can systematically establish a desired target state (alignment with your own processes) and track it (monitor compliance). Usage of the framework ensures that the business meaning of concepts on either side of the integration process is the same, thus ensuring that the integration does what is intended.

One last example: the creation, marketing, and trading in financial instruments. The markets they are traded in are extremely innovative in coming up with products tailored to very specific needs. These are typically highly sophisticated, and their inner workings are accessible to but a few people who understand the market risk associated with trading in them. It will be genuinely difficult to come up with a risk model for these products. There are situations where you will be incapable of fully understanding a problem, let alone the structure and reason about it. This is despite the fact that financial instruments are often composed of others, thus revealing their structure to the observer. As a matter of fact, in many such situations structuring the risk is not the first choice, but using completely different techniques such as exposure limitation or hedging.

Speed and flexibility are crucial in these markets. The proverbial first-mover advantage can mean money lost or won. As such, it would be flat-out silly to subject the designers of complex financial instruments to a rigid regime of rules, constraints, and regulations on the grounds of principle. Not only would you very likely miss out on some nice business opportunities, but you would also miss out on learning how to get better.

The world of managing risk and compliance for financial instruments is a good example of an *ill-structured* problem, meaning that it is full of complexity, ambiguity, and there is sometimes no obvious specification to describe it formally. Such problems can typically be seen from many different viewpoints and require many dimensions along which to describe them properly. To master them is less a question of structuring savvy but of experience or if you will, expert judgement. This makes them hardly accessible to structuring and formalization. Since the financial markets are moving so quickly it is imperative to avoid smothering your staff in red tape. You will want to grant them the flexibility they need to be creative, but only to an extent. You are up for a goal conflict.

Actually, there is another side to the story of financial instruments, and it is about commoditization. You may have noted that it was said that many of today's financial instruments do in fact have structure, and that they are often built on top of other existing, widely-available, instruments. So, there must be some modeling and structuring going on. Can we not make use of that? How does that all fit together? The answer lies in the nature of what (and the place where) something is changing and how to support that process.

Right after a financial instrument has been invented, the risk associated with it is typically not yet understood well. The market sways and swings, and market participants learn how to treat it properly. For example, many accounting issues surround insurance-linked securities, which have jurisdictional dependencies (e.g., US-GAAP versus IFRS/IAS accounting). Ultimately, the risk and compliance issues associated with the instrument are thoroughly understood and they become available as an off-the-shelf product. They may even become traded in a financial exchange, at the time of which they have finally become commoditized. As soon as that has happened, new financial instruments can be built on top of it, and the cycle begins anew.

Although the instruments are not yet thoroughly understood, managing risk (or compliance, for that matter) is a try-and-fix exercise. As they mature, standard products emerge, which can be reused in other settings. However, now that risk and compliance is, for all practical purposes, fully understood, their properties can be used constructively. For example, modeling and simulation tools can be built to compose other products on top of them. These tools in turn make use of said (structural) properties, which are metadata. Modeling, simulation, and design, are in turn highly creative activities, and we go full circle.

This circle happens in many places, both business and IT. Metadata management plays a role in that it supports the management of reusable elements of work (be they software components or financial instruments), once they are standardized. There is a spectrum of volatility: at the one end (immature, poorly understood, highly creative use) people should better be left to themselves than to put them in a straightjacket; at the other end (mature, thoroughly understood, highly mechanized use) it is almost imperative to leverage metadata so as to be flexible, confident, and fast at the same time.

The question is where to draw the line between creative and mechanized. Obviously, the answer has to do with the level of understanding of the objects in focus (components, instruments), their number (few, many, numerous), and the rate of change (quickly, slowly). Answering this question is one subject of this book: setting the peculiarities of a domain (financial services) in perspective with the needs of management (performance, risk, compliance) to arrive at a more refined understanding of metadata's value.

As you have seen, metadata management is not *l'art pour l'art*, a purpose in itself. It must create value. And exactly the question of value creation cannot be answered positively in all cases. In fact, sometimes it may destroy value, namely when it introduces unnecessary bureaucracy to your business processes. All its splendor comes at a cost. Therefore, in situations where it is difficult to understand a problem that needs to be managed for risk (or compliance, for that matter) – for lack of knowledge, skill, time, because of political adversities, or whatever – there are factors that can take away a large part of metadata's allure. It can become too costly, and you must balance such conflicts wisely. This book spends a great deal of time elaborating on the question of value creation and the conflicts that come with it.

1.3   Objectives

Having worked in the financial services industry for a while now, and having gone through the experience of designing, implementing, and operating a number of different metadata management solutions during that time, I cannot avoid but call it a mixed experience. I have long wondered about the reasons.

There were successes – some surprising, others more planned and expected. I still remember the evening I met with a former colleague for dinner before a night of cinema. He mentioned to me in passing that a credit product modeling solution I had designed before leaving the company had gone productive and been very much appreciated by business users. I was electrified: although we had been as thorough about the design as was possible, it did not seem to us there were too many people waiting desperately for our solution to be rolled out. Obviously we had struck a chord with enough of them, nevertheless. At the time of designing the solution, I was mostly concerned with a flexible architecture and integration with the software framework on top of which we had built it, but not with the business implications and possible impact on product design. I went home on cloud nine after cinema. The solution (in extended and evolved form) is being used to this day, six years after.

But there were also failures. The objective of this book is – to an extent – to demystify metadata management and explain some of this apparent randomness. In fact, it turns out that there is a host of good reasons why the projects I was involved in turned out the way they did. But this can only be understood when the analysis combines very different and, perhaps not surprisingly, mostly non-technical fields. The first aspect examines activities and their contribution to value creation so as to make them more economical. In the context of this book, we will take a particular look at the leverage effects of metadata management and how they contribute to value creation. The second area is industry peculiarities, i.e. the idiosyncrasies of banks and insurance companies. This sector exhibits its very own set of rules, based on its history, the nature of its value chains, and most notably, the role of national legislation. In particular, this book takes a closer look at some of the constraints that influence solution design.

In fact, there is a colleague of mine who likes to joke: 'May all your problems be technical!' On a positive note, there is a host of reasons to defend metadata management as an indispensable tool in managing complexity and volatility. Another objective of this book is hence to show

how the use of metadata can contribute to an effective alignment, leading to better change, risk, and compliance management. One reason is increasing systemic complexity, a burden that is attributable in part to the surge in the number and sophistication of regulations introduced in recent years, as well as the continuing evolution of products offered to the financial markets. This book will point out how metadata can critically enhance the ability of an institution to manage change, risk, and compliance by structuring the problem and actively managing transformation processes. Another reason is the widespread use of IT in financial services: banks and insurance companies are some of the most avid adopters of information technology. They have thus long streamlined many of their products, processes, and services (specifically in retail business) and achieved great productivity improvements. This in turn makes them perfectly suited to leverage techniques that build on top of those structures, which is at the heart of this book's idea: systematically managing and aligning the IT supporting the operation of a financial services company with its stated business goals, and continuing to do so in the face of change.

The problem of managing the complexity occurring in financial services is not a recent phenomenon. In fact, it has been around for plenty of years. Yet, many of the (sometimes excellent) publications on the matter have focused on but one side of the coin, either the business or the technology viewpoint. My experience is that this falls critically short of some of the problems you face in this area. Therefore, the overall objective of this book is to tread the line between business and IT, to provide you with a fresh view on things that combines insights from both areas. The most important of these ideas are explained next.

1.3.1 Value proposition for a vertical domain

Imagine a large bowl of spaghetti. Depending on where you poke your fork in, you may have a hard time extracting just enough spaghetti to fit into your mouth. The larger the bowl, the more likely you will end up with a huge pile of spaghetti on your fork, impossible to consume in one bite. However, if your host piles a smaller amount of spaghetti on your plate the whole exercise gets a lot easier. And as you may well know, the more you have eaten the easier it gets.

For a systematic understanding of our problem we must have a way of structuring it. When trying to understand the structure and rules underlying an area like financial services we need to do kind of the same: distribute spaghetti on plates, and adjust the amount of spaghetti to the size of the plates. This is the principle behind *divide and conquer.*

In IT, people often refer to a *domain* when talking about an area of knowledge or activity, like operating systems, relational databases, software development, or more business-related areas like risk underwriting, claims management, credits, payments, investment, or financial accounting. Domains are used to group the concepts used in the real world and their relationships into a coherent whole in order to manage them systematically, independent of others. This aids their management in just the same way that spaghetti plates help you find a group of spaghetti small enough to swallow.

There is a difference to spaghetti bowls, however. Domains are used to arrange and structure your view of the world. This structure often determines which relationships between the concepts you regard as interesting and which concept belongs where. By delineating domains in a specific way you emphasize certain aspects, while de-emphasizing others.

Traditionally, when the real world can be looked at from two fundamentally different viewpoints, people have distinguished so-called *horizontal* from *vertical* organization of domains. Putting things a little simply, a horizontal domain organization tries to maximize your own satisfaction, that is to put concepts into domains the way you prefer. On the other hand, vertical domain organization puts the other (possible) viewpoint first and arranges concepts in the way a person with that point of view would do.

Obviously 'horizontal' and 'vertical' are relative terms. Why all this complication? Value creation is best analyzed when arranged around the concepts dominant to the business process under study. Now, as one moves away from the purely technical (read: IT-related) world closer to business, it becomes less and less helpful to use technical concepts. Since the relationships between the concepts in a business domain are often different from those exhibited in a technical domain, the traces of a value chain can no longer be followed properly.

This book takes a vertical domain viewpoint. In my experience this is indispensable for understanding the levers of value creation at the disposal of business. On the flip side of the coin it helps tremendously in identifying areas where the use of metadata does not add value.

1.3.2   Tradeoffs in large multinational corporations

As was mentioned already, one focus of this book is on large, multinational, globalized companies. This is important for two reasons.

First, such firms are bound by the typical constraints of organizations beyond a certain size, which grew in a more or less uncontrolled fashion over an extended period of time. All of these constraints *decrease* our freedom in designing solutions:

- *Strong division of labor:* people in large companies tend to specialize. New techniques are not introduced by waving a magic wand. It takes time for people to understand what is intended.
- *Business heterogeneity:* there is a multitude of exceptions, niches, and variety in the business. When everything is special, abstracting from it becomes difficult.
- *IT heterogeneity:* banks and insurance companies adopted IT a long time ago and invested substantial amounts of money in their applications. These are not easily done away with and must be treated as monoliths, which does not always conform with plans. Hence, problems must be managed at very different levels of granularity.
- *Politics:* it is a matter of fact that quite a few decisions in an organization are not taken purely based on rational facts. Given the far-reaching consequences of leveraging techniques such

as metadata, political problems are to be expected. They are indeed so important that they must, in my opinion, be addressed strategically.

Second, large multinational corporations are particularly struck by the travails of globalization, which *increase* complexity:

- *Publicly held:* the way they are financed, and because of the critical role data plays in financial markets, means that public companies are the subject of much regulatory scrutiny and reporting requirements, much more than privately held firms.
- *Substantial size:* bigger multinationals are typically conglomerates of dozens, sometimes even hundreds of legal entities. They operate in their specific legal environment, which not only concerns regulatory or legal affairs, but also financial management issues like taxes.
- *Spanning jurisdictions:* legal entities, by definition, must fulfill certain legal obligations stipulated by the authorities. The financial services industry is among the most heavily regulated, which can dominate the way in which a firm's operations are structured: organizationally, in terms of products, or the way its business processes work.

The combination of forces influencing the design of a (successful) solution for a large organization is unique, and yet occurs often enough that it merits dedicated treatment. This is one objective of this book, namely to picture the tradeoffs effected by these forces, and outline a constructive way of dealing with them.

1.4   Scope

This is a conceptual book. It is not concerned with technology or implementation, at least not significantly. It is mostly concerned with business processes and data, and how both are supported, stored, and manipulated by applications, respectively.

Obviously, this book is about the financial services industry, banks, and insurance companies. You may find time and again that some statements would be applicable to other industries as well. I will not dwell on such similarities.

Geographically, or should I say, jurisdictionally, this book is international by design. It addresses the problems of multinational corporations, trying hard not to assume anything is common that in fact varies between countries. Many problems elaborated inside this book are driven genuinely by jurisdictional developments. The focus will be put on important financial markets like the United States, the European Union including the United Kingdom, Japan, and Switzerland.

This book covers both wholesale and retail business. Naturally, not every aspect can be covered exhaustively, so I will restrict myself to a sample of problems that can easily be extrapolated to other areas, such as investment banking, reinsurance, primary insurance, or retail banking.

As a general rule, the book will cater to the needs of diversified companies, that is those with a wide-ranging, non-correlated portfolio of business activities. This does not mean that pure investment banks or specialty reinsurers are not part of the picture. In fact, you will later see that statements calling for specialization will be made in the interest of value creation. However, the point of view *generally* taken will be that of a large, diversified financial institution.

Likewise, the issues of risk and compliance management are a wide field. I would like to reiterate my statement that there are plenty of good books available. Furthermore, there is a plethora of regulations and frameworks that have been issued by national and international authorities, often based on laws agreed by the respective parliaments. Not all of them can be covered. Hence, this book will address selected pieces of regulation that have or can be expected to have a large impact.

Finally, value creation will be analyzed at a qualitative level only. The main reason for this is that coming up with quantifiable benefits depends wholly on the properties of the environment. This will be impossible to do, at a general level, in a book like this. Also, I believe that mathematical accuracy pales in comparison to the, well . . . qualitative differences in value creation that one can observe between, say the various lines of business in a financial institution.

This book takes a reactive perspective on change management. For the purpose of this text, it is always events elsewhere that trigger change processes. Initiating changes and managing them accordingly is a totally different field and will not be covered.

Of the specific types of risks, legal, political, and reputational risks will receive limited or no treatment. The main reason is that whereas the above carry at least some relevance for (operational) risk management, they require their very own ways of handling, which are not readily accessible to support by metadata. By the same token, risk management entails not only risk control, but also risk diversification and avoidance. These are out of the scope of this book as well. The obvious reason is that risk avoidance is a way of getting around a specific risk, at least in part. As will be shown later, the main focus will be on modeling things potentially imperiled by risk and trying to understand concrete perils and risk levels using metadata. Risk diversification (as in portfolio management), on the other hand plays an important role in managing investment and insurance risks, but has been extensively covered by publications elsewhere.

The value proposition, as has been said before, will not be covered at the quantitative level. By extension, covering the quantitative aspects of risk management (during risk assessment) would bloat the contents of the book as well. It would also probably not add too much insight to material presented at the conceptual level, anyway. Again, please turn to appropriate literature elsewhere.

Many of the recommendations that are to follow are based on a model in which meta-data management is carefully planned, executed, and monitored. Especially when it is used to support understanding (e.g., as in descriptions of the business meaning of data or processes), there is at least one other model that can be used, namely so-called *social tagging*, which is a community-based, cooperative mechanism for classifying and documenting things. Typical examples of social tagging include the photo sharing platform Flickr and the online (book) retailer Amazon. Both offer their users ways of adding pieces of data to objects served on their site, such as book ratings or comments on Amazon, or descriptive keywords on Flickr. There are two reasons for not covering this model of managing metadata:

1. The dynamics of social, community-based interactions are only slowly being understood, so it would be a little early to cover them here. Furthermore, it is difficult to scale them since they are based on cultural homogeneity and decentralization, whereas this book focuses on large, hetrogeneous organizations and central control.
2. Value in social tagging is (also) created through network effects, the use of which has a completely different underlying economic model than the two main effects presented here, namely productivity and quality gains.

It should be mentioned that there are situations where social tagging is preferable to the planned model. For the sake of simplicity such scenarios are not considered. For all practical purposes, social tagging should be considered complementary to planned approaches, and as such you may add these mechanisms on your own where you find them helpful.

1.5   Who should read this book?

This book will appeal to three groups of people, corresponding to three organizational functions:

- *Information technology*, organizing the furtherance of applications for the benefit of the corporation, specifically in the form of an integrated framework to align its capabilities with strategic business goals.
- *Risk management*, setting standards on the systematic identification, evaluation, acceptance, reduction, avoidance, and mitigation of risks in which the corporation engages, as well as enacting effective controls to ensure compliance.
- *Compliance management*, responsible for ensuring the conformity of operational business activities with internally formulated or externally given rules, specifically with regards to regulatory authorities.

In terms of organizational level, this book appeals to the first two or three lines:

- *Chief officers*, managers representing one of the above functions at the executive board level, taking decisions of strategic impact.
- *Senior executives*, direct reports of chief officers, responsible for running the day-to-day operation of select parts of an organizational function.
- *Specialty managers*, people who have profound expertise in a specific area, typically serving in a consulting role to senior executives and chief officers.

This book primarily intends to address the following points of interest to the above groups:

- Chief Information Officers (CIOs) and senior IT executives learn how to achieve change goals and track progress systematically. They will understand where and how metadata management ties in with IT processes, what the levers of value creation are, and how they relate to overall value creation in a financial services organization. Furthermore, they get a picture of the downsides and practical problems and how to mitigate them. Finally, they learn how to start a comprehensive process towards metadata management.
- Chief Risk Officers (CROs) and senior risk managers learn the nature of metadata and its use in structuring and modeling risks. Specifically, they learn how the management of operational IT risk can be systematically improved by establishing and maintaining risk portfolios described by metadata. In addition they learn how metadata helps them gain better insight into risk data in general. They will also understand the impact on the organization, applications, and operative processes, as well as the pitfalls.
- Chief Compliance Officers (CCOs) and their senior managers learn how governance, compliance and metadata are related. They formulate and adopt regulations in a methodological fashion. Specifically, they will understand how regulatory alignment can be established, properly assessed, and re-established once deviations are discovered using architectural alignment of IT with stated rules. They will also understand the limitations of such an approach, the costs incurred, and practical mitigation measures.
- Chief Business Engineers (CBEs) and business architects learn their supporting role, the impact of a particular way of scoping and designing architecture, domain model, and metamodel, and how this impact affects the organization's ability to manage change, risk, and compliance actively. They also learn how they themselves can use metadata to improve the results of their own work. This especially applies to capturing and analyzing existing IT portfolios (*as is*) and setting targets for their evolution (*to be*). Finally, they manage to limit the adverse effects on the work of projects, developers, and business users.
- Product managers learn to better understand how to leverage the power of metadata in designing, deploying, and changing products in a complex and continuously evolving environment. They will understand the prerequisites that IT systems must fulfill in order to

support them, but also the organizational setup required and skills needed. Furthermore, they learn how to reduce complexity in the right places, and yet maintain the ability to handle it in others.

Obviously, people working in teams directly supporting the above groups will also find the book useful for the same reasons. As a kind of secondary goal of this book, the following groups of people will find reading the material helpful:

- Business analysts will understand how metadata affects their work, what is asked from them to support it, and what criteria are important in this.
- Methodologists will learn how the processes of analysis, design, construction, and operation are affected and can be supported by metadata to improve productivity and quality.
- Expert business users will see how they can improve their efficiency and effectiveness when faced with complex tasks. They specifically will understand metadata quality deficits and how to handle them.

Finally, there are the specialists in all the different domains (programmers, underwriters, etc.). I do not list them here, because they are typically quite detached from much of the above, but they may use the material for information purposes.

1.6   Contents and organization

This book is divided into three parts. First, it illustrates the peculiarities of metadata management and its use in architectural alignment. Second, it outlines how and where metadata management creates value, namely by supporting an efficient response to change, improving the ability to ensure compliance and regulatory alignment, and supporting the management of risk. Third, it casts a light on the practical problems (the mechanics, if you wish): dealing with business and technical evolution in its various forms, managing quality, and planning, extending, and sustaining the success of a metadata-based solution.

Chapter 2 takes a reactive, process-oriented perspective on the management of change in a corporation. Business processes are structured into core, support, and steering processes. Metadata management is presented as an IT support process controlling and supporting the adoption of change in a company's IT. The two main facets of metadata management are described: metadata as a reification of how models are related, and metadata management as a process that couples change adoption activities. With this, you achieve a separation of concerns at the data level, while requiring an integration of concerns at the process level.

Chapter 3 presents alignment as an activity that uses metadata by reifying how compliance is achieved, and then actively managing that metadata as part of governance activity. The chapter emphasizes the interplay of architecture and metadata, describing how architectural building blocks relate to metamodel abstractions, and how that can be used to ensure compliance. It is highlighted how metadata can be made a strategic tool in the planning and implementation of structural changes. Finally, the important practical issue of handling exceptions to the rules is given room, with the text explaining how to deal with them from a data and process perspective.

Chapter 4 concerns itself with making the organization more efficient and effective in responding to change, in a word: to achieve productivity improvements. The different cost factors arising through the use of metadata management are discussed and juxtaposed with the realities of the financial service industry. The effects of typical changes on the IT landscape of companies are discussed, leading to the result that only a targeted use of metadata management creates significant value. The main message is that a bank or insurance company should seek performance improvements through metadata management only in its company-specific way of adopting technology. Several case studies illustrate how others have used metadata in this way, such as credit product design, using business rules in trade automation, and model generation in asset management.

Chapter 5 looks at the risk management process and describes how you can make use of metadata to manage risks more successfully. First off, it explains why IT today plays a bigger role in managing risk than ever before. It then goes on to illustrate what effects the use of IT has in managing risk, both direct and indirect. It also emphasizes the risks IT itself introduces. With this picture in mind, the chapter claims that the role of metadata in managing risk lies in the support for risk transformation, data quality management, and architectural alignment. Several case studies illustrate the practical use of metadata, ranging from data quality management in data warehousing to operational risk management in architectural governance.

Chapter 6 gives a brief overview of what compliance means in terms of regulation, governance, control, and audit. Then it takes a look at the regulatory landscape in different jurisdictions, and discusses the nature of different regulations. From there, it explains what role IT can play in supporting compliance management. The contribution of metadata management to this is explained. A number of case studies from anti-money-laundering, SOX- and US-GAAP-compliance, taxes, privacy, and documenting the opening of relationships complete the picture.

The first practical issue is handling evolution, which is at the heart of Chapter 7. The activities in this area are listed and explained, such as metamodeling, organizing impact analysis, or change propagation. In all this, the challenges of real-life large organizations and how to overcome them are woven in, such as dealing with division of labor, dealing with impedance, retaining and regaining consistency, or grouping changes. The various tradeoffs of solution templates are discussed.

Chapter 8 looks at how metadata quality deficits affect its utility. Because metadata management is a support process, any deficit in its intelligibility, completeness, correctness, consistency, actuality, or granularity has a characteristic impact on the core processes it ties into. Ways to detect such deficits and countermeasures for tackling them are explained from a risk management perspective. Side effects of such countermeasures are explained.

Chapter 9 deals with the question of how to ensure the continued success of metadata management in typical big corporations, despite such usual phenomena as politics, lack of ownership, or limited awareness and understanding. Ways of identifying and recruiting owners, as well as alleviating their fears are listed, also with respect to other stakeholders. The chapter also discusses the challenges in scaling metadata management to global scope. Awareness and understanding, the issue of training people, and making them use metadata appropriately, are problems that receive coverage as well. Finally, the issue of company politics is examined, its nature illustrated, and the reason why metadata management gets so tied up with it is explained. Different political maneuvers are discussed, highlighting both the offense and defense of playing politics.

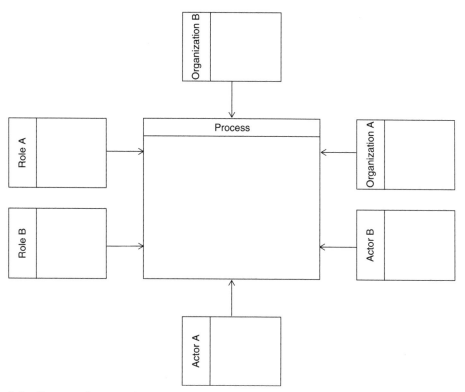

Figure 1.1: Context diagrams feature a single process, which sets the scope of attention. Outside actors, such as roles or organizations with which the processes interact, are grouped around it

Finally, Chapter 10 puts forth a vision of an institutionalized corporate function for combined change, risk, and compliance management. It revolves around using models for a more systematic management of change, using the mechanisms of enterprise architecture and metadata management in union. The tasks of such a corporate function are described. In closing, the main lessons (some dos and don'ts) learned from this book are summarized, and a forward-looking statement concludes the book.

The notation used for diagrams is as follows. The *context diagram* (see Figure 1.1 for an example) is used to illustrate what environment a business process is embedded in, and how it interacts with that environment. It sets the scope of the discussion by defining what is considered part of the problem and what not.

The *process diagram* (Figure 1.2) describes the events triggering activities in processes, the sequencing of activities, and their completion in the form of result events. Process diagrams specify how processes are executed.

The *data diagram* (Figure 1.3) is an entity-relationship model that illustrates the main data elements and their relationships at a high level. Data diagrams are not complete, but merely serve to highlight the most important connections.

The *data flow diagram* connects processes and data (Figure 1.4), and highlights the most important interactions of two independent processes via the data that they exchange. A data flow diagram can be used to illustrate what data originates where, and what route it takes between processes. Its function is to describe the sequence of interactions.

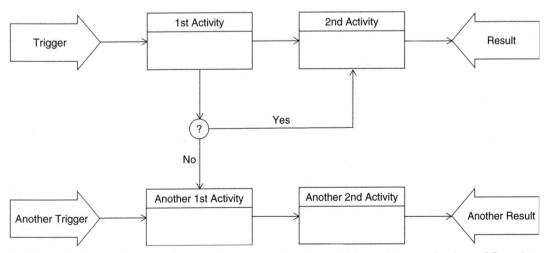

Figure 1.2: Process diagrams illustrate the events triggering activities and the results thereof. Branching is used where necessary, with the labels on the branch describing the choice

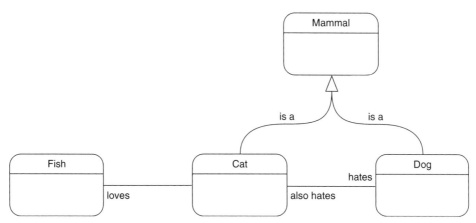

Figure 1.3: Data diagrams describe the structure of the data being used, that is entities and their relationships. Where necessary the relationships are labeled to describe their meaning. The triangle signifies the 'is a' relationship, meaning that the entities subsumed under it are treated the same way by processes as the entity above

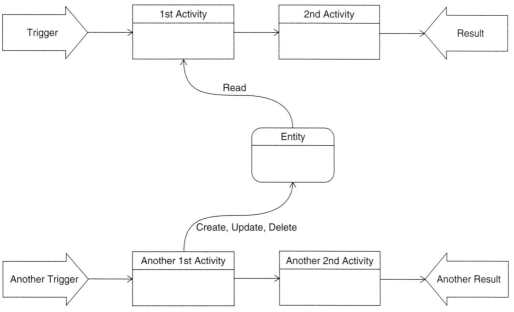

Figure 1.4: Data flow diagrams describe the interaction between data and (at least two) processes. Each process shows an end-to-end activity sequence from trigger to result and which entities it uses (reads) or manipulates (creates, updates, deletes). The direction of arrows thereby indicates which way data is being used. Later diagrams will not label arrows. Data diagrams are used to illustrate how processes are coupled to each other through the data they exchange

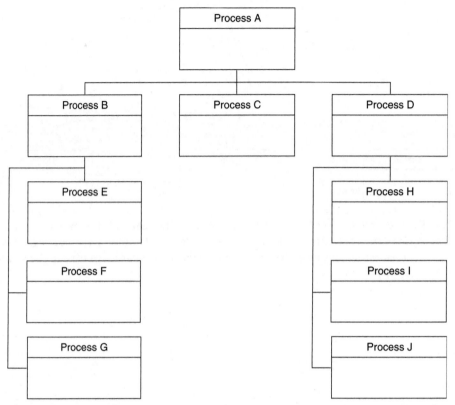

Figure 1.5: Process hierarchies illustrate which processes and activities belong together. A process in a lower layer 'belongs to' the one above, meaning that the subordinate is primarily executed as part of the superior one

Finally, the *process hierarchy* specifies which process is part of another process (Figure 1.5). Typically, activities can be subdivided along some criterion, and the process hierarchy is there to illustrate that subdivision. With it, you can see which activities are part of others.

Part I

Changing the Way You Change

2

The Role of Metadata in Supporting Change

And if you're so meta that you're completely unimpressed with how meta [the movie Adaptation] is, then you're only reinforcing the movie's point: You've become so meta-consumed by metaculture that you're no longer able to take pleasure in art, to laugh at your own foibles, to appreciate true brilliance. [It] is a movie that eats itself whole and leaves the audience with nothing, and we're supposed to go home happily, clutching our little souvenir naughts as if they actually added up to something.

Stephanie Zacharek on Salon.com

2.1   Overview

- You will want to consider metadata management when the cost or risk of adopting changes and ensuring compliance has become prohibitive.
- Metadata management can help you by structuring changes and their impact, and systematizing the handling of structured changes versus unstructured changes (and their respective impact).
- To do this, you isolate the sources of change as they present themselves, and reify them into separate models. Metadata helps to derive the impact sometimes automatically, a process that is based on a metamodel.
- Metadata management is an IT support process. It is triggered by changes to objects across their lifecycle, and ensures appropriate updates to their metadata and effecting appropriate impact on other objects where required.
- What is 'meta' and what is not is relative. Nothing is 'meta' per se, or not so for that matter. You choose to consider it based on where changes bite you most.

Aligning Business and IT with Metadata   Hans Wegener
© 2007 John Wiley & Sons, Ltd.

2.2 Managing change adoption: when change impact begins to bite

Any financial institution operates in an environment that influences the way it works (see Figure 2.1). Regulators require reports on specific topics to ensure fairness in the market and stability of the industry. Tax needs to be deducted and forwarded properly to the state. Investors demand the disclosure of reports on a company's financial well-being. Customers must be kept happy by putting out new services or offering them at more competitive prices. The financial markets move here and there, requiring adjustments in investments. Technology, specifically IT, evolves, offering opportunities to do things more efficiently or more effectively.

When changes happen outside a corporation, they can have an impact on its inner workings. Many of the business processes in financial services have been automated by (and most of the data is stored in) applications. Thus these applications capture, in some form or another, the way the company works and how it presents itself to and interacts with the outside world. Therefore, when the external world changes, that can have an impact on the internal workings of data, processes, or applications (see sidebar 'Reactive versus proactive change management').

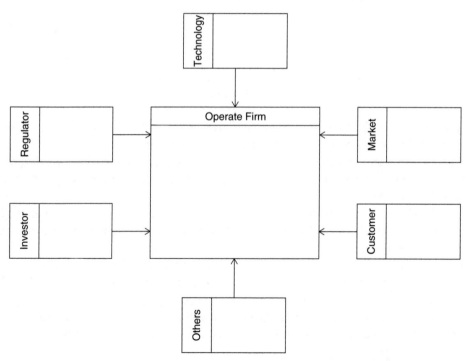

Figure 2.1: A financial services institution is subject to a multitude of influences

Reactive versus proactive change management

You may have noticed that I emphasize external changes leading to an internal impact. This is a reactive perspective, which means that control of the course of events lies outside your own sphere of influence. The outside world exerts a much bigger influence on how you organize your company than you do. The proactive approach to managing changes entails influencing the outside world in order to ensure that certain events do happen or to keep them from happening. I think that, although some areas lend themselves to a proactive approach (product marketing would be a good example), taking on a purely reactive perspective is sufficient for the change management challenges financial corporations meet.

This challenge in itself would not be major news. However, two continuing trends in the financial service industry have recently made them a force to be reckoned with.

First, a continuing trend in industries relying heavily on IT is *automation* and *integration* of business processes on the basis of applications. Financial services are no different in this regard. The number of applications can easily range in the hundreds, and the number of dependencies they share – interfaces, processes, organizations – breaks the thousands barrier quite often. One company I know sports well beyond a thousand dependent applications that support or run the business processes, and that is counting only those running on central servers, but not Excel spreadsheets (an apparent favorite of finance and risk professionals) or Access databases. In a word, this web of applications and dependencies gets quite close to resembling a spaghetti bowl. By the way, that company now has about 10 000 employees; others I have seen have more than 60 000, so complexity there is even higher.

Integration and automation normally save money, improve quality, and often lead to better responsiveness. But on the other hand, stronger integration also means that when something goes wrong, the pain will be felt in faraway places: the fault is transmitted seamlessly through the maze of dependencies. Stronger automation in turn means that you may not even take notice before it is too late, because it happens in the virtual world. Thus, as scale grows, the risk of error, omission, or just sheer forgetfulness increases. Beyond a certain size, no single person can understand, let alone control, the complex maze of dependencies that a large organization typically exhibits.

Second, the number of factors constraining banks and insurance companies has grown substantially in the past few years, and investor scrutiny has done its share in raising the level of sophistication that companies must master to pass the test. They now enjoy considerably less liberty in how they operate than five or ten years ago. However, it is not only the sheer number of regulations to comply with or risks to manage, but also the increasing international span that financial operations have attained. It means that constraints can interact or even contradict each other, which makes it increasingly difficult to manage change with the certainty you need to say: 'We have things under control.'

Internationally operating banks and insurance companies have long passed the tipping point, and the impact of changes has begun to bite noticeably. The impressive cost of many a SOX compliance project speaks for this fact. Managing such changes has begun to keep financial institutions busy, and more seems to be coming their way. They must, for a living, understand and sometimes even control that maze. Or, to continue the metaphor used in this book's Introduction: straighten out the spaghetti. But how to do so? The solution starts with the way they look at the problem.

Some changes hurt more than others (see sidebar 'Scoping and relevance'). Those that tend to hurt more are where a lot of complexity and volatility are involved. Humans are really terrible at performing repetitive tasks over a long period of time. Apart from that, we do not like it. We are also really bad at memorizing large chunks of data when they are quite similar. We forget, confuse, and overlook things we should not. To put it shortly, we have real difficulties in the following situations:

- There are numerous objects to be dealt with.
- They exhibit many dependencies.
- There are frequent changes to this maze of objects and dependencies.

Scoping and relevance

With some changes you have no choice but to accept and change accordingly; regulatory reporting and tax deduction requirements are but two such examples. Other changes present no urgent case and you may decide to let the occasion pass or take it up later. It is a good idea to distinguish consciously between changes as they occur and select those of relevance. Systematically managing all changes that occur can require a lot of work, and you may get bogged down in bureaucracy. Some changes may not require the entire company's attention and can safely be handled by those who are closest to the problem. Establishing thresholds and criteria for deciding what is relevant to scope your efforts helps focus on the really important issues. Good examples for thresholds are expected cost impact, risk profile, whether regulatory requirements are concerned, or where an expert concluded that something merits attention.

This may sound rather abstract. I would like to illustrate what is meant with an example: for SOX compliance, a company must typically keep track of its business processes, legal entities, data, and applications relevant to the production of financial statements. The number of

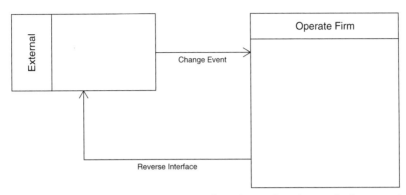

Figure 2.2: External change events alter the interface that a firm has with the outside. In order to handle the impact, the organization must find a systematic way of arriving at the new state. The same holds when the firm is an internal organization and the 'external' actor is some other internal actor

these objects can easily range in the tens of thousands – much more than one individual can memorize. In addition, many processes depend on applications (or vice versa, for that matter), because they are supported by them. There are frequent changes to this network as well: at any given time, the corporation evolves, which gives rise to changes. However, from a SOX perspective, a consistent, correct, and transparent account must be given of how the company has produced its financial reports and whether there were any material issues to be pointed out. This is an inherent conflict of interest, because consistency, correctness, and transparency are challenged by changes, which have a tendency to erode existing order.

The challenge is illustrated in Figure 2.2: an external change can lead to an internal impact; the more numerous the number of objects to change internally, the more complex their dependencies, and the more frequent the external changes occur, the higher the costs and risks attached. In these situations a mechanism to ease the adoption of change is needed.

Metadata management can come to the rescue. Some changes have a uniform impact on a company's internal workings – its processes, data, or applications. In metadata management, we split the adoption of changes into two parts:

- *Structured:* Those parts of a change, as it presents itself to you, which you can easily categorize, classify, relate to each other, or describe and validate with formal rules are captured, along with their properties; an automated mechanism then uses these descriptions, categories, and so on to compute the structured part of the adoption work you need to do.
- *Unstructured:* The remainder part of the change, which does not lend itself to formal capture and methods, is handed to human beings who then figure out manually how the adoption needs to be handled.

Ultimately, structured and unstructured parts are combined to adopt a change. This combination process can take many shapes and forms, and run from very simple to highly sophisticated. A portion of Part III of this book is dedicated to describing what methods are at your disposal in this step.

We thus achieve what is illustrated in Figures 2.3 and 2.4: without metadata management, the adoption of a change may lead to a substantial amount of manual work, which is not structured

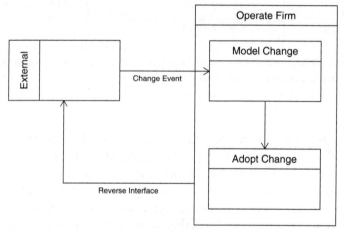

Figure 2.3: Change management without metadata somehow arrives at an internal model commensurate to the change. Then the organization adopts it

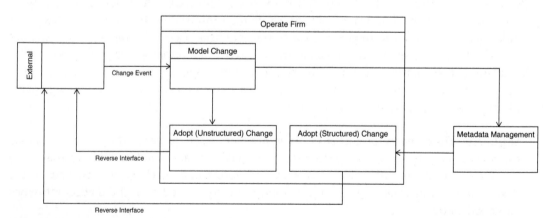

Figure 2.4: Change management with metadata makes a clear distinction between the structured and unstructured part of a change and its adoption. The structured part is then handled with the support of metadata management

systematically. With metadata management, however, we bring changes into a structure of our choosing and then use that structure to automate change adoption. By achieving a high degree of automation we can realize substantial savings, yet at the same time increase quality.

In order to make things more tangible, lets extend the above example. In SOX compliance, we are interested in documenting who authorized changes to applications. However, only those applications that might have a material impact on the financial results are of interest. This can include large mainframe applications, but also spreadsheets with risk calculations on an actuary's desktop. Quite a few applications will not be relevant to SOX. Keeping track of both can be difficult, especially in a globally distributed enterprise.

In one company I know, people used the following hybrid technique: the company ran an inventory of all server-based applications. This inventory was extended to hold, for each application, a marker whether the latter was relevant to SOX. Whenever an existing application was phased out or a new one added, dedicated process activities ensured that the application received its marker. When a statement of compliance was due, all SOX-relevant, server-based applications could be derived automatically. However, for the desktop applications, manual work was still required, which came in the form of line managers asking people around. That worked as well, but at different costs, much more slowly, and with less safety. It required additional measures to mitigate against the risks incurred.

You may think that, ideally, we should structure 100 % of the change and achieve 0 % unstructured implementation work. That is, I am afraid to say, not universally true, but depends strongly on your goals and the environment within which you operate. Part II of this book will talk about that in detail. For the moment just keep in mind that it does usually not work that way.

2.3   The essence of metadata: reification of data

In order to structure change adoption, we need to organize our corporation. One popular way is to look at the *data* that is being processed. For financial services organizations, this is an almost natural way, as they mainly process data, not goods. When looking at data, we emphasize what is being handled, not how or in what order. That data may come in the form of an account balance, a credit score, or the claims for an insurance contract. All these pieces of data are used in business processes such as payments, credit underwriting, and claims management, respectively. To these processes, all that counts are the said pieces of data, which they store, manipulate, erase, or consume. Hence, when an application that supports claims management is designed, it will typically handle data related to the field of claims management: loss events, exclusion clauses, coverage limits, deductibles, and so forth.

As a result, the concerns of managing reserves, taxes, or payment of claims will receive less attention, if any at all. (As a matter of fact, many design methodologies make a point of limiting their scope such that the essentials of the problem at hand are carved out prominently.) Therefore, the design of the solution – the application – may not represent these concerns explicitly, let alone appropriately, in its design. That goes not without consequences: sometimes (or, perhaps more appropriately, quite often) it happens that something about an application must be changed. Imagine that a new statute on reserves has been introduced. The design of the application provides few or even no hints as to where or what must be changed in order to reflect the requirements of the new statute. The hints are not there because one did not leave them when the application was designed.

Applications are but one example of missing data. You can replace them with just about any abstraction. SOX projects have proven so tedious and expensive in part because companies took little or no account of their business processes. When SOX implicitly required them to do so, the processes had to be captured, classified with regard to their relevance, and related to each other so that deficiencies (that might have a material impact on the company's published financial results) could be appropriately handled by process-level controls. These would also apply to the claims management process, as above.

Any such piece of data, be it related to managing reserves or to SOX, must be managed in addition to and separate from claims management itself. It would not make much sense, let alone be practical, to try to wedge every concern existing in the company into one viewpoint: that of the application design. This would burden the design to an extent that people would not see the forest for the trees. However, something to that extent seems necessary, since claims management does indeed touch aspects of reserves and SOX. The trick lies in having one without avoiding the other.

2.3.1   Model separation and data reification

What essentially happens when one designs an application, a business process, or an organization, is that a model of reality is built. This model reflects what, to us, are such important aspects of reality that we want to make sure that certain things about them can be ensured. For example, when a payment process is designed, we want to make sure that we cater for the risk of non-payment due to insolvency, fraud, etc. That is why there are the processes of clearing and settlement. When an application is designed, the integrity of the data it stores will be important to us, which is why we use relational integrity constraints in databases.

Often it is not possible to devise one single viewpoint from which all the forces affecting a design can be resolved easily. Sometimes it works, but quite often complexity rises too quickly, and we get lost in the details, or people disagree what might be the 'right' way of modeling things and the effort gets stalled. (Do you remember the times of 'enterprise data models?') Therefore, it is time to abandon that idea and start to design solutions from different viewpoints *at the same time*: instead of trying to integrate the many different concerns affecting the design (resulting in one unified model), we willfully ignore the interactions between these concerns and separate out different models. These models each insist on their own viewpoint on the world (Figure 2.5).

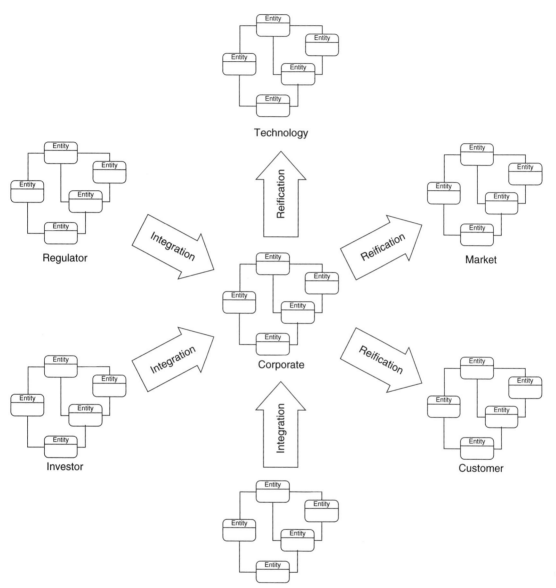

Figure 2.5: During reification, we isolate and externalize specific concerns of a model into another model to manage them separately, from their own viewpoints. Metadata is then used to integrate them into a unified whole

By separating different models we solve one problem, but create another: how and where is the reconciliation of these many different viewpoints supposed to happen? This is where data comes into the picture: models express the structure of the world as we want to see it. Different models may exhibit different elements, relationships, and constraints, but since they are all just models, we can devise a mechanism to relate them to each other. This mechanism is based on yet another model, called a *metamodel* (see sidebar 'Epistemological versus ontological view').

Epistemological versus ontological view

A common theoretical explanation of what metamodels are comes from philosophy: by looking at the world, we obtain an understanding of it based on our own or someone else's observations. This is called the epistemological view. By reasoning about the underlying laws governing the world, we create an ontological view. Hopefully, the epistemological and ontological views are consistent. For the domain of modeling, the model corresponds to the epistemological, and the metamodel to the ontological view. Epistemology and ontology are 'hip' words that you can use during cocktail conversations to impress your audience, but be prepared for your conversation partners to fall asleep or walk away.

'Metamodel': A model of how (other) models can be related to each other.

Based on a metamodel, an algorithm can get us automatically from one model (viewpoint) to the other. For that, the algorithm uses data that describes how they are related, which is accordingly termed *metadata*:

'Metadata': Data that describes, based on a given metamodel, how (other) models are related to each other.

Establishing a metamodel means to *reify* the relationships between the concerns we care about. The step of reification is important, because it enables us to manage the integration of concerns actively: when a claims management application has to comply with SOX and reserve statutes at the same time, while taking care of its actual core business, success comes from giving all three concerns a place of their own right (models) and integrating them systematically using metadata.

It should be noted that reification is not the only mechanism with which changes in complex settings can be managed. Simplification and isolation are two alternatives: by simplifying our models, we can take away some of the complexity that haunts designers and, possibly, achieve an integrated viewpoint on reality without sacrificing the idea of a unified model. By isolating parts of a model, we can manage changes to it in one place, eliminating side effects in

Figure 2.6: Reification, simplification, and isolation all address different reconciliation challenges along the dimensions of method of reconciliation and number of concerns to be reconciled. The challenge at the bottom right you should not strive to take on

faraway corners of the remainder of the model. Simplification effectively transports complexity back into the human world (where it is handled manually), whereas isolation effectively locks complexity into a safe place (where it is handled locally) so it will not emanate from there. From this point forth it should be assumed that before reification, all opportunities for simplification and isolation have been exhausted. Figure 2.6 illustrates what is meant.

Take an example from the banking world, credit products: whether you are taking out a loan on your house or financing your car, the rules will be different. For a home loan, different legal clauses apply and different types of collateral are permitted. In Switzerland you may post your 2nd pillar pension (which is private but partially paid for by your employer) as collateral, but in Germany you cannot. Financing your car may require the bank to ask you for different types of collateral and insist on certain clauses. The clauses themselves may be mutually inclusive or exclusive, and the rules when they are will change over time. Due to a change in Swiss legislation a while ago that was intended to protect consumers, banks were required to inform their clients specifically about when it was illegal to grant credit to individuals (namely when they would become over-indebted). Each new contract had to be signed with that specific clause included. Given all the different types of credit products, banks had to adapt their contract forms, but only for consumer credits, not those granted to institutions.

In this situation, a bank will have been glad to have known from their databases which credit products are of type 'consumer' and which are not. They will have been even more glad to reify the notion of a 'clause' in a form, so they could simply add the new legally required text to all their consumer credit forms.

But what actually happens when we use models in such a way? What are we doing when we reconcile modeling viewpoints, and what does that have to do with change?

2.3.2   Model evolution, mapping, and integration

There are basically three different ways of using metadata, namely for *model evolution, model mapping*, and *model integration*. Evolution, mapping, and integration are essentially part of the same story, and the techniques required for them are identical. However, I would like to keep them conceptually separate, because they address different needs.

'Model evolution': Taking one specific modeling viewpoint and one model as its starting point, focuses on transforming the model such that it addresses changes in the real world that have occurred over time and must now be reflected *by* the model.

'Model mapping': Taking two specific modeling viewpoints and one model as its starting point, focuses on transforming the model such that it can be seen from the *other* viewpoint than it was designed from.

'Model integration': Taking two specific modeling viewpoints and two models as its starting point, focuses on merging the models in such a way that both can be mapped to a *third*, unified model.

Evolution is typically seen when changes occur within your realm of control. All that is required is for you to decide what an appropriate change in the model is in order to reflect the changes in the real world. For example, when your company changes its profit center structure to react to business needs, business associated with old profit centers must be updated to reflect the new ones. You are free to choose an appropriate (new) profit center model, but it must update the (old) profit center associations.

Mapping is used when one viewpoint exerts a dominant force over the other. For example, when your company acquires another company, the business processes, organizational structure, and applications of the acquiring part will typically take precedence over those of the other. Consequently, the latter will have to align its own way of doing business with that of the partner, which may mean migrating data, adapting business processes, or reorganizing teams. Another good example is regulatory changes: when regulators require new or different reports about a corporation's activities, it must adapt to that requirement and map its own (internal) models to the outside (external) ones.

Integration is used when there is no dominant viewpoint, but several equally important, or viable if you wish, viewpoints. Integration is achieved by choosing (designing, identifying, developing, etc., you name it) a unifying viewpoint to which the existing models are mapped. This may be considered a generic case of mapping, with an artificial viewpoint coming in from the outside. However, practice shows that integration is typically 'messy,' to an extent that the unified viewpoint is not easily identified, but more likely to be discovered over a longer time period. Hence, methodological concerns (i.e., how to arrive at the desired goal) play a much larger role in integration than in mapping. For example, in a merger of equals, the merging companies will have to settle for a joint viewpoint about how the combined enterprise will operate. However, due to the many dependencies, this will not be decided once and then implemented. There may also be more than one 'ideal' way of looking at things. In fact, the notion of 'optimal' may be elusive in such scenarios. Instead, an initial viewpoint will be defined and evolved over time as knowledge grows. As another example, consider the financial electronic commerce formerly known as business-to-business. In this area, standards are sometimes not as hard-fast as in other industries. Take, for example, the ACORD range of (insurance) standards. They provide formally defined models, but these must be reconciled with the exchanging companies' (internal) viewpoints, which typically requires these partners to settle for a joint understanding, or interpretation if you wish, of the standard. In this scenario, strategic company goals, market politics, and other concerns come into play. Needless to say, this has little to do with a rational calculation but requires a methodological approach to converge towards an integrated viewpoint, irrespective of why and where deviations from the ideal occur.

All three cases are instances of model transformation, yet they focus on different types of changes. Your choice of technique depends on how much control you exert over the modeling viewpoint; that is, how things may, or perhaps more accurately, are to be seen.

2.3.3   Understanding and executing change

There are two ways to put metadata to use: passively and actively. As you will see later in this chapter, this corresponds directly with the type of process within which you use it. However, for the moment let us focus on why we use it in such ways, and what makes the distinction so important.

First, passive metadata: this comprises metadata that is used or created to support the understanding of the nature and impact of changes. Examples include:

- Compliance: where in the company are we not yet aligned with a given requirement? As an example, take process-level controls in Sarbanes-Oxley: by designating certain processes as relevant to the act, we can check them and thus assess alignment. Nothing about the processes themselves is changed.
- Risk: what is the inherent risk of engaging in a certain activity? As an example, take portfolio management in investment: by using a market model, the composition of the portfolio is analyzed for sensitivity with respect to certain market movements in order to identify viable investments. The market model is used to assess the portfolio, but nothing about either is changed in any way.

- Quality: does an object under scrutiny meet certain requirements? As an example, take data validation in electronic commerce: based on the data model agreed with an outside partner, data delivered can be checked for correctness and consistency. The model determines what is correct and consistent, it does not lead to the creation of anything.
- Structure: what is the impact of a given change on an object of interest? As an example, consider the separation of the Czech Republic and Slovakia: by using data about the composition of the market and our business, we can decide whether it makes sense to split our business units by country or by line of business.
- Semantics: what is the meaning of the terms and words with which we are dealing? As an example, take the business terminology used in accounting: by documenting the requirements of the US-GAAP, accountants in an insurance company can understand how to treat certain types of assets or liabilities in the different accounts. The documentation only provides a basis for such an understanding, it does not steer or control it.

Second, active metadata: this comprises metadata that is used or created to effect the adoption and implementation of changes. Examples include:

- Configuration settings: how are things linked together? For example, order routing in equities trading requires the direction of the flow of incoming orders to market makers based on the type of order, available market prices, or expected speed of execution. The configuration of a routing application determines what takes precedence over the other; that is, for instance, whether speed beats price or vice versa.
- Business rules: which rules apply in the operation of the business, and what are their characteristics? For example, consider trading once more, namely taxes to be paid after trading a certain type of asset: by grouping assets into classes, the machinery can be fed business rules based upon which taxes are automatically deducted and set aside.
- Data mappings: how is data that is captured based on one model to be transformed into the representation of another model? For example, during the merger of two companies the customer base of one merger partner may have to be migrated to the customer base of the other partner. Chances are that the two data models are not the same. A mapping of representations may perhaps map the currency codes used in one model to those in the other.

The distinction between passive and active metadata is relevant because humans play a different role in its creation and consumption: both types are created by humans, but whereas passive metadata is exclusively consumed by humans, active metadata is mostly consumed by machinery. Consequently, the scope of where you may actually be able to identify, capture, and maintain metadata is different, as are the quality requirements for its management.

2.4 The essence of metadata management: coupling processes for systematic change

2.4.1 Different types of processes

One popular way of organizing a corporation is built around business processes as the main abstraction. Processes are readily understood by both technical and business people alike, which is critical to getting an insight into the implications for both sides. Processes also give way to an event-oriented focus, which is natural to understanding a reactive activity like change adoption. Finally, they are extremely helpful in scoping. This becomes critical when the design space needs to be set, thus helping to assess value creation properly.

Functional organization emphasizes arranging similar practices or disciplines in the same way – like procurement, development, or sales – , whereas *process organization* looks at what business data is dealt with and manipulated as part of that corporation's operation, such as orders, contracts, or liabilities.

Processes have as their focus the creation of value for their customers. This aids the optimization of value creation for the parties who ultimately receive the goods or service offered. Since any corporation of reasonable size interconnects a multitude of processes, people have come to distinguish different types. These types serve to emphasize their characteristic differences, which aids in selecting, managing, and optimizing them:

- *Core processes* are concerned with creating immediate value for customers. They are the visible face, be it an (external) company or an (internal) unit. Examples include underwriting, investment, or payments.
- *Support processes* generate (internal) goods or services that are required to execute core processes in an efficient and effective manner. This specifically includes activities required to provide the resources for creating those goods and services, like buildings, people, or applications. Examples include legal affairs, human resources, or information technology.
- *Steering processes* are concerned with cross-cutting concerns to maintain, direct, and develop other processes in the interest of increased efficiency and effectiveness, like controlling, budgeting, or scoping.

The division of processes into core, support, and steering processes is recursive. This means that a support process can be carved up again, resulting in core (support), support (support), and (support) steering processes.

It is generally accepted that information technology constitutes a support process (Figure 2.7). It is less commonly agreed, though reasonably safe to say, that information technology itself can be divided into the following processes:

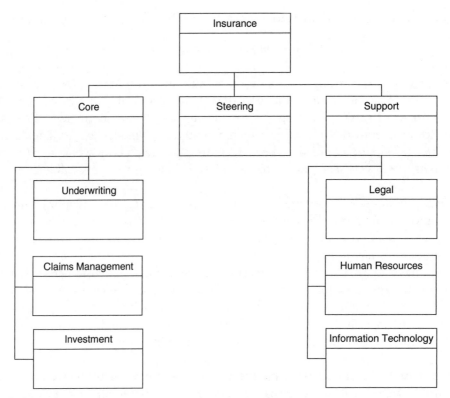

Figure 2.7: Generic process hierarchy of an insurance company

- Core: development (build) and operations (run) of applications (solutions).
- Support: architecture, procurement, project management.
- Steering: financials, governance, procurement, human resources.

These processes form the context within which metadata management must be embedded. The next section explains how and where that actually happens.

2.4.2   How business, IT, and metadata management are coupled

Metadata management is an information technology support process that ties in with other processes in characteristic ways. It always operates within a context where the following processes are present (Figure 2.8):

'Introduce Object (Process)': Officially starts the lifecycle of an object.

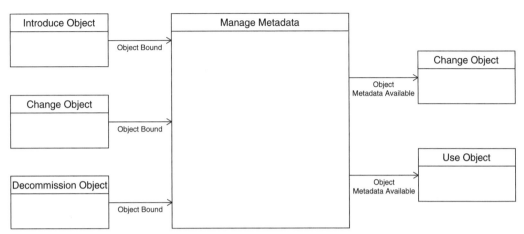

Figure 2.8: The context of metadata management activity. Once an object subject to metadata management is bound, activity starts and finally results in the availability of metadata for downstream processes

'Decommission Object (Process)': Officially terminates the lifecycle of an object.

'Change Object (Process)': Across an object's lifecycle, this process changes the state of the object.

'Use Object (Process)': During an object's lifetime, this process makes use of the object within the frame of its designated purpose.

Object here means anything you care enough about to manage it explicitly. If there is no object, there is no need to capture metadata about it. Events occuring as part of introduction and decommissioning thus effectively demarcate the frame within which metadata management takes over responsibilities.

Some examples may better explain what the above processes are about: the acquisition of a legal entity, the closure of an insurance contract, and the deployment of an application all introduce new objects. The lifecycle of a legal entity begins with its acquisition; that of an insurance contract with the start of its contractual validity period; that of an application at the point of deployment. Similarly, the sale of the legal entity, time passing the end of the insurance contract validity period, and the ultimate deinstallation of the application mark the respective end of lifecycle.

Metadata management supports different uses of and different changes to these objects, all from different viewpoints. From the viewpoint of financial reporting, for example, it will be of interest whether the legal entity contributes significantly to financial results of the owning company, maybe by merit of it being a wholly owned subsidiary. Corresponding metadata may cover the relationships between reporting processes and to the legal entities that may have a material impact on reported figures. This will in turn be used in financial reporting, ensuring capture of all material deficiencies per legal entity, propagating them up the reporting chain to arrive at an aggregated deficiency result to be included in the annual report for SOX compliance. From a risk viewpoint, the insurance contract leads to exposure to different perils, with associated terms, limits, deductibles, and so on. This can be used by a risk management tool to monitor and adjust capital allocation and reserves. The tool will use metadata to compute required reserves from the interplay of perils, limits, deductibles, or location. If these turn out to be no longer justified, the metamodel used in the computation needs be adjusted. This happened, for example, after September 11, 2001, when insurers discovered that this new form of terrorism caused claims across a multitude of lines of business (life, health, property, business interruption, casualty), rendering void their terrorism cover models, which were often based on fire insurance risk models.

The role of metadata management is to ensure the appropriate selection of metadata (including the definition of the metamodel), and to capture and maintain that metadata on behalf of its consumers across the lifecycle of the objects concerned. In this context, metadata management organizes metadata such that, across the lifecycle of an object, certain key properties are ensured. First and foremost, all of the above triggers must lead to activity that updates the required metadata. As a result, said metadata is made available and can be used in other processes. Thus we finally arrive at the definition of metadata management:

> 'Manage Metadata (Process)': Selects, captures, and maintains metadata about objects, with the objective of controlling and supporting changes to objects.

Metadata management is an IT support process (Figure 2.9). It is obviously part of IT. However, it is not part of the core activities, which is to build and run IT solutions. It is also not a steering process. It merely supports IT practitioners in their adapting to changes. More specifically, note that building applications is the central activity during which the model of the application is created, and running it is where that model is used. The model is stable for the duration of use, which is why any changes to it require a new release of the application be built. However, if those parts of the model that change more frequently or have an intricate impact on the application design can be reified and externalized, they can be managed separately on a different schedule and even, where desired, by different people. What thus effectively happens is that different core processes related to change (change application, change insurance product, change regulatory rule, etc.) with different occurrence frequency can live side by side without getting into each others' way. This opens up new possibilities in designing processes for the frequency of the events they need.

This last point is important. Traditionally, application development is a single process that takes into account all the viewpoints relevant to its design, to arrive at a single model that caters to them. This is not only difficult from a modeling perspective (i.e., how to reconcile

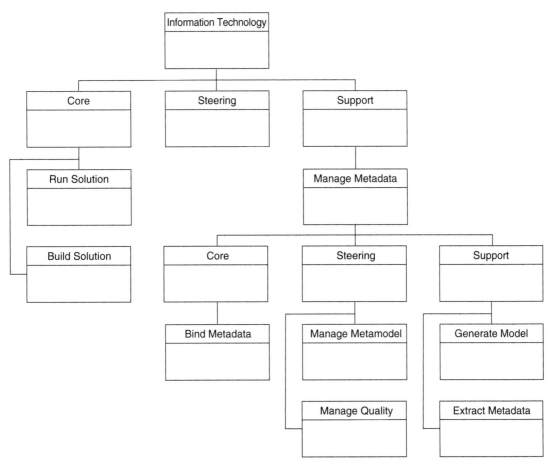

Figure 2.9: Metadata management is an information technology support processes, supporting the core processes of building and running solutions

all different viewpoints) and from a change management perspective (e.g., to decide when some desired change can finally be implemented because we have to wait for a new release each time). It is also less than optimal because the processes, people, roles, and responsibilities required to cater to the different viewpoints are all crammed into one effort: building an application. With metadata management, however, this is wholly different. Now we can set up separate processes, organizations, and models that each cater to the specific needs of their viewpoint. The application needs only provide the technical mechanisms to integrate them via metadata management techniques (which themselves are sufficiently stable not to interfere with the core of the application).

Of special interest therefore are the events that trigger activities to *bind* metadata, and the results that need to be achieved to reach that said goal:

'Object Introduced (Trigger)': The object has begun its lifecycle. Metadata about it can now be captured.

'Object Bound (Trigger)': The state of the object (may have) changed and can henceforth be considered frozen with respect to the viewpoint for which the metamodel was conceived. It is now safe to capture and store metadata about the object.

'Object Decommissioned (Trigger)': The object has reached the end of its lifecycle. The metadata captured about it can safely be removed.

'Object Metadata Available (Result)': Signals the (renewed) availability of up-to-date metadata about an object after it was bound.

Metadata management is part of IT. It relates to the business by way of its support for a closed loop of metadata capture and use along the lifecycle of objects. Figure 2.9 shows a real-life example of the context in Figure 2.8, the maintenance and analysis of product classifications in applications. It was taken from the worldwide standard for master data management at a reinsurer.

First of all, the objects: there are two of them, applications and attributes. Applications (like a data warehouse or an underwriting application) use master data attributes. The underwriting application may store particular contract terms, for example the types of peril covered by the contract, whereas the data warehouse may calculate key figures, such as the total exposure for a given peril across the contract portfolio.

The list of values in an attribute is subject to change. For example, new perils like 'genetically modified organism' or 'nanotechnology' may have to be covered for industrial liability insurance contracts. When the company decides it wishes to do so, that constitutes a change of type 'introduce type of peril.' As a consequence, the applications using the attribute 'type of peril' may have to be changed. Consequently, an impact analysis must be performed to establish the cost of change and plan it. Once that is done, the new peril type must be propagated to the applications using it so that it becomes available. Timelines, rollout plans, etc. must be defined and followed up on.

In this situation, we need metadata from the viewpoint of dependencies – which application uses which attributes – and membership – which value belongs to the particular attribute 'type of peril.' Once it is available, it is possible to assess the (potential) impact of changes to the attribute on applications using it, and systematically propagate the change throughout the application landscape. As part of the metadata management process, which here is more appropriately called 'manage business terminology' (because master data is modeled using business terms), we record the list of values in the attribute 'type of peril,' the dependencies, as well as the portfolio of applications. If we considered more than just the 'type of peril,' we would also record the portfolio of attributes (as is actually the case there). In any event, once we have this metadata available, we can support changes to applications and attributes at the same time.

Back to the coupling of IT, business, and metadata management. Each time a new application starts using our particular attribute (an IT event), or when it ceases to do so, metadata management kicks in. The same applies when some change is applied to the 'type of peril' (a business event). Metadata management (de- and re-) couples both business and IT in the following systematic way:

- *Separation of concerns (at the data level):* IT and business can change independent of each other. To an application it is now of lesser concern which exact peril types are of importance to business. Similarly, business need not worry about ensuring that each application in the company uses the most current list of perils. More specifically, both parties' models of the world are effectively decoupled.
- *Integration of concerns (at the process level):* when a change in either realm occurs, metadata management ensures that all necessary steps are taken to adopt the change in all applications and attributes affected. More specifically, both parties' change processes are effectively coupled, though change impact typically flows in only one direction: from business to IT.

It is important to note what has happened here: you are now capable of establishing a model of the world from your own viewpoint, irrespective of what other viewpoints there may be. Metadata management ensures you can do so without compromising your ability to change this and that about your model, *and* safely adapt changes from some other viewpoint.

Coming back to the example at the beginning of this chapter, the benefits are clear: the applications of a corporation are the manifestation of the company's model of the world. However, that model is influenced by a multitude of other viewpoints (regulatory, risk, technology, customers, etc.), which make change management, well, a little difficult. Metadata management gives us the concepts and tools to manage the situation systematically: first, we decouple the viewpoints so that they can be treated separately. Second, we establish the change events that (may) have an impact on our own and other's viewpoints. Third, we design and set up the processes for managing the changes as they come along. The next section highlights the details.

2.4.3   Constituent processes of metadata management

How does metadata management achieve what it does? As you can see in Figures 2.9 and 2.11, you can divide metadata management into core, steering, and support processes as follows:

'Bind Metadata (Process)': After a change to an object has occurred, capture and store metadata about it for later use.

Binding metadata is an activity that can take many different forms. Sometimes it will simply be captured manually. This is mostly the case when metadata is inaccessible or beyond one's control. In a few cases, however, it will be available in a different form, in which case it can be transformed. And then there are those cases where metadata can be extracted from the model data itself, an activity that is called metadata extraction:

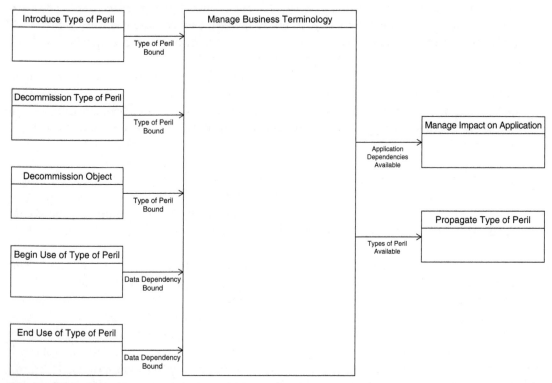

Figure 2.10: Metadata management activities in business terminology management as seen by the data language. Activities and lifecycle events not shown are the introduction and decommissioning of applications

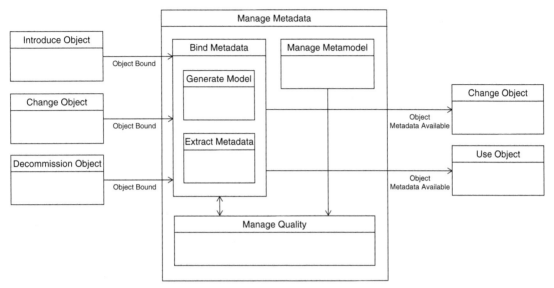

Figure 2.11: Interplay of metadata management processes and their embedding in the business context

> 'Extract Metadata (Process)': Given an object and a model about it, extract from the object metadata by taking its properties as seen by the model, using them (and, optionally, additional data provided elsewhere) to infer properties as seen by the metamodel.

A typical metadata extraction activity is to generate a conceptual data model from a given physical data model. In this case, the mapping between the two is inferred from the physical model, perhaps using input from the original designer to disambiguate situations where different mappings are possible.

> 'Manage Metamodel (Process)': Based on the goals and scope of a given effort, maintain a metamodel that supports the evolution, integration, or mapping of given models.

> 'Manage Quality (Process)': Ensure that, given stated quality criteria, the metadata complies with these criteria.

Managing the metamodel and metadata quality are the central activities in managing metadata. The metamodel describes what form the metadata may take. It describes what constitutes valid, actual, consistent, complete, or useful metadata. In the quality management process, this is used to ensure that all metadata stored complies with these rules or, if it does not, will be corrected to do so again within a reasonable timeframe. I emphasize the quality management aspect so much because it is a crucial element in most (if not all) metadata management solutions. Quality deficits must be systematically managed, because your sources of metadata will usually not be 100 % reliable. If you do not tackle quality deficits from the start, you risk losing your customers.

> 'Generate Model (Process)': Based on stored metadata, automate the adoption of changes to objects.

Model generation is perhaps the most popular form of metadata use, especially in developer circles – code generation being one of its best-known instances. Formally, I consider it not to be part of metadata management itself: it is a particular form of using metadata. However, since the activity would never exist without metadata in the first place, and also because the case of metadata extraction is kind of comparable, I include it here.

How do all of the above processes work together in managing metadata? To understand that, consider Figure 2.12. Once we have a metamodel, we can use it for managing metadata quality

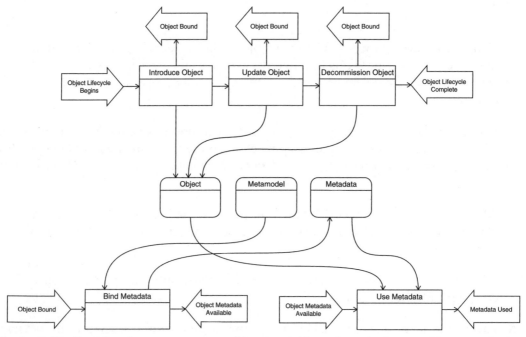

Figure 2.12: Data flow between processes. Metadata is always bound when an object experiences a lifecycle event. The origins of the metamodel are not shown to keep the diagram simple

(which typically reads, but sometimes also creates, updates, or deletes metadata when required to restore quality). Metadata is brought into existence by binding it manually or automatically (metadata extraction). From then on, assuming it has the appropriate quality, it can be used to change objects manually or automatically (model generation), or simply understand what they are about. As such, the status of a object can be changed not only by (external) events, but also by metadata management activity.

This is the previously mentioned closed loop: binding metadata (passively) uses objects and (actively) creates metadata; objects can be (passively) changed by external events or (actively) by using metadata. Hence, by mixing and matching active and passive use of data and metadata in a manual or automatic fashion, metadata management puts itself in the middle of the change management process. It supports the adoption of changes by first systematically separating, then coupling different viewpoints.

2.5   What is 'meta'? What isn't?

Based on my selection of examples so far, you may hesitate to identify a particular piece of data as 'meta,' or in fact not 'meta.' In fact, there is no such thing as an intrinsic 'meta-ness.' It is a relative property, a matter of your choice. The choice is oriented along the lines of your own core process. If you consider certain objects that your core processes deal with as 'out of scope' (e.g., because you have no control over their lifecycle), but the cost and risk of adopting changes in them or ensuring compliance is high enough, then you may want to consider reification. Metadata is then something for you to consider. It is mostly a question of the value proposition. Part II of this book is dedicated to discussing where this is most likely to pay back.

In some areas, tradition has come to define what is considered 'meta.' In IT, for example, the structure and composition of data models, software package dependencies, or configuration settings are considered metadata. However, that is a software developer's viewpoint, who regards the construction of a software product as his or her core process, and data about what is being produced as secondary. To a software architect, however, the product itself may be of secondary interest. Instead, he or she will focus on managing the portfolio of software products from the view point of component reuse or operational risk by using data models, software package dependencies, and configuration settings directly. To this role, this data is not 'meta' at all. The software architect supports the software developer in the achievement of his or her goals, but their respective relevant data and processes are orthogonal.

I have found this aspect of metadata management to be the most difficult to convey. This has, in part, to do with precedent: technically minded (IT) people rarely hesitate to use the 'm-word' liberally, whereas I have seen too many business people's eyes glaze over rather quickly as soon as it is used. It just seems odd to them. However, the notion of a portfolio is not alien to them. I have therefore come to prefer describing metadata to business people as data that is used to manage portfolios in a structured fashion, and metadata management as the process of doing so in a controlled way. They often understand this description and the 'm-word' need not be used.

I would also like to point out again that not everything that can be reified should be reified. Relevance is a function of many parameters, and you should not forget the costs attached. Therefore, although something may rightfully be considered 'meta,' it does not immediately follow that it has to be elevated to that status. Distinguishing different levels of abstraction is a conceptually tricky business, and some problems are just not big enough to merit this extra expense.

3

Aligning Business and IT: the Role of Metadata, Strategy, and Architecture

Language has an enormous influence on our perception of reality. Not only does it affect how and what we think about, but also how we perceive things in the first place. Rather than serving merely as a passive vehicle for containing our thoughts, language has an active influence on the shape of our thoughts.

William Kent in *Data and Reality*

3.1 Overview

- Alignment is of interest along the dimensions of cost, risk, and compliance. It must be ensured across the lifecycle of a solution and re-assessed before, during, or after changes.
- Alignment requires two models, designed from the solution and compliance viewpoints, respectively. They are bridged with a metamodel that reifies how compliance can be achieved.
- Managing exceptions is required when bureaucracy is to be avoided. The metamodel used for alignment may offer many specific modes of alignment, but one generic, catch-all mode is required to handle exceptions.
- Alignment with architecture, specifically to support the adoption of standards, is supported by metadata. Architectural building blocks and their relationships become abstractions in the metamodel.

Aligning Business and IT with Metadata   Hans Wegener
© 2007 John Wiley & Sons, Ltd.

- Evolution of a solutions portfolio towards standards is supported *ex-ante* by helping to identify standardization opportunities, while helping to identify *ex-post* solutions that are not compliant.
- Business and IT model design quality influences the effectiveness and usefulness of metadata. Metamodeling cannot completely compensate for a lack of separation of concerns.

3.2   Change, alignment, models, and metadata

Each external change that leads to internal impact requires you to reassess how far the new status quo is still in alignment with the stated goals of the corporation. Triggers can be found in many places, for example the merger with or the acquisition of a competitor, the adoption of a new technology, or the evolution of the products and services offered. Of course, for the adoption of a change to be a reliable process, you want it to be executed systematically so to reduce risks and avoid needless effort, especially when the scale is sufficiently large.

Alignment can be required along a host of dimensions. In this book, performance, risk, and compliance will be looked at:

- *Performance:* Relates to improving the (financial) input necessary to obtain a certain output (the cost) as well as reducing the (production) time (the latency) required before it is obtained. In many ways, this is about achieving efficiency gains.
- *Risk:* Tries to assess, control, transfer, and avoid exposure to events that may lead to (financial) loss.
- *Compliance:* Controls company activities such that existing rules and regulations are followed. Minimizes the risk of lawsuits because of a violation of regulatory duties, and public embarrassment because of immoral or unprofessional conduct. Compliance can be seen as part of managing operational, legal, or reputational risks.

Risk and compliance have become of greater concern to companies recently, but performance, especially cost savings, has always been on the agenda.

Alignment means that viewpoints need be integrated to establish a compliant whole. This 'whole' (which, for obvious reasons, I would like to call 'solution' from this point forward) can be many things: an application, a business process, a legal entity, or just about anything you may choose. 'Compliance' in turn means that the rules and requirements (as seen from a specific viewpoint and/or alignment dimension) are fulfilled by the solution in its entirety. For example:

- You may want to reduce the cost of changing the terms of your loan contracts to less than 100 000 USD end-to-end (inception to implementation). The solution in this case is

a loan contract's list of terms, and compliance means that the upward cost bound is not exceeded.
- The delay from recognizing a new type of peril worthy of capture to its appearance on the entry forms of all the company's applications is less than three weeks. The solution is the list of perils, and compliance means the deadline is met.
- The residual system risk of operating a particular application is smaller than 100 000 USD/year of losses at 99 % confidence level. The solution is the application, and compliance means that the risk is lower than the stated limit.
- A given application is 'secure'. The solution is the application, compliance may mean that all cross-tier communication is encrypted, users are strongly authenticated, and all access to the system is managed via roles and granted by the data owner.

It is important to note two things. First, a solution has a lifecycle. It comes into existence, does its job, is perhaps altered, extended (in a word: evolves), and finally, some day it is decommissioned. These events mark changes in its composition and state, which are subject to governance, that is a reassessment of its alignment. Second, a solution is dealt with from an individual, scoped-to-purpose viewpoint. An application is built for a specific purpose, a contract term serves some stated need, and a peril may have to be recognized for a technical reason. That viewpoint is typically not identical to the viewpoint from which alignment is required. The latter usually takes on a holistic, company-wide perspective. Therefore, the process of managing the lifecycle of the solution and the process of aligning it with goals and statutes must find some form of coexistence and, for it to be actionable, be based on some form of method.

Here is how: we need to make sure that the model used for constructing (in the case of an application) or organizing (in the case of human activities like business processes enacted by people) a solution respects faithfully the regulations with which it needs to be compliant. For that to be verifiable in some sort of process, and for it to be based on a methodical approach, the rules stipulated by a regulation need to be reified (in a model) as well. All that remains is to answer the question of how the two relate to each other. That is, what *form of alignment* has been chosen.

You arrive at two different modeling viewpoints plus an integrating third, the metamodeling viewpoint: an individual, solution-oriented world; a governance, cross-cutting perspective; and the alignment viewpoint (Figure 3.1). But what have we thus achieved from the point of view of systematic alignment?

- Two viewpoints have been effectively separated: the solution is constructed in (relative) isolation from the concerns of the governance viewpoint. This separation of concerns helps keep them manageable and intelligible. More specifically, the models corresponding to the viewpoints can be expressed in a fashion adequate to the problem they intend to serve.

- Where necessary, bridges between both models are erected and expressed in the form of a metamodel. It reifies the specific ways both worlds can relate to each other. More specifically, the mapping offered between abstractions of the individual and governance viewpoint will cater to the ways in which the corporation treats both.

What effectively happens here is that *we reify the peculiar ways in which a solution can achieve compliance* with respect to a particular realm of governance in the form of a meta-model, and capture the particular way a solution does so in the form of metadata, thereby making it accessible to systematic assessment and exploitation. But it goes beyond that: by emphasizing or omitting abstractions, the designer of the metamodel makes it possible for the corporation to understand, steer, and correct the stance it takes with respect to alignment in general.

Why would that be of interest? First of all, as soon as data about alignment is available, systematic 'to be' versus 'as is' comparisons become possible. This is immensely helpful in transition management, as it makes explicit the difference between where we stand and where we want to be. With the constant flux of changes affecting corporations today, keeping track of the many concerns is a continuous exercise in transition management. Another reason for being interested is that alignment takes on a tangible nature. If you can demonstrate to an investor that you are able not only to produce a compliance report for current regulation, but also demonstrate how big the gap is to upcoming regulations, their confidence in you will almost certainly rise. Finally, by providing to designers 'prêt-à-porter' abstractions for describing the alignment of an envisioned or existing solution, it makes it easier for both the governor and the designer to express and assess compliance.

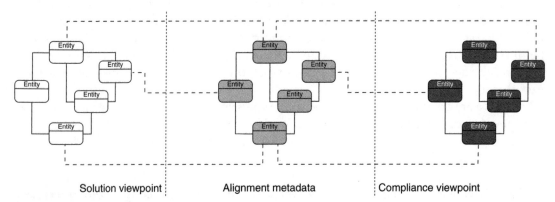

Solution viewpoint   Alignment metadata   Compliance viewpoint

Figure 3.1: Alignment requires three models, one designed from a solution viewpoint, one from the compliance viewpoint, and the alignment metamodel. Each has its own model elements and relationships (solid lines), while only the alignment metamodel maps corresponding abstractions (dashed lines)

Metadata can objectify and make transparent in what manner and to what degree your company aligns itself with a given compliance viewpoint. Transparency and, to a certain extent, objective facts are invaluable tools in demonstrating that you are indeed on top of things.

But that is just the data side of things. From a process perspective, the exact same pattern is applied (Figures 3.2 and 3.3): a solution is designed, constructed, organized, or brought into the world in some other fashion. The associated activities correspond to a project or initiative. It delivers a result and then concludes. Delivery is the trigger to bind alignment metadata. Depending on whether any lack of compliance is detected after the fact (*ex-post*) or prevented before the fact (*ex-ante*), the metadata is used right away or later.

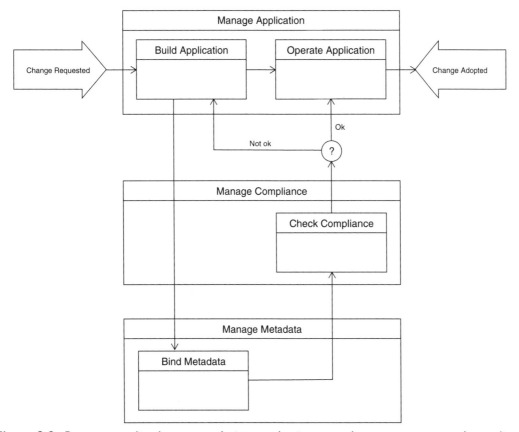

Figure 3.2: Process coupling between solution production, metadata management, and compliance management *ex-ante*. When compliance is checked before a solution is introduced, metadata management acts as a gatekeeper. Events triggering metadata management activity have been omitted for clarity

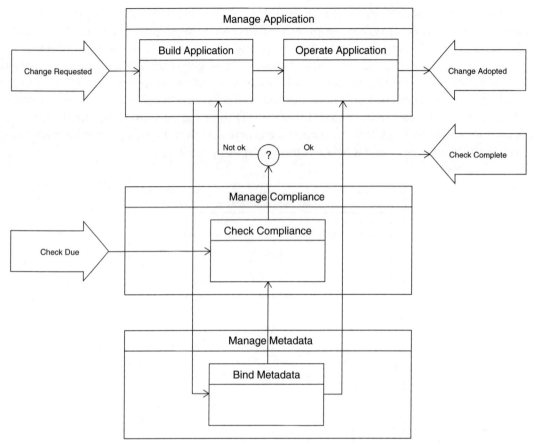

Figure 3.3: Process coupling between solution production, metadata management, and compliance management *ex-post*. When compliance is checked after the fact it acts as a kind of depository, and corrective action is taken separately instead of on the spot. Events triggering metadata management activity have been omitted for clarity

3.2.1 Layers of abstraction: business versus IT

A specific challenge is ensuring alignment between business and IT. This is more of an internal task for a company, but an important one, because so many business processes are enacted and almost all of its relevant data stored by applications. Metadata management can play a supportive role.

In a way, all that it takes is to transfer the above considerations to the world of IT. What previously may have been a regulatory authority now becomes your company's business gremium; what formerly was the company now becomes your IT. Changes are triggered by business decisions, which IT needs to map to its own way of thinking.

Hence, in order to align business and IT, we need two modeling viewpoints, which refines our perspective on the corporation (Figure 3.4):

- The *business model* emphasizes the concepts important to the business. This includes the company's core processes, which are closest to the heart of what creates value for customers, but also steering processes that align its activities with the needs of external factors, such as regulators or investors.
- The *IT model* focuses on the technical means to support the business efficiently. It specifically aligns itself with the business model and the (external factor) technology. For example, IT may want to reconsider previous technology decisions in the light of newly available products or techniques.

The IT model will (predominantly) allude to technological concepts and the business model to financial industry concepts. Aligning both means bridging the two worlds and providing a *trace* as to what corresponds to what and where. For example, we may want to know which application supports which business process and during what activity in order to change them systematically towards new requirements.

By separating business and IT, we achieve two things. First, we can more clearly assign responsibilities for internal activities according to their nature. Technology decisions can now be driven from within the IT department, because the nature of these questions is much clearer. The IT model makes explicit what IT cares about, just as the business model makes clearer what is important to business. We decouple business and IT. Second, activities related to alignment with external parties can be assigned more clearly to one or the other area of responsibility. IT will care about progress in the technology arena, about the most recent standards and methods that make them more effective. Business, on the other side, to a large extent does not need to worry about this particular problem. We put the responsibility where the knowledge is.

We only need to get the alignment right, which is a task to be supported by metadata management. In terms of the business process and data perspective, IT is at a great advantage. Most of what it produces can be clearly delineated, described in a systematic fashion, and analyzed for its properties. In addition, and this is a very helpful property, it is made effective in a single, defined step when a change in the IT world is made permanent. For software, this moment is deployment; for data, this moment is a transaction. Therefore, for alignment between business and IT, this is the very point where metadata can and must be bound.

You may have noticed that by separating the two different modeling viewpoints we have effectively introduced a division of labor: methodologically, modeling activity will concern itself with different goals for the business and IT viewpoints. The people involved in these

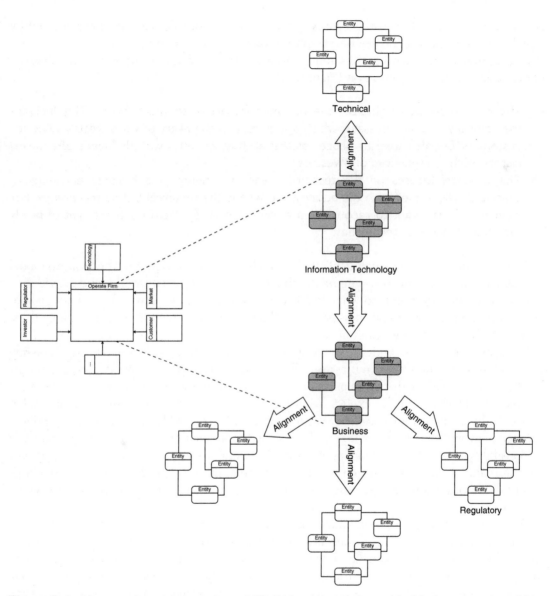

Figure 3.4: Alignment between business and IT within a corporation, and with the external world

activities will typically have different skills and use different methods to formalize requirements. The choice is somewhat arbitrary, because one may just as well prefer three or four viewpoints (see sidebar 'Handling more than two viewpoints'). Essentially, this is a question of how far you want to drive it. A time-honored principle is not to over-specialize. With each new viewpoint you introduce a new specialty, methodology, and a set of skills required to master it. This can get very complex, because for each specialty you need an organization that backs it with experience. Typically this is not what is desired, which is why I will keep with this coarse-grained division.

Handling more than two viewpoints

There are quite a few ways to further subdivide viewpoints. For example, in IT architecture, it is possible to distinguish between data, process, application, technology, and operational architecture, which requires you to manage five different viewpoints. Some companies do this, but I know of none that manages to keep them all in sync. Factually these companies manage five isolated viewpoints that somehow touch but rarely truly integrate with each other.

Another popular way of subdividing viewpoints is along the lines of standards, which sees technology-neutral, technology-specific, company-neutral, and company-specific viewpoints. Technology and company are proxies for IT and business, so essentially this carves up both the business and IT viewpoints into two. I personally think that this works reasonably well for IT, but on the business side of things it soon gets difficult to form abstractions.

From a conceptual perspective there is no reason to stick with merely two viewpoints, but something seems to break down along the way as the number of viewpoints rises. The net effect is that the rigidity required when juggling so many of them jeopardizes its success.

3.2.2   Dealing with reality: managing exceptions

An important challenge in governance in general and alignment in particular is to avoid the bureaucracy trap: by formalizing relationships between different viewpoints, we emphasize (or disregard) certain aspects relating to how they correlate. Of course it would be desirable to capture, manage, and analyze metadata at the lowest level of detail. However, the more detail we emphasize, the more we force participants into a straightjacket, because they must provide all the detail requested in order to describe their particular way of alignment.

Sometimes, however, bureaucracy is not even the problem. A solution may rightfully claim that it would not be appropriate to force it into compliance. There is a multitude of reasons for granting exceptions. Here again the question comes up how to describe it.

We need to strike a balance between the principal need to describe alignment, while providing leeway for exceptions. This is typically decided on an individual basis, for which reason there cannot be clear-cut recommendations, but the tradeoff is normally between these two concerns:

- *Comprehensiveness of assessment:* The more detail you obtain about a solution, the easier it becomes to objectify assessments. The less detail you have available, the more assessments will depend on the professional experience of the assessor, or a body of tradition in that profession (like case law).
- *Quality of metadata:* The higher the cost of providing metadata, the more people will attempt to cut corners. At the extreme end of the spectrum it can become political and lead to complete unavailability of metadata. But even when you can enforce it, the metadata provided may not be as accurate, timely, or consistent as you may require.

What we need therefore is a systematic way of going about exceptions. In order to handle exceptions gracefully, we need to achieve the following goals:

- *Effectiveness:* It must be possible to describe the alignment of a solution with a piece of regulation quickly and at minimal cost.
- *Intelligibility:* It must be possible to understand what needs to be aligned and how with little effort.

How does it work? First of all, in the data dimension, any metamodel you design will be based on the concepts you want to know something about. These concepts will ultimately be used to describe the alignment of a real-life solution in a formalized way. Some parts of that solution may not perfectly align with the regulation at hand, or the metamodel may not be detailed enough to describe the particular way in which it does in fact align. You must therefore be capable of describing these differences.

Figure 3.5 depicts the changes required over our previous attempt (shown in Figure 3.1): there are no changes to either the solution model or the compliance model, but the alignment metamodel is extended. Besides the regular (or, if you wish, foreseen) ways of aligning a solution, which describe a *particular mode of alignment* with clearly understood semantics, there

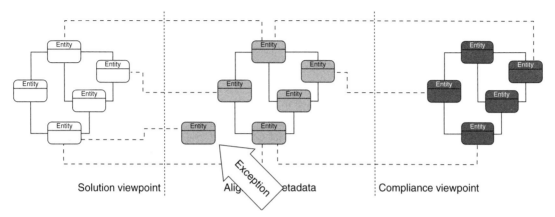

Figure 3.5: When dealing with exceptions, a solution or one of its model elements (left) may not be able to align itself with a compliance model element (right). The alignment metamodel should, however, be able to capture this case as well so that it can be handled systematically (middle)

is now an additional way, which captures *all other modes of alignment* with loosely or not at all defined semantics. If you want to, exceptions can be handled as part of the latter, or as part of yet another mode of alignment.

By extending the alignment metamodel this way, we provide a 'catch-all' mode that reverberates in the process dimension: capture of alignment metadata works as before, though one has to provide for activities that authorize exceptions. However, its use in compliance is different when it comes to automation: any alignment mode with clearly defined semantics can also be automated. The catch-all mode, however, is accessible only to humans, which is why that corner of our metadata universe will typically not be processed by machinery. This is what Chapter 2 referred to as *unstructured* change adoption (see page 27).

Exceptions and catch-all modes of alignment are important practical tools to keep the metamodel simple, intelligible, and effective: for all modes that can be described formally, ready-made abstractions with clear semantics can be provided, making the provision and assessment of compliance statements a breeze. For all other cases, catch-all concepts provide for the flexibility we need. The balance between formality and flexibility is where its usefulness lies. The handling of this has importance for (metadata) quality and sustainability management, which Chapters 8 and 9, respectively, will talk about in more detail.

3.2.3 Alignment modes and managing change on different layers

This section takes a brief detour on modes of alignment that relates to change management: by describing the IT model of a solution in terms of the model it implements, we correlate concepts of one viewpoint with those of another. Depending on the situation, this correlation can be simple or complex. It can often be reduced to a few cases:

- *1-to-1:* One element in the IT model corresponds to one element in the business model. This is the simplest case. When you change a business model, you know to change just the IT object corresponding to the one in the business world.
- *1-to-n:* One element in the business model corresponds to (potentially) many in the IT model. You need to be careful in the case of changes in the business world, because there may be dependencies between the (many) IT model elements which you have not reified, and which may lead to inconsistencies there.
- *n-to-1:* Assuming changes always trickle through from business to IT, this case should not occur. However, it sometimes does (see Section 3.4.1 for details).
- *m-to-n:* This is the most difficult case, in which arbitrary correlations exist between business and IT models. In both ways, a change can potentially lead to inconsistencies and misalignment.

Obviously we would like to see 1-to-1 correlations all the time, because the more complex the dependencies are, the more difficult impact analysis becomes. But that this is not always possible. However, what you know is that if you were able to ensure that solutions were to (re)use abstractions and solutions that get us closer to such a 1-to-1 correspondence, that would be a great advantage. This is the realm of architecture governance, and hence it is of interest how metadata can help.

3.3   Architecture: structure, compliance, and the management of portfolios

A metamodel reifies and metadata expresses the peculiar way in which a solution aligns itself with a particular compliance concern as seen from a given viewpoint. As such, metadata management is of interest to architects. Architecture (in IT) is a bit of an elusive term. An architecture is a means to describe solutions in terms of their characteristic traits from a particular viewpoint. To do that, an architecture identifies building blocks (e.g., software component, data element, process activity) and their relationships (e.g., method call and object state, entity composition, process triggers, activities, and results). It defines rules and constraints on building blocks and relationships.

An architecture describes two things: first, the correspondence between (business) requirements and the (IT) building blocks; second, the peculiar way in which a (proposed) solution relates to and uses those building blocks. This is an important tool in aligning business and IT:

- Building blocks are the smallest abstractions from which we build solutions. By ensuring that the concepts used in building blocks correspond closely to the concepts used in business, we lay the foundation for constructing solutions that align well with the business.

- Relationships compose, group, connect, order, or otherwise tie together building blocks to shape a solution as the business (or IT) require it. By using relationships, one expresses the particular way in which a solution makes use of the architectural building blocks.

As such, each architecture holds in it the essence of a *language*: building blocks form the 'terms,' while relationships form 'sentences' built on top of them. And here is where the use of metadata comes into play: although we may want to express all sorts of sentences as we see fit, only a few of them will be permitted. Which sentences are allowed and which are not is dictated by the rules of the architectural language. These rules govern the use of terms and the structure of sentences. Metadata and metamodels can be used to ensure alignment with the architectural language rules as follows:

- Offer the architectural building blocks and relationships as model abstractions (terms and sentences to describe the solution). These become part of the (alignment) metamodel.
- Define rules that govern the usage of metadata (a concrete statement of compliance), and use it to validate the consistency and correctness of a solution model.

When such metadata is available, we can collectively manage an entire *portfolio* of solutions for alignment with a given architecture. We can analyze weaknesses of the existing architecture and run scenarios to find room for improvement. We can guide the re-alignment of solutions that were built on an earlier version of the architecture (see also sidebar 'Architecture, Methodology, and Metadata').

Architecture, Methodology, and Metadata

The route from (loosely defined) requirements to (formally specified) models is taken using the methodology bus, so to speak. Given a list of requirements, a methodology organizes them in such a way that different design goals are achieved, such as reuse, performance, or others. In this, the methodology makes use of the architecture or, more precisely, the building blocks: put simply, it reduces requirements to a number of building blocks that are used by the solution design in a specific way that fulfills said requirements. For example, an object-oriented design tries to fulfill requirements by reducing them to a number of interacting objects that reuse other objects in different ways (composition, inheritance). An entity-relationship design reduces everything in the world to . . . well, entities and their relationships. Metadata can reify the particular way in which this reduction is accomplished. In fact, I regard metadata as a natural side-product of the analysis and design phase of any solution you design. Quite often, design tools are not equipped to support this view, but it would be only a small stretch to imagine them doing so. In any event, architecture, methodology, and metadata are natural team players.

On the flip-side of the coin, we can automate the validation of compliance rules: by making the structural rules of an architecture explicit in the metamodel, and by making the concrete alignment of a solution accessible as metadata, a machine can easily check it for compliance.

The great value of reification lies in tying together different strands, namely the solution-oriented and the compliance-oriented viewpoint, and making the alignment between both accessible to systematic inspection and analysis at the portfolio level.

3.4   Supporting evolution towards and adoption of standards

One particular way of ensuring close correspondence of business and IT with each other, or with respect to the outside world, is to base the concepts codified in models on agreed standards. They can play a great role in lowering cost and risk of misalignment. There is a plethora of organizations and standards available; the question is which to choose.

Before a company seeks to align itself with a particular standard, be it internally established or externally agreed, it faces a dilemma: what is the economic utility of a given candidate standard? A standard makes certain assumptions about how it is to be used, which products support it, and so forth. Do they suit the company's goals? A proposed standard also has a certain maturity, network of adopters, and exhibits some level of detail. Will it make a difference for the better? Think of the latest technological invention claiming radical efficiency gains. Can the vendor be trusted to support the product in ten year's time? What about the skills required to operate it? Should we wait until a major overhaul of the IT landscape is due, anyway? But this is not all. Company-specific standards especially are often not 'invented,' but more likely 'discovered' as they emerge from collective experience. In terms of standards adoption, a company will want to be prudent in its pursuit of standardization opportunities; ideally, it will want to actively support this process somehow. To do all this, a company wants to be

- careful to allow for some evolution and maturation of a standard before officially adopting it;
- but relentless in its drive to align existing solutions with the standard, once it has become established.

Put differently, a company will want to wait while it can, and push forward quickly when it needs to. Again, metadata management can help make this easier. The first thing you need to define is the portfolio of solutions within the scope of your concern, and then obtain metadata about how they align with existing standards. For example, you may want to understand which application in the company supports which business process; the list of applications is the portfolio, the association of applications and business processes is the alignment metadata.

Once you have obtained this overview, you can start to use it systematically. One common task is to identify overlaps, which hint at reuse opportunities and potentially inconsistent implementations, that is: cost and risk. Assume that a dozen or so applications support some business process at the same time, and assume further that there are substantial overlaps. The architecture people single out one application, which is to support the business process exclusively, but is reused by other applications.

Now imagine the job is done. Of course, most of the dozen applications are still claimed to align with the business process; at least that is what our alignment metadata tells us if we do not change anything. However, that would not be telling the exact truth. If the architecture people take a look at the metadata again, they would not know that something has changed, possibly assuming they have to go through the whole exercise again.

What needs to change? There needs to be a new relationship between applications (that is, reuse) which needs to be reified in the metamodel, giving life to new metadata (the dozen or so, except the one using the single application supporting the process) and abandoning old metadata.

What have we achieved with this? We have introduced a new relationship, expressing a new way of aligning a solution with a standard. However, this is a *new* kind of standard: a reusable application was previously unknown, and we have just established it. This is important: the process of establishing a new standard on top of others can be supported by two uses of metadata:

- *ex-ante standardization:* metadata supports the identification of overlaps and standardization potential;
- *ex-post standardization:* metadata supports the alignment of solutions that are non-compliant.

The exact same scheme can be used for external standards. There, however, *ex-ante* activities are normally omitted, since the alignment metadata of outside actors is not known.

As such, alignment metadata can be made a crucial tool in supporting the *planning and implementation* of strategic decisions related to structural change, particularly in IT: because metadata shows the way that solutions align with standards, evolving the standards landscape and re-aligning solutions with it becomes much more controllable, and sometimes even fun.

3.4.1   Top-down or bottom-up? How changes reverberate through models

So far I have only talked about changes that occur in one model and then reverberate through to the model of another viewpoint. A corporate buzz classic is along the lines of 'business drives IT,' or vice versa, depending on who you talk to. I do not think either is true but actually a mix of both. This makes directing the flow of changes more difficult.

Consider this situation: in many areas (investment and asset management are good examples of this) software tools are purchased for their unique value proposition. They do something of high interest to the company particularly well, and so it comes to depend on that solution. In fact, the very way in which the tool works creeps into the way that the business works (enterprise resource-planning software is a good example, though not from investment or asset management). Therefore, the separation between both viewpoints is blurred, and as a consequence, changing both independently is no longer strictly feasible. People become painfully aware of this when the product is abandoned and a different one introduced. Suddenly the IT change reverberates through the business model as well, causing frictional cost and putting the effort at risk.

This actually happens quite often; sometimes it is a matter of sloppy work, but most often it is because the ideal (complete separation) is difficult to achieve. For example, numerous times I have witnessed colleagues purchasing a particular product before they have even started thinking about the essential business problem, confusing it with a purchasing decision. Regrettable, but real-life. Anyway, I want to illustrate two things:

- Sometimes even metadata cannot really help if changes occur to models that have been poorly separated at the design level. More specifically, if the model elements mean more or less the same from each viewpoint, what is the point of mapping them? And why bother to capture metadata when all it can help separate is the non-essential model elements of both viewpoints.
- The direction of change propagation between models becomes unclear. Is it from top to bottom (business change drives IT change) or vice versa? Where should you start? More specifically, assessing the impact and planning the propagation of a change becomes difficult.

Therefore, insofar as metadata management is concerned, not much can be achieved if the viewpoints and models have not been clearly defined. *The success of metadata management depends on good (model) design.* I mention this because, as will be shown again and again in this book, in financial services this precondition cannot always be met: the problem itself is sometimes ill-defined. But help is on the way. There are intelligent ways of curtailing the effects of such problems.

3.5 Aligning business and IT: using a global data language

This section uses the case of a global standard for data management at a large reinsurer. It is based on business terminology, and aims to support the systematic management of changes by aligning business and IT such that 'semantically correct' integration of applications becomes possible.

The data language serves a wide business audience and many processes, from underwriting to product modeling to the production of the annual report. As it exists today, the data language defines how IT and business work together to achieve cost and risk reduction in application construction and change management.

3.5.1 Business versus IT perspective

The data language framework is an IT governance tool for the corporate architecture team (Figure 3.6). It deals with *content standards* and *architectural rules* and, most specifically, introduces a *compliance* concept that describes what the alignment between business and IT means exactly.

Here's how it works: a business analyst captures business requirements in the form of a model that describes how data and business processes tie in with each other. Both of these are

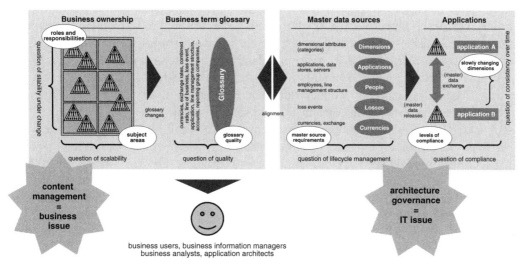

Figure 3.6: The data management framework has two main realms: content (left) and architecture (right), which correspond to the business and IT viewpoints. On the content side, terminology is at the center of attention, regulating how changes are made. On the architecture side, the master sources and applications are in focus, regulating how alignment with content is achieved and compliance is checked

described in terms of the business language. These terms are captured as part of the analysis phase of any effort introducing or updating a solution.

Business objects are captured in the form of a data model, activities in the form of a process model. The particular method used (a proprietary form of *Catalyst*™ – a business analysis methodology developed by Computer Science Corporation) assumes that an end-to-end process manipulates and changes the state of at least one, possibly many, business objects. Therefore, the following types of business terms occur in an analysis (Figure 3.7):

- *Categories*, which serve to group or segment business data, such as lines of business, currencies, or countries, and their values.
- *Business objects*, that is entities of importance to business, such as clients, employees, or loss events, and their instances.
- *Calculation parameters*, which are used to compute values of other attributes, such as interest rates, translation factors, or exchange rates.
- *Measures*, which express quantitative properties of objects such as monetary amounts, magnitudes and so on.

Processes have triggering events that cause activities and ultimately lead to a resulting event. As a side effect, the status of some of the above data elements is changed; the status corresponds to a trigger or result event such as 'submitted' or 'published.' Each of the process concepts, that is triggers, activities, and results, are business terms as well.

From a business perspective, this is what needs to be captured to formulate requirements in a model of the business. From an IT perspective, however, things are a little different. The data is stored and manipulated in relational databases. Therefore, the above business terms do not map exactly to model elements in the technical world. For example, the status of a business object is typically an enumeration that is stored as an attribute of an entity. That attribute has no corresponding concept in the business world, it is a purely technical object. Also, business objects can be subtypes of each other. An employee of a (retail) bank will also normally be its customer, but that does not mean that there will be two different concepts in the technical model (one for employee, one for customer). On the contrary, there may be four: an entity called 'customer,' featuring an attribute 'customer type,' and two values of that attribute, 'employee' and 'regular.' So, the mapping in these cases is 1-to-n instead of 1-to-1. However, in many cases it is in fact 1-to-1.

3.5.2   Systematic alignment with master sources

For each business term, there is a corresponding master source that stores the data corresponding to the term. For example, in the geography database you find data for 'United States of America' (a value) and 'Country' (a category). In the human resources database you find 'Vice President'

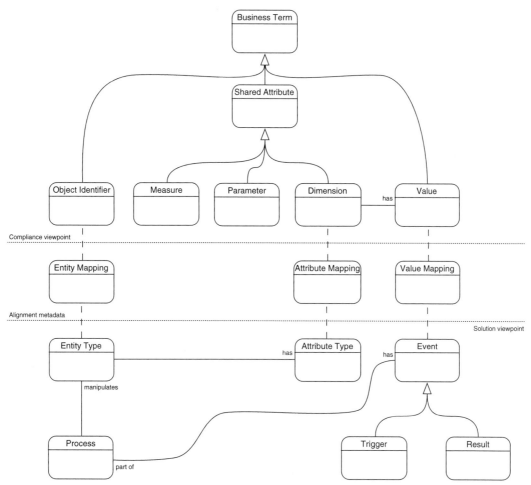

Figure 3.7: In a compliance assessment, the solution model (bottom) is checked against the terminology used by the compliance model (top) of the respective domain. The task of the solution designers is to map their (solution model) abstractions to those of the complience model by relating to the existing (data) standards. The task of the governance unit is to identify and maintain those standards and ensure their (re)use.

(a value) or 'Rank' (a category). The currency database in turn sports 'Exchange Rate' and others.

Each master source undergoes an acceptance process (which is managed by the architecture team) that ensures the data held corresponds to the business notion, in a word: that obtaining data from that source is the 'semantically correct' thing to do for an application.

The business terms are stored in a glossary available to all employees, along with the associated master source. The term describes the business significance behind the concept evoked by the term name. The master source describes the technological concept to be used to align an application with the business concept. This provides ready-made building blocks in the form of content standards, and yet for a technical world.

Alignment works as follows: as part of changing an application, projects undergo an architectural review, as part of which they submit an *compliance statement*, which essentially provides the alignment metadata. They list the business terms they intend to use in the application and where they want to obtain them from. The *compliance assessment*, again performed under the auspices of the architecture team, ensures *ex-ante* that business and IT are aligned, at least when it comes to data.

The data language is already being used to align the business itself with external standards like ACORD, ISO, CRESTA, and others, which is a very powerful way of reusing the concept in other contexts. By extension, of course, alignment of the IT world will be ensured as well.

3.5.3   Dealing with exceptions: compliance levels

Compliance with the data language has been designed to cater to the real-world needs of a multinational corporation. Specifically, the existence of legacy and the complexities of cross-company data exchange must be taken care of. For example, contractual obligations in some units force the company to use exchange rates from a particular data stream provider (of which there are, of course, many). Internally, however, another provider has been set as the standard. Or, as mentioned before, data exchange in certain business areas is based on ACORD, while partially different terminology is being used internally. Therefore, the data language recognizes three different types of compliance of an application with respect to a business term:

- *Full compliance*, which stipulates that the term is taken (unchanged) from the designated master source.
- *Interface compliance*, which claims that there is a mapping between the (internally used model of the) application and the (externally visible model) standard as established by the master source.
- *Non-compliance*, which states that no alignment has been achieved.

Full compliance and interface compliance are specific modes of alignment, whereas non-compliance is the generic form (the 'anything but the others' case) covering the exceptional case (no alignment) as well. This achieves an optimal balance between effectiveness and intelligibility: submitters of a compliance statement can very effectively describe what they are doing (one statement per business term), while the whole scheme is still simple (only two alignment choices).

Based on this notion of compliance, the portfolio of applications is managed for alignment with the business when it comes to data. A systematic analysis of the distribution of compliance levels may for example be used to assess the operational risk of data quality deficits. A master source that is used by many applications may require specific hardening against system failure. At the same time, terms not being used by (many) applications may require a rethink and be removed from the content standards list. The possibilities are endless.

3.5.4 Managing changes and automating their adoption

The master sources also store the relationships between business terms, for example which values belong to a category, or which of them is more generic/specific than the other. Hence, we have reified not only the business concepts in the form of terms, but also their relationships in the form of (structural) metadata.

This makes impact analysis and change adoption (although not a piece of cake) more of a systematic endeavor: think of the breakup of 'Czechoslovakia' into 'Czech Republic' and 'Slovakia.' From a business terminology perspective, this means that two new values are added to the attribute 'Country,' while one is removed. An application that obtains the countries from the official master source will be able to detect and load the new ones and deactivate the outdated one, respectively. New data can be entered based on the new countries, and old data may now be migrated.

The structured part of managing this one change comprises adding and removing the terms to 'Country.' From there on, the machine can take over and handle the adoption of the change in the category. However, the data migration still needs to be mastered. Here it gets a little messier: for example, how will you divide up the data you have stored? It may be an easy thing to assign loans to the new countries based on the residence address of the customer, but what about re-assigning contracts of companies that now have branches in both countries? Here automation may end, and the way forward may be unstructured. At some point later, when the mapping is clear, automation (and more metadata) can be used again.

Part II

The Value Proposition

4

Improving Performance

There is only one road to follow, that of analysis of the basic elements in order to arrive ultimately at an adequate graphic expression.

Wassily Kandinsky

4.1   Overview

- Performance improvement with metadata management is achieved through automating the model generation process.
- The relevant costs of employing metadata management are the cost of constructing the model generator, the friction cost when incorporating manual work, and the metadata extraction cost.
- Ideally, one-off costs for construction are quickly offset by leverage effects when adopting changes.
- Realistically, financial services lie on a complexity continuum from entirely commoditized to fully customized, thereby influencing construction cost and change frequency.
- Substantial performance improvements are possible in areas of heavy use of disaggregation and reintegration and long-term trend analysis.
- Scenarios likely to lead only to improvements in exceptional cases include mergers and acquisitions and outsourcing.
- The financial services sector exhibits strong national divisions in the retail sector and a large degree of globalization in the wholesale sector. Both provide unfavorable conditions for achieving performance improvements across the sector.

Aligning Business and IT with Metadata   Hans Wegener
© 2007 John Wiley & Sons, Ltd.

- Consequently, when it comes to using metadata management for business change problems, a company's strategy should be to seek performance improvements only in its company-specific way of adopting technology for a specific business domain.

4.2   Reducing the cost and improving the speed of change

In earlier chapters I pointed to the cost-saving and speed-increasing effects of metadata management. Costs are saved by automating activities that were previously executed manually, thereby also increasing the speed of performing them. Now it is time to go into the details.

Before I do that, a note on the term 'performance improvement:' at its core, the approach presented here is based on reducing manual work. There are, however, other ways of improving performance, such as eliminating waste (activities that do not add value) or simplifying the problem (changing the scope). Reducing the friction between manual and automated tasks can play a role in this. Furthermore, culture, organizational structure, and strategic goals influence performance profoundly as well. This book will not concern itself with any of these aspects, since they act in a complementary fashion to metadata management. It will also not concern itself with the role of metadata management in supporting such techniques besides alignment for risk and compliance. However, please keep in mind that they are also at your disposal while you read the text.

Typically, once we automate change adoption activities they are also performed faster. Hence, lower cost is a good indicator of higher speed. This is not always so, as it is perfectly possible to achieve high speed by throwing more resources at the problem. However, this normally increases the likelihood of uncoordinated effort, raising the specter of friction costs. Hence, just assume that low cost means high speed.

The topic of cost leads us back to Chapter 2 and the structuring of change and impact. Metadata management aids the adoption of changes by dividing both change and impact into structured and unstructured parts and partially or fully automating the former. It is important to distinguish *fixed* and *variable costs* in the equation. Fixed costs are one-off investments that are hopefully low enough to be amortized by a high enough number of change events where we reap the benefits of metadata management, minus the variable costs we have to pay each time such an event occurs.

Looking back to Figure 2.4, we can illustrate variable and fixed costs, the results of which are depicted in Figure 4.1. Generally, the following cost factors arise (see Table 4.1):

- *Extraction cost*, which arises from capturing metadata after objects are bound. For example, when a product has been designed it must be documented whether it combines other products and in what way. Or, an application may have dependencies to other applications, which must be captured.

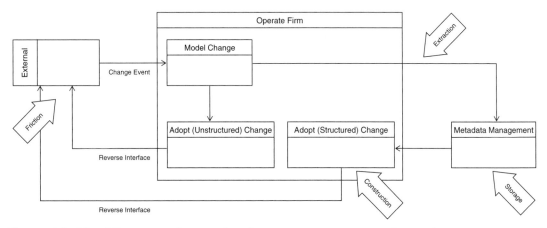

Figure 4.1: The different cost factors of performance improvement with metadata management and where they occur in the change adoption process

Table 4.1: Cost characteristics of change adoption in manual, ideal, commoditized, and customized scenarios

Scenario Factor	Manual	Ideal	Commoditized	Customized
Extraction	N/A	low . . . medium (unit)	low (unit)	medium . . . high (unit)
Storage	N/A	low (fixed)	low (fixed)	low (fixed)
Construction	N/A	medium . . . high (fixed)	medium . . . high (fixed)	medium . . . high (unit)
Friction	N/A	low (unit)	low (unit)	medium (unit)

- *Storage cost*, relating to the provision and maintenance of a metadata repository. For example, a simple database may suffice for the purposes of a small unit, but to scale that to a global enterprise will often require sophisticated configuration management, access control, workflow support, and other niceties.
- *Construction cost*, arising from the design of the metamodel and its associated model generator. For example, an engine mapping a business model to a technical model must be designed, validated, and tested.
- *Friction cost*, which occurs when structured and unstructured efforts are combined to arrive at systematic change adoption. For example, depending on the technique, generated code sometimes needs to be manually corrected, because it interferes with manually crafted code produced earlier.

All these variable and fixed costs must be compared against the cost of performing change adoption wholly manually, therefore the question needs to be asked: under what circumstances does metadata management improve performance?

4.2.1   In an ideal world

In theory, we would want to achieve what is described as the 'ideal' case in Table 4.1: the only substantial cost factor is construction, that is the provision of a mechanism to map one model to the other. This fixed cost can be medium to high, but unit costs are generally low. The cost structure that plays best into the arms of metadata management can be characterized as follows:

- The *frequency of change events* is high.
- The *number of objects* to be integrated (on either or both sides) is high.
- The *number of relationships* between objects is high.
- The *model integration is simple* compared to the models mapped.

In such a setting, the investment would pay off rather quickly, in large part because the added cost of using metadata management is generally low. In other words: in an ideal world we would be able to simplify change adoption dramatically, while not investing too much in our ability to automate it. The *leverage effect* would be substantial.

We said that 'in theory' such a case should be found. The obvious question is, how frequent or rare is it? Are there any settings where we can get close to the ideal? The tentative answer is: there are such settings, but they are rare. For the rest we have to live with shades of gray. How light or dark the gray gets depends very much on the characteristics of the models and, by extension, the real world behind them that you are trying to represent. And it is here where some of the more interesting facets of financial services come to light.

4.2.2   In the real world: customization versus commoditization

Generally, you could picture the world of financial services as a blend of *customized* and *commoditized* areas. Commoditization tries to achieve economies of scale through standardization and automation, whereas customization tries to achieve economies of scope through tailoring products to the needs of customers. Commoditization requires a lot of *commonality*, while customization breeds a lot of *variability*.

For example, using an automated teller machine allows the bank to cut costs by automating the process of handing out money. Likewise, using the Internet as a communications channel allows an insurance company to sell policies without the hassle of having sales people travel to the customer, let alone pay commissions. On the other hand, a private banker catering to the needs of the well-off would go to extremes to tailor the products to their desires, since here it is not the number of transactions but the volume of assets (and, of course, fees) that brings in the money. In the same vein, advisory business in investment banking or reinsurance for large risks typically exhibits a low transaction rate but high complexity and value for the company.

'Customized' and 'commoditized' can be considered two extremes of the complexity spectrum: a one-dimensional projection of many different factors that contribute to it. The number of objects to be integrated and the number of relationships between objects is different. In a commoditized setting, the number is typically low whereas in a customized one it is more likely to be high. The run-of-the-mill retail banking customer will normally just be offered a handful of options for his or her savings account, while the well-off customer may have access to the full range of investment products. But this is not the only difference: by its very definition, a customized setting offers little room for abstraction, so it will be difficult to reify concepts in a model (see sidebar 'The spectrum of model generation techniques').

The spectrum of model generation techniques

To cater to the needs of different levels of complexity in model mapping, different techniques have been developed for model generation. Each of these techniques allows for a certain degree of leverage. At the least complex end stands simple parameterization, where individual values can be controlled, flags switched on and off, or options selected from a predefined list. It can for example be used for specifying simple data mappings, such as different code representations. In the middle of the complexity range lies feature modeling. Whereas parameterization permits control over the concrete values of properties, feature modeling allows the conscious distinguishing between common and variable (optional versus mandatory) properties and the formulating of interdependencies between these properties to ensure consistency. For example, a particular type of credit may only allow for particular types of collateral. At the top end of complexity lies full-fledged metamodeling and metaprogramming. Pretty much anything about a solution can be changed flexibly. All concepts of the implementation are reified in a model and can be altered at will. This technique provides maximum flexibility, but also the least amount of (guaranteed) leverage.

So, how can these settings be supported by metadata management when it comes to improving performance? Going back to Figure 4.1, we see that it can be difficult to design a model mapping where the leverage effect does not get lost partially or vanish completely. In a customized setting, this may lead to the extreme case in which construction costs are not only high, but become unit costs, because the construction process needs be repeated each time something changes. On the other hand, a commoditized setting can provide fertile ground for using metadata management, because it can be performed at a comparatively low cost. However, this only holds when the frequency of change events and the number of objects affected are substantial. That may not always be the case. If you take the handful of savings account options, why not adopt changes by hand? Here integration may be a better technique, because it offers consistency without the extra level of complexity that a metadata-based solution requires; the construction and extraction costs especially can be saved.

In a word, we must not prescribe metadata management as a cure for all ills. On the contrary, careful consideration is necessary in which areas to use it, because of the risk of low economic efficiency. Therefore, we must distinguish precisely and think hard about the area in which we intend to employ metadata management. And in doing so, we get back to the topic of viewpoints.

4.3   From technology-neutral to company-specific viewpoints

The topic of customization and commoditization can be looked at from many different viewpoints. For IT people it is of interest where and how applications are affected by changes, because it is of interest to business people how their business is affected. So, if we decide to take a deeper look at the value-creating capacity of metadata management, where should we dig deeper?

A good way of dissecting a corporation is along the lines of the divide between business and IT; that is, along the divide between *company* and *technology* (Table 4.2). Furthermore, it has proved helpful to distinguish traits that are specific to an individual company or technology, and traits that are generic across different companies or technologies. This helps to separate common and variable aspects. We thus identify the following layers of abstraction:

- *Technology-neutral*, which reifies things common to all technology, such as the representation of function, information, and so on. For example, programs can be structured in procedural, functional, logical, or object-oriented fashion.

Table 4.2: Using different viewpoints helps to identify common and variable aspects, thus helping to find an ideal approach to managing change. The division into four layers is traditional, even though you are open to work with more or less of them

Company-specific
Company-neutral
Technology-specific
Technology-neutral

- *Technology-specific*, that is those abstractions that concentrate on how a specific technology organizes itself in order to solve a specific technical problem. For example, data warehouses are a specific way of extracting, organizing, and provisioning information for analytical purposes; relational databases are a specific way of storing and retrieving information.
- *Company-neutral*, corresponding to things common to companies in a given industry. For example, payments, clearing, settlement, underwriting, claims management, investment, and so on commonly occur in a financial services company. Likewise, customers, policies, coverages, credits, assets, and so forth are also to be found in most such companies.
- *Company-specific*, which reifies the specific way a company aligns itself with the needs of the industry: how it lures customers, how it manages itself internally. For example, the particular products a company sells or the information it stores to manage its own risks are company-specific, as are the way its processes work.

For certain industries in particular, company-neutral models for information and processes can be found. Some were established by industry bodies and adopted selectively, whereas others have become widely used de-facto standards. For example, ACORD, FIX, and ISO 15022 were established by industry bodies, with ACORD focusing on (re)insurance and FIX and ISO 15022 focusing on securities trading. SWIFT on the other hand has become the de-facto standard for (international) payments. Likewise, technology-specific standards can be found, established by a body (think of the structured query language, SQL), market players (think of Oracle, Microsoft, or IBM), or just internally (technology platforms in large companies). In a company, all four layers are established, built upon each other, and the company picks and chooses which standard to adopt and which to put aside based on its preferences. By doing so, it chooses whether it wants to differentiate itself from competitors (product leadership) or to pursue cost savings (price leadership).

In each of these decisions, a company is on its own. Hence, the question of where exactly a company should (let alone will) find potential to improve performance with metadata is still out in the open. Therefore, as the final step, let us see if we can identify significant variability and complexity that *generally* affects companies. And to do that, we need to look at where changes typically occur.

4.4   Sources of substantial change and impact

Before we discuss to what extent and where metadata management helps financial services companies improve their performance, we must assess the most likely sources of frequent or large-scale changes. These are the most likely to generate a substantial leverage. Furthermore, there are seemingly minor changes that also create substantial impact. These should be identified as well. And obviously, my choice of scenarios here focuses again on representatives. You should always apply it with the key insights from Section 4.3 in mind.

4.4.1 Mergers and Acquisitions

When a company merges with or acquires another, almost the entire way in which both companies work is at stake. In such settings, a mix of both sides' processes, information, products, locations, and so on survive the shakeout. These need to be integrated to arrive at a single, unified model of the new company.

The details depend on the size of both companies and the overlap between the two. For example, if an investment bank merges with a commercial bank (as happened with J.P. Morgan and Chase Manhattan in 2000), the expected overlap would be small with respect to large parts of the customer base, marketing processes, and so on. However, if a large universal bank merges with another large universal bank (as happened with UBS and Swiss Bank Corporation in 1998), we would expect both to undergo a profound transformation. So, in mergers and acquisitions it is important to understand what part of the business and IT will overlap, requiring consolidation, and to what extent.

This leads to two extremes of the merger spectrum: on the one hand, we have the case of a large company engulfing a small specialist boutique. Integration problems would be expected to be marginal, unless the newly acquired entity became a core part of the joint enterprise. On the other hand, we have a giant merger of equals, which questions practically everything both companies have previously taken for granted.

A solid set of metadata about itself will aid in increasing the performance of integrating other companies' operations, especially when a company pursues an acquisition-based growth strategy and goes on a buying spree. However, this will only be the case if:

- The strategy involves buying alike competitors, not firms complementary to the existing business portfolio.
- The size of the counterparty is similar, equal, or even bigger in size, not substantially smaller.
- The frequency of such mergers, or the expected duration of the pursued strategy, is considerable.

The above applies to the models specific to the company. Company-neutral models, by their very definition, should be reasonably equal to ensure that simple integration (and elimination of redundant capacities). For example, two banks entertaining the same payments, trading, or settlement processes would normally eliminate one each. Data, on the other hand, is always a concern, because it contains the state of the business. It would normally not be eliminated, but mapped from one company's model to the other, using metadata along the way.

4.4.2 Disaggregation and reintegration

In order to appeal to a different customer segment, a financial services company may decide to offer products that can be flexibly adjusted to their needs. If these products are based on existing ones (that is, not entirely new), the company must perform the step of *disaggregation* and *reintegration*, which involves taking the existing product apart (conceptually, that is) and putting it back together so that its exact composition is no longer fixed, but can be changed via parameters. This is a common business practice to achieve economies of scope. It makes existing offerings accessible to a wider audience and allows the company to diversify (thereby reducing its business, market, or insurance risk).

From an architectural point of view, the granularity and relationships of the (technical and business) *building blocks* are changed. For example, consider an insurance company that sells motor insurance to retail customers. It discovers that certain customer segments (e.g., experienced drivers, younger people, women, men, public servants, drivers owning red sports cars) have a different propensity to cause accidents. To increase its market share, good risks (e.g., public servants, women, experienced drivers) are lured with lower premiums. However, to do that the company must change quite a few things in its business processes and applications. Customers must be segmented by type; the pricing process must use that type in its calculations; underwriting systems must be allowed to distinguish customers, etc. Or, consider the *bancassurance* model, where retail customers are offered combinations of products from banking and insurance. The combined product has a different granularity than the ones it builds upon. In a word: when disaggregating, we require a more fine-grained, more complex model of the business, and the building blocks are typically smaller. When reintegrating, we reuse existing building blocks, thereby relating them to each other, perhaps even constraining the nature of those relationships further.

In any event, this should be metadata management heaven: complex models with many abstractions and relationships, high rate of change, wide range of potential impact, and so on. And indeed it is. However, there is a caveat: how often will you need it? One-off transactions of complex, tailor-made products may not benefit directly from metadata management. Their development is not made faster, because the bulk of the work lies in finding out what the customer needs and what the company can offer. On the other side, in asset management and also increasingly in some corners of retail banking and insurance, companies find themselves ever more pressed to tailor their products to the needs of customers. A better longevity promises to pay back the one-off investments in constructing a metadata-based solution.

4.4.3   Brokerage

Brokers are financial intermediaries acting as an agent for buyers or sellers, charging a commission for these services. Brokers mediate in intransparent or illiquid markets as well as when complex transactions need be made. They create value by finding counterparties willing to buy or sell at the indicated price, thereby acting as grease to the market wheels. Brokers do not perform *transformation* tasks, that is keep a part of the capital brokered for themselves.

For example, insurance brokers sometimes compile insurance 'programs' for very large objects by liaising with numerous insurers to cover the risks on the object. An individual insurer may not be willing to stand in for the total sum insured, but perhaps for a specific layer. The broker's task is to bring together a consortium of insurers that, as a group, cover the entire risk. Dealing with the insurers via the broker relieves the buyer of insurance from having to know all insurers, their products, or specific terms and conditions. In equity trading, as another example, brokerage means to route orders to a market that offers the best possible price, allowing the broker to charge an extra fee for this service. By matching buyer and seller together, value is created.

The main task in brokerage is to bring providers and users of financial capital together, thus providing a one-stop shop service for clients. Part of this task requires the structuring, packaging, and integration of a single (assumedly large) request such that market participants can be searched and found. However, there are numerous challenges to the task. For example:

- orders are, by their very nature, often not of the same size or composition;
- not all markets offer trade in the same capital classes;
- the fees these markets charge for their services are different;
- brokers may use other brokers or investment banks themselves, trying to optimize their costs;
- for various reasons a market, broker, or investment bank may be shut down, not available, or banned at the time.

Therefore, brokers are often faced with the daunting task of managing this complex maze of constraints for themselves. The trouble is that all of the above factors are beyond the control of the brokers themselves. In a word, they need to manage changes to these environmental conditions systematically.

Brokers hold an information advantage over their trade partners. This advantage is their main source of revenue, which they ingrain in their business processes. Some brokers, especially in equity brokerage, have ingrained the processes in applications in that they use expert systems, neural networks, or simpler mechanisms to match buyers and sellers. In order to work, these applications must be capable of adapting to the changing conditions within which they operate.

Imagine an equity brokerage house holds business relations with the main Italian, Swiss, British, and American markets, and offers to find the best price (taking currency conversion fees into account) for orders for its clients. The routing of orders will be subject to the many constraints and conditions mentioned above. Each will change on its own schedule. However, the central routing (algorithm) will have to contend with all these changes *while* maintaining to the outside (ultimately, the client) an image of seamless integration.

As you may have guessed, this is an ideal field for systematic metadata management to bring its leverage to bear. Wherever electronic brokerage takes place, the contribution of metadata management can be summed up as follows:

- The language capable of describing the rules governing markets (e.g., fees charged) and the properties and structure of capital (e.g., asset classes traded) is captured in a metamodel. Metadata is administered to *reify changes to such business rules.*
- An automated (central routing) process matches buyers and sellers based on the metadata and metamodel, optimizing for achieved price and cost. It integrates different viewpoints, *reifying the broker's information advantage.*
- To the outside client the broker exposes yet another viewpoint, *offering a unified model of the domain.* Metadata supports the mapping to this model as well.

Metadata management will help best when the structure of the financial capital traded and/or the markets where trades are executed, are highly commoditized, that is to say: they can be reduced to (a few) joint structural commonalities. Yet their variability should still be high enough to merit the extra effort.

Brokerage involving a lot of interaction, which is the realm of humans, will not benefit from metadata in a substantial manner. The insurance brokerage task above, especially when the risks become complex and diverse, will typically be completed by a human in a multi-step process, consulting with the client to change the request if a perfect match cannot be found. Except when it acts as collateral to the decision process, metadata will play a negligible role in this. This does not mean that metadata should not be used when a negative response (no match found) is possible. In fact, in equity brokerage it is more than normal that orders are returned to the client (yet the fee charged), because no trade partner could be found. What it does mean, however, is that the successful completion of the brokerage process depends less (or) not at all on metadata.

4.4.4 Outsourcing

Outsourcing means to hand over responsibility for parts or all of a business process so far managed internally to another company. In IT outsourcing, the other company typically takes over responsibility for a particular layer of the IT architecture, for example networking, hardware, operating systems, storage systems, database management, and the like. However, there are also more sophisticated scenarios where the other company takes over the responsibility for entire applications, such as enterprise resource planning packages.

On the face of it, outsourcing is a one-off effort, and therefore not of interest to metadata management. However, you may want to reconsider that thought. A company that wants to maintain a certain flexibility will be likely to choose the degree of outsourcing carefully and progress slowly, layer by layer. There are also responsibilities that cannot be delegated, or you as a customer may want to stay in control (knowing versus believing). First off, outsourcing requires a company to accept a certain degree of standardization on the part of the outsourcing partner. Maybe only a select number of types of hardware are in the offering, or the permitted configurations for the database management platform are not 100 % as desired. Negotiations for exceptions and all that aside, the principal problem is: if the outsourcing company wants to remain flexible at a certain abstraction layer, a mapping to the layer provided by the outsourcing partner must be performed. And it is here where substantial variability can occur (or not occur, for that matter).

For example, take the case of a bank that is too small to operate its own IT. It will outsource the development and operation of some or all of its business applications to a central provider, who can pool resources and skills. This is common practice in many countries. However, in order to maintain its own stature in the market, the bank may still want to distinguish itself from others by offering different products. Or, it may want to maintain its capacity to switch providers at a later stage. This requires it to reify the mapping from its own models to the technology-neutral or technology-specific models offered by the provider. This is what happens in customization: individual parameters are the simplest form, and it can range up to very sophisticated configuration exercises (think of SAP).

But not all outsourcing should be considered to hinge on flexibility issues. For example, many business processes in banking have been effectively outsourced even though it is not termed that: clearing, settlement, and payment are performed by companies independent of particular banks, for example SWIFT in payments, or Clearstream and the National Securities Clearing Corporation in clearing and settlement. There are many more such providers in other areas. Many banks use them, but they are often not in a position where they can choose from a wide range of providers. Hence, their flexibility is limited, and by extension the variability for which they need to prepare.

4.4.5   Analysis of long-term business trends

One particularly company-specific problem occurring due to frequent changes is that of *long-tail business*. What is that? In long-tail business, a company takes on liabilities whose real extent typically becomes clear only a very long time after the contract was closed, sometimes decades. This is very important in some areas of insurance. For example, professional liability (lawyers, medical malpractice, or directors and officers) and industrial liability (asbestos, gene-technology, nano-technology, or various pharma scandals) have such tendencies, as do annuity-type insurances (longevity risk).

Long-tail business requires the analysis of very long *time-series* of data to identify historic trends. For example, mortality trends affect the setting of reserves (and future prices) for annuities. Trends in litigation affect the magnitude of prospective claims for asbestos-related health impairments.

All of these trends occur slowly. This means that the models based on which data was captured has changed many times since it was first entered. The situation is compounded due to the sometimes complex nature of a trend analysis (many influence factors to be considered). In a word: in long-tail business, the problem is not the frequency of changes, but rather the duration across which these changes occur, leading to a similarly high total number of changes: small changes, high impact.

The performance improvement issue here is the construction and execution of mappings. Over the lifetime of such a trend analysis system, many model changes will have occurred, and many new data sources integrated (think mergers and acquisitions or external data providers). Each of these will require the calculation of new projections, based on updated data. For example, if it occurs that a particular type of medication exposes the insurer to higher liability risk than originally thought, this new peril must be recognized in the analysis data. It requires to re-classify and re-calculate (the data for) original contracts. More specifically, a new class of medication needs be introduced and assigned to the appropriate contracts.

In this setting, using metadata for computing mappings puts it to an excellent use. Not only do we increase the consistency and transparency of the whole process, but we can also automate part of the mapping process. A metamodel that reifies the evolutionary steps that data can perform (e.g., category splits and merges) helps to automate the reclassification of the stored data itself. Thereby we simplify and expedite the steps to be taken by humans.

Note that to a certain extent many risk management practices use or even depend on trend analysis. Examples include the management of credit and financial market risk, or underwriting risk for natural catastrophes (think climate change). They have different characteristics with respect to time horizon (how for back analysis is performed), change frequency, and model complexity. Consequently, the value of metadata management for these varies as well.

4.5   Financial services: not a 'one-size-fits-all' industry

Returning to the statements in the previous sections, we will now finally take a look at particular areas of financial services. More specifically, we will look at the structure of the industry in different countries and market segments to draw further conclusions on the value of metadata management.

The *wholesale business*, which includes the likes of investment banking, financial advisory, or reinsurance, is effectively globalized. The complexity of products and services offered is typically very high, the transaction rate comparatively low. Companies vie for customers by providing highly customized offerings that cover the full product and service range of what the market has to offer. Here the ingenuity of the product designer creates value, rather than the cost of producing and selling the product. Accordingly, the opportunities for performance improvements are likely to be found only in the company-specific layer. Portfolio management is one such case in point where trading or diversification strategies can make a big difference.

As opposed to that, *retail business* appeals to the customer masses and is still very much nationally divided. This has to do with regulatory constraints, customer behavior, and ownership patterns. Barriers are erected to entry in offering products in other national markets. Therefore, the value created by reusing and combining products is not significant, making disaggregation and reintegration *across* national boundaries quite unlikely. But even when barriers are removed, customers are careful if not unwilling to consider foreign companies. In the *European Union*, for example, a conscious effort is being made to remove barriers by lifting limitations on some areas of insurance and banking, such as allowing companies regulated in the United Kingdom to offer products on the German market. However, so far success was limited, which has been explained by customers' general reluctance to move to a different bank or insurance, even if prices are lower.

Another problem is ownership structure. Many *state-owned and mutual banks* in Germany, Austria, and Switzerland do not really compete against each other, because they have carved up the market nicely. Although they still compete with publicly-held banks, it reduces the necessity for diversification and, by extension, the need for flexibilization of processes or products. This is exacerbated by state guarantees, which allow them to offer products at cut-rate prices. In Italy, mutual banks tend to cross-hold stakes in each other, making mergers and acquisitions difficult.

But even when one discounts for the mutuals, a high number of mergers and acquisitions is not a very likely scenario in the near future. In the United States for example, regulatory changes in the 1980s led to relaxed branching restrictions and resulted in a series of mergers. The number of banking organizations was cut by half. However, an overwhelming majority of organizations are still small community banks with total asset size in the order of up to USD 500m. Yet, the total volume of assets is held overwhelmingly by banking giants with an asset size beyond USD 10bn. This is basically a two-pronged system that has been relatively stable for a while now, and does not seem to be headed for change. In contrast to that, the German mutual and cooperative banks hold the majority proportion of total assets in the country.

But even within a jurisdiction, massive change at the product level is not seen as overly likely. A good example for this is bancassurance: combining insurance and banking products has been tried with mixed success. In Germany, Switzerland, or the United States it has so far not generated the benefits hoped for, or it has even failed (in the case of Credit Suisse/Winterthur or Citigroup). France, Belgium, Italy, and Australia have been more successful. Some say that this model is not much more than a cross-selling opportunity (e.g., marketing life and household cover to a mortgage customer or car insurance to a car loan customer). Therefore, at the product level, complexity is still often constrained to individual lines of business, offering little room for disaggregation and reintegration.

4.6 The big picture: a mixed bag

So, what are we to make of this situation? There are two lessons: one, the structure of the financial service sector has a strong impact on where the specific value-creating effects of metadata management can be brought to bear. Two, integration is sometimes a better idea than reification because of limited variability in the layers that are not company-specific.

Consequently, as a general rule *the strategy of a bank or insurance company should be to seek performance improvements through metadata management only in its company-specific way of adopting technology.* There are too few opportunities for pursuing a strategy of comprehensive, large-scale use of metadata. The company-neutral layer does not exhibit significant-enough variability to justify the extra cost of reification.

Product combination and customization in both banking and insurance is fertile ground for metadata management. Making order routing in brokerage more flexible is another opportunity

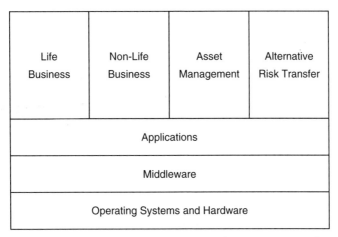

Figure 4.2: In the financial services industry, it is best to take a two-pronged approach to metadata management: the models relating to technology (operating systems, middleware, applications) are best cut horizontally, whereas the business domains are best cut vertically. Metadata will then support their integration. The example shown here is one for reinsurance. It can be applied alike to other areas

for bringing its strengths to bear. However, and this is a sobering conclusion, there are many areas of variability and volatility where we cannot find good reason to claim that metadata management creates significant value. Again, this depends on concrete circumstances, but as a general rule your approach should be conservative.

You may have noted that I have so far mostly left out the technical layers. There are opportunities, and these do not depend on the industry or company within which they are exploited. I shall not elaborate on them, since there is a lot of literature available on techniques like software product-lines, aspect-oriented programming, model-driven architecture, and so forth.

From a design perspective, this leads to a two-pronged approach: for the technical layers, metadata management is used for cutting across a horizontal domain, whereas for the business layers it is used across a vertical domain (Figure 4.2).

4.7   Case studies

4.7.1   Using business rules for trade automation

Trading is a complex activity. The number of financial instruments, tasks, rules, exceptions, markets, and above all the volume of trades, is huge. Add to that the multitude of regulatory requirements, and you see that trade automation can help to reduce the cost of the end-to-end process.

Consider the equity trading platform of the investment bank in this case study. Management by means of simplification was not a solution because this bank offers services to a wide range of clients, from normal run-of-the-mill investors to institutional clients, high-net-worth individuals, and acting as a bank for banks. (Over-)Simplifying the offering would alienate a significant portion of its customer base.

Integration, likewise, was not an option because this bank acts as a hub between the client and numerous markets, brokers, and other counterparties. The complexity of an overarching model would be too big to swallow, and it is not at all certain one could be found, given the number of independent stakeholders.

Naturally, reification was the way to go forward. The (company-specific) rule language that was built addresses the following concerns based on the characteristics of client and order (Figure 4.3):

- *Routing:* forward the latter to an appropriate market, broker, or person, optimizing for achievable price within the specified order constraints.
- *Stoppage:* cease automated processing for orders that may imperil price or require costly manual intervention.

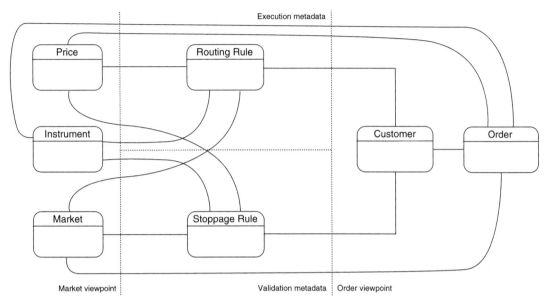

Figure 4.3: Data diagram for equity trading. Note the many different viewpoints that are integrated by the business rules

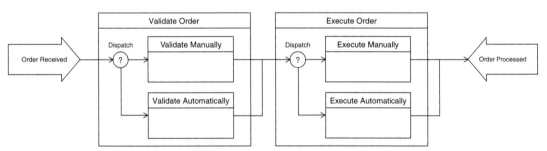

Figure 4.4: Process diagram of the trading process. This is a drastically simplified illustration: reality is much more complex, taking into account all the variability (markets, instruments, etc.) that exists

For example, some clients pay extra for order repair, manual handling, or special (manual as well as automated) execution strategies. The rules also cater to the needs of two different trading roles, *sales traders* and *trade executers*. They are responsible for order validation and execution, respectively (see Figure 4.4), but they have different needs when it comes to the question of which orders should be handled automatically and which manually. For example, sales traders are more client-focused and sometimes want to stop orders for a certain (kind of) client, because their orders frequently fail to pass validation. Trade executers, on the other hand are more market-focused and may for example want to stop orders above a certain quantity for low-volume listings to avoid moving the market, that is raise or lower achievable prices substantially.

Furthermore, although most rules are stateless (i.e., always evaluated the same way given the same input), others are stateful. The bank uses them to achieve better prices, for example by using historical data about markets, brokers, and other counterparties.

Another area of trade automation concerns so-called *corporate actions*. These are changes in the equity composition of a company, like stock splits, mergers, and acquisitions. These corporate actions can be announced, but even more importantly, they can become effective at any time. This becomes especially tricky with *multi-day orders*: large order listings are split into multiple smaller chunks so as not to move the market. Therefore, they are distributed over a longer period of time, thus exposing them to the possibility of a corporate action becoming effective during the execution period.

The problem with corporate actions is that they affect the entire chain of activity, from order handling to settlement to (historized) market data. For example, assume you scheduled an order of 100 000 IBM at USD 100.00. Then, half way through execution, a stock split of 1:10 becomes effective. Afterwards you should see an order of 1 000 000 IBM at USD 10.00, with 50 % of it already executed.

This is clearly a case of a data mapping to evolve the model of the world in the bank's applications. Since it affects different applications in different places, this activity obviously merits the use of metadata, albeit very simple metadata: a basic metamodel consists only of a successor mapping describing how the stock is split or merged (see Figures 4.4 and 4.5).

4.7.1.1 Critical success factors

I like this case study, because it illustrates just how complex modeling challenges can become. Although the full range of variability cannot be presented here, what should have become evident is that finding the appropriate balance between automation and manual task performance is crucial. And it is here where the simplicity of the existing rule language proved a blessing as well as a curse. It is possible to formulate rules rather quickly and cover a decent percentage of cases, thereby saving the bank money. Currently the bank is moving towards a more sophisticated rule model to enable business to maintain them for themselves. This includes being able to formulate more complex rules. However, it turns out that quite a few business users have problems envisioning the impact of their rule changes. As I have seen in other places myself, even just using first-order Boolean logic can cause trouble. The ultimate results of this bank's endeavor are still out in the open, though.

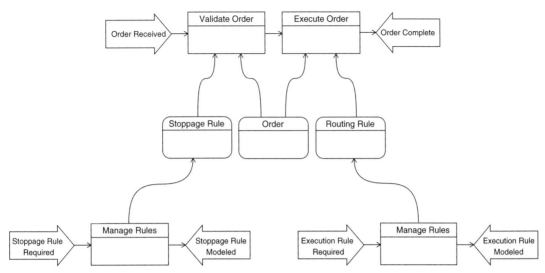

Figure 4.5: Data flow diagram for the business-rule-based trade automation. The diagram has been strongly simplified, taking an order as surrogate for all other trade-related data (market, instrument, price, customer)

Due to the complexity of trading activity, the cost structure is not ideal. There is still quite some manual intervention required, which is not unusual for a equity trading. Yet, it does spoil the value proposition a little (Figure 4.6):

- *Extraction:* low unit cost (direct administration of rules).
- *Construction:* medium fixed cost (provision of business rule engine).
- *Storage:* low unit cost (business rules in a repository).
- *Friction:* medium unit cost (manual intervention is still required a fair bit).
- *Manual:* medium unit cost (fair share of cases that still need to be handled manually).

There are issues with the existing solution, however. First of all, performing an impact analysis without specific relationships between the rules proved difficult. It was sometimes not easy to figure out whether new or updated rules would contradict, be redundant to, or otherwise interfere with the rest of the rule base. Also, the bank did not establish (rule) lifecycle management as part of its processes, which led to dormant, outdated rules that were no longer being taken care of.

Note, by the way, that the decisions being taken by the automated routing algorithm, including the business rules used therein at the time, are all logged. This is indeed used for legal and compliance reporting, for example to provide statistics about which rules were used

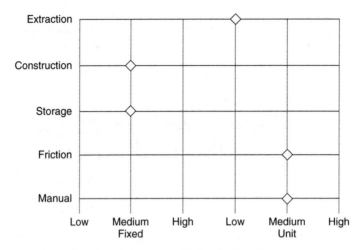

Figure 4.6: Cost structure of trade automation with business rules

when and how, as well as what the rules themselves looked like. Note also that without the rules being reified in some way, the original source code of the trading system would have to act as evidence. This is so obviously expensive to analyze that a rule-based solution seems like the best way of addressing the trade automation challenge.

4.7.2   Speeding up the design process in asset management

In this case study, a globally active asset management firm has developed highly tailored solutions for its customers. Customized investment portfolios are offered to high-net-worth individuals. Where desired, a customer can specifically express preferences for his or her portfolio, based on which individual benchmarks are measured and strategies executed.

The company wanted to achieve economies of scale by reducing the cost of implementing customized portfolios and investment strategies. However, with the substantial number of financial instruments, this mass-customization proved a challenge: how can complexity be managed at a lower cost? Or, put differently, how can the required economies of scale be achieved?

The existing portfolio management application could not be replaced for reasons of cost and risk. As such, the architectural building blocks for executing investment strategies had to be taken as (sort of) given. Disaggregation at this level was not an option. Therefore, the approach chosen instead was to build on top of it, but to represent this layer in a way that the construction of a more flexible, malleable solution is facilitated.

Reusing the architectural building blocks of the existing portfolio management system proved a challenge in itself: these building blocks also change (even though relatively

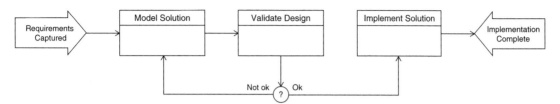

Figure 4.7: The design process is relatively simple. Assuming that requirements stay constant, a solution is designed until the customer is satisfied and has validated the design

rarely), and so change had to be weathered in the development process for the new solution (Figure 4.7), not only in the requirements, but also the implementation substrate. This can cause substantial friction costs, but in this case it was different due to the way model-based tools were used.

4.7.2.1 Reuse and reintegration of the existing solution

The key to this representation was reification. First, the business object model of (all) financial instruments was captured as metadata, based on the EMF (Eclipse Modeling Framework) metamodel, which corresponds to a subset of the UML (Unified Modeling Language). What practically happened was that the Java classes of the existing implementation were extracted using EMF. Once the financial instruments were reified, the old service interfaces were formally described in metadata as well (the metamodel again being UML). These were now to be reused and reintegrated in a systematic way (Figure 4.8).

Up to this point, only the data and service model of the old portfolio management system had been extracted. With the available technology, this step incurred only low costs. In the next step, the envisioned new portfolio management system was designed on top, adding a new level of flexibility by using the available metadata in the construction process. This is where substantial time-savings were achieved and benefits realized.

One of the salient features of the new portfolio management system was the generation of investment strategies from generic investment patterns and investment constraints. These are based on metadata about the financial instruments. The business logic for executing these customized strategies was built on top of the existing interfaces, using executable UML and metadata about instruments and interfaces to generate code.

In order to construct strategies, portfolio managers accessed the repository of instruments, patterns, and constraints through a custom-built design tool and put them together as needed. Since many aspects of the tool depend on the composition and properties of said instruments, patterns, and constraints, metadata was again used to generate code for the user interface and link it to the business logic (Figure 4.9). Essentially, a portfolio manager would then *parameterize* patterns and constraints as he or she sees fit.

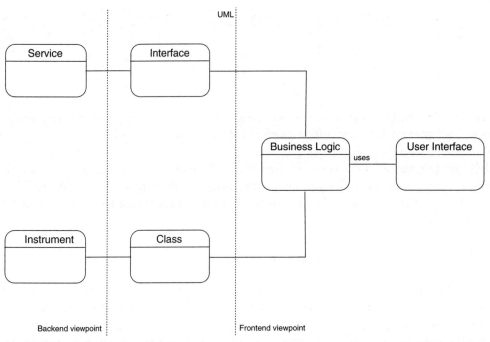

Figure 4.8: This data diagram illustrates the separation of concerns achieved with UML: it decouples the developers of the existing solution from those of the new frontend. In addition, it reifies the financial instruments and services of the existing solution, allowing the latter to work independent of the former

4.7.2.2 Critical success factors

The solution was a success, although a qualified one. In the design phase of the project, business requirements could be explored substantially quicker than previously. Much of the development team was bypassed and the team responsible for the metadata-based solution could interact directly with business and demonstrate (prototypes of) the envisioned solution, fully functional, on site. The time for design roundtrips was reduced because costs were as you would ideally expect them (Figure 4.10):

- *Extraction:* low unit cost (extraction of the financial instruments model with EMF).
- *Construction:* medium fixed cost (provision of investment patterns and constraints, creation of the model generator).
- *Storage:* low unit cost (metadata in a repository).
- *Friction:* low unit cost (full roundtrip support from EMF, see below).
- *Manual:* low unit cost (fully automated solution).

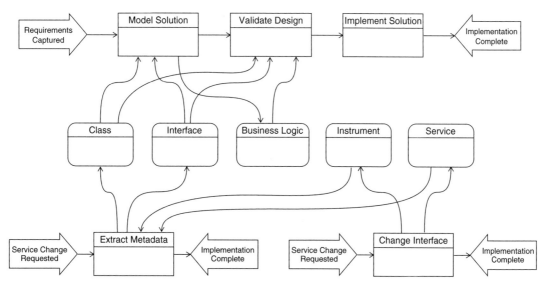

Figure 4.9: This data flow diagram illustrates the interactions between three processes: development of the existing platform continues (bottom right). Changes to it trigger the extraction of metadata (bottom left). The development of the new solution uses the metadata to model business rules (top) and implement them. The data flow to the implementation step has been omitted for clarity. They resemble those of the design validation step

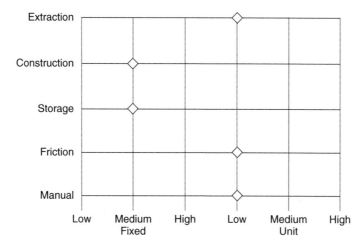

Figure 4.10: Cost structure of the portfolio management construction platform

With this degree of automation, a corresponding speed-up in the design process was observed. A noteworthy feature is that this solution supports complete roundtrip-engineering, even under changing conditions. If, say, the financial instruments model changed, EMF takes care of integrating changes seamlessly. This relieves developers from tedious manual tasks, further cutting costs.

However, and this is where the success must be qualified, the existing development team did not feel completely comfortable with this solution. Their main concern was that 'business might mess up,' hinting at doubts about the ability of non-IT staff to model the solution appropriately without major IT involvement. Justified or not, this was attributable to risk considerations, for example, architectural concerns and questions about how to test such a solution. In the light of these concerns, a decision was taken to develop manually by IT staff what had already been modeled (in executable form) by business staff.

The lesson here is that the operational risk of handing to business modeling activities which were previously executed by IT people must be taken into account. It is an open question as to whether the savings are worth the risk (I believe they often are), but it can turn into a political issue rather quickly and you better be prepared. More about that in Chapter 9.

4.7.3   Credit product parameterization for private and corporate clients

In this case study, an internationally operating bank wanted to establish a new, standardized credit process to streamline operations in the home market for private and corporate clients. One goal of the project was to enable business to change terms, rates, and conditions flexibly without requiring IT involvement. For example, applications should not have to be redeployed when the interest rate or limits changed. The obvious idea was to become quicker in offering new credit products to the market.

The approach chosen is classic metadata management (Figure 4.11). In a central process, product management takes decisions as to how the credits to be offered should be constructed, for example:

- what interest rates apply;
- what types of collateral are acceptable;
- to which kinds of customers would the credit be offered;
- how payback is organized.

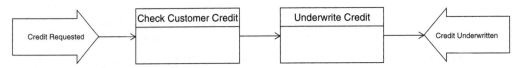

Figure 4.11: The process of underwriting credit is relatively simple

These terms, rates, constraints, and conditions are then captured in the form of parameters. These parameters are provided as a reusable *service* to applications, which access it at run-time to obtain the specification of the *currently valid* product offerings. With this specification available, a contract can be formulated, printed, and signed by the client. The metadata provided by the service is administered in yet another application by an individual skilled in its use.

4.7.3.1 Process coupling via service-orientation

The construction and operation of solutions (applications) is a wholly separate process, executed independent of product management (Figure 4.12). The link is established through the reusable service, which acts as a conduit between both processes as follows: every time the application calls the credit parameter service, it *binds* the credit being offered or sold to the currently valid terms, rates, and conditions. The coupling between the processes is rather loose (a service call), which makes it very easy to design an application for the business process it is primarily intended to support, without undue interference from the parameter change process.

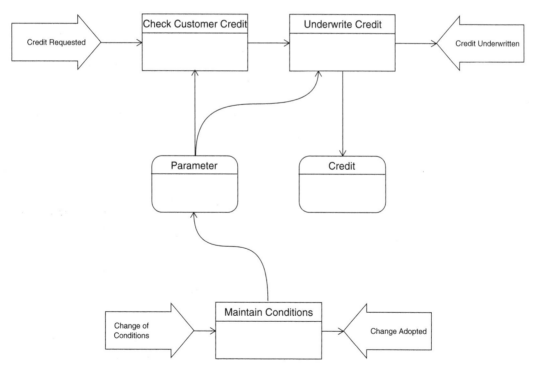

Figure 4.12: The data flowing between the credit underwriting process and the maintenance of terms and conditions is, again, rather simple

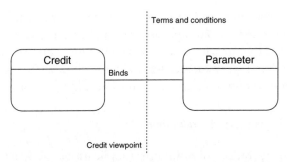

Figure 4.13: The data diagram for the credit product parameterization solution is rather simple as well

Two considerations were important in the overall approach and the design of the service. First, the service had to be integrated with an existing application, which was already in use. The integration made sure that the service, which was completely new, had a chance of actually being used (before attempting reuse). To achieve that, the technology employed to implement the existing application was also used for the administration front- and back-end. Second, the expressiveness of the metamodel had to be attuned to the tolerable operational risk. Because this way of coupling processes was new to the bank (in this area), and also because changes to metadata went directly live, a decision was taken to limit the expressiveness of the metamodel (see Figure 4.13). The bank refrained from modeling business rules or even more complex features of credit products. The result is that only simple parameters are permitted to be 'modeled.' Consequently, changes remain that cannot be handled by calling the service at the opportune time. Instead, traditional application development and deployment are necessary to get the job done.

Today there are about 200 parameters that can be changed freely, being disseminated through the service to about 25 applications. Obviously, not all applications use all available parameters, but the parameters cover all credit products available at the bank for that market.

4.7.3.2   *Critical success factors*

One important contributor to success was the simplicity of the metamodel. It alleviated fears that changes to the metadata might have wide-ranging effects that are difficult to undo in case of errors, typos, or other accidental misuse. Furthermore, applications only obtain the parameters *once* and then work from there on their own. This way there is no (or only very limited) need to maintain metadata consistency over time, just at individual points in time. Finally, the simplicity allowed a business person to administer the parameters, which grants business a certain degree of IT-independence while not compromising overly on metadata quality.

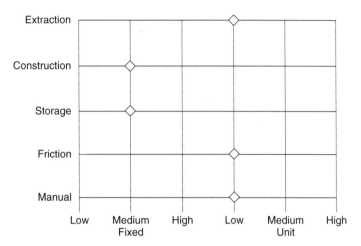

Figure 4.14: Cost structure of the credit product parameterization solution

The second contributor to success was the tight integration with the existing application. Because of that, the administration tool and the service almost 'inherited' the credibility from its mothership. This helped establish them without need for intensive lobbying. Also, and this is more a technical argument, developers could transfer their technology skills from previous exposure to the application.

The cost structure is depicted in Figure 4.14. It is close to the ideal scenario, although it must be said that the change rate is only medium:

- *Extraction:* low unit cost (administration of parameters).
- *Construction:* medium one-off cost (establish the service).
- *Storage:* low unit cost (parameters in a repository).
- *Friction:* low unit cost (integration of manual application changes and automatic parameter changes that occur combined as part of the same change).
- *Manual:* low unit cost (fully automated solution).

Despite this, the investment in a metadata-based approach will still pay off.

5

Managing Risk

Those who live by the numbers may find that the computer has simply replaced the oracles to whom people resorted in ancient times for guidance in risk management and decision-making.

Peter Bernstein in *Against the Gods*

5.1   Overview

- The demand for company-wide, systematic risk management has increased the need for an integrated approach. IT is of particular relevance in the area of operational risk.
- Risk management is a cyclical process that establishes tolerance levels for different (identified) risk types and then goes on to measure, mitigate, and monitor risks within that tolerance range.
- The regulatory landscape on risk management, particularly capital requirements, is very heterogeneous. Basel II and Solvency II are set to become standards for market and credit risk management in banking and insurance, respectively.
- IT holds direct and indirect benefits for risk management. It plays a role in measurement and monitoring as well as mitigation by computing exposures and reliably executing processes.
- IT also introduces new (operational) risks, which need to be controlled as part of building and running solutions.
- Three areas of risk management are specifically susceptible to change and need support from metadata: risk transformation, data quality management, and change management.

5.2   Why risk has become a concern to IT

In the last few years, risk management has become more of a concern to senior executives. Certain areas, particularly those in banking facing the financial markets (investment, asset management) and of course insurance, have a long-standing experience base and established trade practices for managing risk. However, other areas such as information technology, regulatory affairs, or corporate communications, have recently woken up to the call to order as well. Especially the topic of operational risk has become more prominent, and some companies still have to catch up with the practice leaders in these areas.

Part of this is attributable to changes in the political climate. Today it is inconceivable for a company to be lenient on internal oversight and get away with it. It is just as inconceivable that its reputation is put on the line by riding roughshod over the concerns of individuals or interest groups outside the company. As such, a more systematic management of this topic is now considered a must.

What may have changed the landscape even more profoundly, though, are the new industry regulations requiring an integrated approach to risk that directly affects the requirements for capital to be held. The new Basel Accord on capital requirements for banking (Basel II, for short or, as it is incomprehensively called, 'International Convergence of Capital Measurement and Capital Standards: a Revised Framework') and its upcoming insurance counterpart, the 'Solvency Margin Requirements for Insurance Undertakings' (Solvency II, for short) regulate the capital required to balance the risks in which a company is engaged. They demand that corporations enact a comprehensive, systematic, and company-wide scheme for managing *all* their risks. This raises the level of urgency to catch up with risk management practice leaders for previously more lenient corners of the company.

IT is one such corner, and catching up particularly pertains to operational risk management. Since IT is merely a support process to a financial services company, this type of risk is at the focus of considering the likelihood and impact of losses due to glitches resulting from IT activity. The question here is: how can you make IT risk management comprehensive, systematic, and company-wide? Where do operational IT risks occur? And, finally, what does metadata have to do with all of this? To explain, we first need to quickly dive into what risk management is all about.

5.3   Risk management in a nutshell

5.3.1   The risk management process

Risk management is a process. Its aim is the identification and assessment of exposure to the risk of (financial) loss, and the selection and implementation of appropriate measures for dealing with such exposure. Risk management can also be seen as a propensity to fail

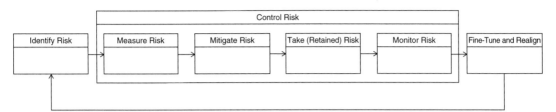

Figure 5.1: The risk process is cyclical. As long as the identified risks stay the same, taking risks is preceded by measurement and mitigation and followed by monitoring activity

to achieve specific goals within given constraints, such as quality, compliance, or financial. Risk management operates in cycles. Once risks have been identified, assessed, and mitigating action has been taken, the status quo is monitored and reviewed on a regular basis in order to react to the evolution of the risk landscape. The risk management process is summarized in Figure 5.1 and the activities are examined in turn in this section.

'Identify Risk (Process)': Determine the different types of risks to which the corporation is exposed and set tolerance levels for each.

Risk identification sets the starting point for all subsequent activity, which is why it is so important to identify *all* types of risks to which one is exposed. This can be tricky. There have been numerous occasions where companies discovered to their dismay that something had been overlooked. This is why the process needs to be cyclical and assumptions reviewed and overturned where necessary.

The tolerable level of risk depends on the appetite and capacity of the company to take on risks. Note that this is not about measuring what extent of risk is actually being taken. It is merely to set principles and boundaries for subsequent activity. For example, as a matter of policy an insurance company may decide not to cover industrial liability for operating nuclear power plants, producing nanotechnology devices, deploying genetically modified organisms into the wild, or it may only provide cover up to a certain limit.

'Control Risk (Process)': Based on an estimate of the extent of risk being taken through a particular exposure, check it against defined tolerance levels and take mitigating action where necessary.

A financial services operator that trades on its own book, sells derivatives, or provides insurance to its clients, must make sure that controlling risk happens within the frame of tolerance set by policy. Thus, controlling risk includes three activities:

'Measure Risk (Process)': Based on qualifiable and quantifiable characteristics of an exposure, assess *ex-ante* whether it fits within established tolerance levels.

'Mitigate Risk (Process)': For risks outside the boundaries of risk tolerance, attempt to reduce exposure so it becomes acceptable.

'Monitor Risk (Process)': Some risk factors such as fluctuations in the financial markets like exchange rates or equity prices lie beyond the control of the corporation. Here, *ex-post* measurement of said factors provides a new assessment of the extent of exposure, possibly requiring mitigating action or more capital reserves.

Depending on the type and magnitude of exposure, mitigating risk is a complex activity and encompasses a mix of techniques. Most of the latter can be boiled down to the following:

- *Risk avoidance* is the most extreme form, where loss exposure is never acquired. For example, some insurers have stopped underwriting industrial liability or directors and officers insurance in the United States. Institutional investors have long been (although not so much anymore) reluctant to invest in hedge funds. Or, more sadly, people with critical illnesses are often turned down by health insurers.
- With *risk transfer*, the risk taker obtains partial or full cover from a third party against expected losses. For example, stock or interest rate options can protect the owner against unwanted moves in the equity and bond markets. Reinsurers protect primary insurers against large losses. And, more recently, reinsurers protect themselves against some of these losses by transferring them to the capital markets through insurance-linked securities. The most extreme form of risk transfer happens in the area of investment and asset management. Here it is the normal order of business to combine financial instruments in ever more complex ways to hedge risks, and to appeal to the very specific needs of customers.
- *Loss control* tries to reduce the frequency or severity of loss events. Effectively, this technique changes the nature of the risk engaged so that it becomes more palatable to take on. For example, terms and conditions (the dreaded fine-print) help to exclude certain covers in insurance contracts. Banks now routinely limit the volume of positions traders can hold so that, should one of them run into the ground, the potential loss exposure is not fatal for the company.

Note that loss control is different from risk control. Whereas risk control tries to find out whether a particular risk is considered beyond the tolerance level of the corporation, loss control may ensue as part of a negative answer and lead to the risk being structured in such a way that it becomes tolerable.

Finally, all risk not mitigated against is considered *retained*. After risk has been successfully controlled, and business goes on as usual, the only remaining risk management activity is therefore:

'Fine-tune and Realign (Process)': Based on earlier experience and observation, revisit the assumptions made earlier about the risks landscape and adjust them where required.

Summing up, the cycle works somewhat like a sandbox: the company defines a 'safe area,' within which the players can move freely without endangering the livelihood of the corporation. These boundaries are set by a high-level gremium (often the board of directors) or even a regulator. But once this is accomplished, different techniques are at the disposal of risk takers to use up the available 'safe area' as much as possible by way of mitigation.

5.3.2 Types of risks

I would like to distinguish *core risks* and *operational risks* (Figure 5.2.) Core risks (sometimes called *external risks*) are actively sought and managed by an institution for profit. They are typically much larger than the operational risks (sometimes called *internal risks*) which occur as part of doing business, but need to be minimized, always taking the cost-benefit-ratio into account. What is considered a core risk differs from industry to industry. For financial services companies, the following are core risks:

- *Financial market:* exposure to changes in market prices, e.g. stock prices, foreign exchange rates.
- *Credit:* risk of loss arising from outstanding contracts should a counter-party default on its obligations.
- *Insurance:* exposure to claims emanating from a cession of liabilities, e.g. property and casualty, life and health.
- *Liquidity:* risk of loss due to a company's working capital becoming insufficient to meet near-term financial demands, e.g. bad capital structure.

Figure 5.2: Taxonomy of risk types. Risks may be named differently, but the general distinction between core risks (taken for profit) and operational risks (minimized as much as possible) should hold up

Operational risk has been defined as the risk of direct or indirect loss resulting *from inadequate or failed internal processes, people and systems, or from external events*. Here are some examples:

- *Processes:* faulty execution, methodological error, faulty booking.
- *People:* fraud, incompetence, rogue trading.
- *Systems:* loss of data, privacy violation, programming error.
- *External:* breakdown of market data feed, hacking, counterparty misperformance.

There is some discussion as to whether strategic, reputational, or legal risks are operational risks. For example, the United States Treasury Department, following the Basel II accord, includes legal risks but not strategic and reputational ones. I will consider none of these three to be an operational risk.

5.3.3   Risk management and regulation

The distinction between risk management and regulatory compliance is not always easy to make, because some risk management practices (particularly holding capital to secure against the risks taken) are already embedded in regulation, and yet not complying with regulatory requirements is an operational risk. This can become a little confusing at times. Furthermore, the question of exactly who has regulatory authority over a financial service operator can become difficult as well.

From a regulator's perspective, risk management has different functions. First, in banking, capital adequacy standards are intended to protect the deposits of consumers and, in securities regulation, the objective is protecting investors. In insurance regulation, the objective is to ensure that insurers will be able to meet their liabilities, which often lie far in the future.

From a company's perspective, risk management tries to optimize profit, that is to find the sweet spot in the field of tension between risk and return. Essentially, its function is to continually evolve and improve the company's ability to make best use of its capital by not letting it lie idle.

The regulation landscape for risk management or, more appropriately, capital requirements, is profoundly heterogeneous. Therefore, only a cursory overview can be given for some of the more important jurisdictions for financial services firms.

The United States traditionally distinguished *commercial* from *investment banks*. That distinction gradually eroded over the years, especially in the 1990s through the so-called 'Section 20 subsidiaries' and was finally laid to rest by the Gramm-Leach-Bliley Act of 1999, allowing financial holding companies to hold commercial and investment banks as well as insurance companies under one corporate umbrella. However, there continue to be two different regulatory regimes for banks, *state-chartered* and *federally-chartered*, meaning that oversight can be exerted by different regulators, each of which may have their own rules. Therefore, when it comes to risk management, only about 20 banks will come under the auspices of Basel II; most (commercial banks) will be regulated based on the old Basel I capital requirements, and some state-chartered banks may even be subject to different rules. Insurance continues to be regulated by the states alone, although the activities of the National Association of Insurance Commissioners (NAIC) have brought some centralization and standardization, especially when it comes to capital adequacy.

In the European Union (EU), with its many jurisdictions, things are no less complicated. First off, the EU does not directly determine national legislation, but rather provides regulatory directives, which are then encoded in law in each member country. The hope is that the spirit of the directive corresponds with the letter of the law. Second, the EU features different banking models: the British model separates commercial and investment banking (as a matter of custom) like the United States. Others like Germany, France, and the Scandinavian countries do not make that distinction and treat all banks the same, including the conglomerate *universal banks*. The EU has long pursued providing a level field for banks to operate across the entire EU, leading to the Capital Adequacy Directive (CAD), the Solvency Ratio Directive, and more. Currently the EU is pursuing the implementation of the Basel II accord, leading to an updated CAD III directive. Regulatory oversight is exerted by national bodies, each enforcing the national law, not the EU directive. As for insurance, the new Solvency II directive is currently under development, and regulates the capital insurance that firms must hold to fulfill their obligations.

In Japan, a single authority supervises insurance and banking: the Financial Supervisory Agency (FSA). The most important regulatory basis for insurance companies is the Insurance Business Law, most recently amended in 1996. For banks, the implementation of the Basel II requirements are planned for 2007.

In Switzerland, things are similar to Japan. Here, however, two different regulators watch over banks (Swiss Federal Banking Commission) and insurance companies (Federal Office of Private Insurance). For banks, the relevant risk regulation concerns the implementation of the Basel II capital requirements; interestingly, the principles of Basel II will be applied not only to internationally active banks (which do cover a huge portion of the Swiss market), but also 'in spirit' also to smaller and local banks. As for insurance, the Swiss Solvency Test (SST), which is modeled after the EU's Solvency II directive, will provide the basis upon which minimum capital requirements will be set.

There are several corners of the industry that are not, or only lightly, regulated but still need to manage their risks properly. Some more arcane funds businesses belong in this area, but also reinsurance. The main reason they have so far escaped regulation is that their customers are assumed to be well-informed and that their operation does not pose a systemic risk to the financial world. Both, however, face the threat that that may change (especially Solvency II and the SST make provisions for reinsurers) and the EU is working on the implementation of a reinsurance directive.

So, now that the risk and regulation landscape has been charted, what are the consequences? Where can IT help in all this? And, once you accept this help, what is the role of metadata in it? Read on.

5.4 The value proposition: risk and the role of IT

In this section I outline how IT can be used to manage risk more effectively. There are two mechanisms by which IT can help in managing risk. They correspond to *direct and indirect effects* on the risk exposure of a company. In addition, using IT introduces new risks, and so those must be addressed as well.

5.4.1 Direct and indirect effects

IT can directly affect risk exposure by reducing the number or magnitude of human errors through automation. Whenever computations or activities need to be carried out in large numbers, repetitively, and quickly, computers are there to take over the task. Consequently, IT plays a role in risk management by replacing humans with machinery, in:

- *Risk identification*, by maintaining inventories (of objects exposed to risk), risk (type) taxonomies, etc.
- *Risk measurement and monitoring*, by computing exposures based on formulas, classifications, parameters, etc.
- *Risk mitigation*, by reliably executing processes in the specified manner, validating rules, checking constraints, etc.

For example, in portfolio management it is common practice to calculate optimal portfolios with simulations. These are based on the type and structure of financial instruments and assumptions about financial market behavior to make investment decisions based on a desired risk-return-ratio. In credit management, creditors regularly monitor for their exposure to other risks that may result in their debtors' default. Credit card companies monitor cash flow patterns and detect potentially fraudulent behavior based on computations of complex measures. In trading, settlement risk is reduced by automating the exchange of assets on-the-spot to avoid the risk of differences in their value later on.

5.4.2 Risks introduced by IT

On the flip-side of the coin, extensive use of IT carries its own, mostly operational (system) risks. Automation can lead to errors made once by humans, but executed many times by machines.

Furthermore, privacy violations through hacking in particular can turn into reputational, sometimes even legal, risks. The biggest operational risk of them all, however, is the failure of IT to deliver the services that support or run the business processes and store business data, for example because:

- data is irrevocably lost due to the company's failure to create backup copies before the data center was destroyed by fire;
- sabotage is made possible due to insufficient physical access control to premises;
- critical applications cease operation for a prolonged time due to the spread of a computer virus.

As such, IT introduces risks that need to be controlled as part of the following processes (also look back to Figure 2.9):

- *Run solution*, by establishing measures that can (directly) detect erroneous, fraudulent, or otherwise unwanted behavior, mostly in data entry; by supporting users in the interpretation of data received to (indirectly) avoid inappropriate action.
- *Build solution*, by validating desired or required properties of an envisioned IT solution, mostly by ensuring structural constraints that guarantee those properties.

For example, business rule engines can capture erroneous data input. Data mining techniques can be used to identify fraudulent behavior. Data design techniques help reduce data quality deficits before they lead to misinterpretation. Construction methodologies aim to ensure that business and IT have the same understanding of the solution to be delivered. Various techniques, for example in the areas of security, performance, and usability, support or ensure their respective goals by guiding modelers in their design of the solution. Finally, solid requirements for management and testing helps to reduce the risk of persistent misunderstandings between business and IT.

Inventories like the list of all applications, servers, or third party software, are an essential part of achieving complete *coverage* of a risk portfolio. When a member of a portfolio goes unnoticed, risk may not be adequately managed. To the risk management process, therefore, inventories are a bread-and-butter necessity. They play an even more important role in managing continuity, security, or availability of IT services. As such, inventories are candidates for systematic change management. However, the handling is relatively trivial from a metadata perspective (just keep stock of things), so I will not delve into this issue.

5.4.3 IT, change, and risk

For all of the above examples, and many other unnamed processes, risk management techniques, processes, and organizations are very often in place, sometimes well-supported by IT. They work reliably. And yet, the environment of some is particularly susceptible to change. With the increasing degree of integration of IT solutions, three areas have become important to financial services firms:

- *Risk transformation:* accepting, re-packaging, and re-selling risk exposure requires the systematic management of data standards, as well as the consistent mapping and integration of data on risk exposures.
- *Data quality management:* the increasingly complex needs of regimes like Solvency II and Basel II require the integration of more and more data sources, each of which is subject to its own changes and designed based on rules, and with methods, of its own. Ensuring the delivery of consistent, transparent, correct, and timely data has become a profound challenge.
- *Change management:* the intricate web of dependencies in typical IT landscapes today raises the risk of accidental impact when changes are introduced. Thorough impact analysis and systematic management of the propagation of changes has become indispensable to ensure the reliable, uninterrupted operation of IT systems.

For these activities, we increasingly need additional risk control, measurement, and mitigation measures. But this time, they must specifically help us deal with change. The role that metadata can play in this is the topic of the next section.

5.5   The Role of metadata management in managing risk

5.5.1   Risk transformation

Many financial service companies act as *risk transformers*. Banks take on risks, repackage them to make them marketable, sell them as *securities*, and thus move them off their balance sheet. For example, credit securitization packages mortgages, car loans, and other assets and transfers the risks (of non-payment) to the capital markets. Transforming illiquid, non-marketed assets into liquid, marketable assets creates value if the bank can achieve a price on the capital markets that exceeds the cost of holding capital against the risk incurred. Complementary to banks, some insurance companies take on risks and transfer them to capital markets as well. In their case it is insurance risks instead of credit risks. For example, natural catastrophe bonds (or cat bonds, for short) transfer the risk of earthquake, floods, or other catastrophic events. Again, the value-creating step is the packaging and selling of parts of the risk portfolio. Transformation is well-established in banking. Credit securitization has been around since the 1970s. In insurance it is more recent, with the historic roots of cat bonds lying somewhere in the 1990s.

Central to the ability of a financial service institution to transform risks is the ability to structure them. In order to give an insurance-linked or credit-based security a price, it must be homogenous enough to perform a risk assessment, which determines the premium to be paid on top. Packaging for homogenity requires you to structure the underlying risks, for example by allowing only AA-rated credit into the portfolio to be sold, or by allowing only insurance contracts into it that exclude certain perils. Once the criteria for the portfolio are clear, a price can be calculated.

As long as your company controls the composition of the risk portfolio, everything is fine. Its structure can be determined, and even if it should change, an according change of price can be computed. However, this is completely different for companies that take on diverse risks from many different sources. For example, if your company offers credit solutions to large corporate customers, it is unlikely that each of the contracts underwritten will be structurally alike. Without further measures it will be difficult to transform these risks and sell them. Even worse, consider the case of reinsurers who take on portfolios of risks. In order to securitize them, each of the primary insurers will have to be called upon to provide (statistical) data about the structure of their portfolio. Without that data, an adequate price will be difficult to compute, and it will be difficult to securitize the risk. Therefore, the ability of the company to securitize risk (and create value) is limited.

This is in fact what happens today in reinsurance: until recently, securitization was sought mainly for (very) large risks as a stop-loss mechanism. The exposure to such large risks was computed based on so-called trigger-based models: instead of determining the detailed composition of the portfolio and its incurred risk, a trigger (e.g., earthquake magnitude) is used as a proxy. However, increasingly securitization is sought for smaller risks to smoothen the primary insurer's portfolio, or to increase its underwriting capacity. It is here where reinsurers are more and more hitting the wall, because they must handle data integration, mapping, and transformation at an unprecedented scale and with previously unseen demands on systematic change management.

Obviously, transforming, mapping, and integrating structures is one of the key strengths of metadata and metamodels, playing a part in *risk mitigation*. In fact, it can possibly be said that, as a financial service institution migrates away from being a risk taker toward becoming a risk transformer, the contribution of metadata management to value-creation will increase. This is particularly true for companies in the wholesale business, which mostly have commercial customers.

5.5.2 *Data quality: ensuring (risk) data makes sense*

The particular issue with data quality in large financial service providers is that data is integrated from a multitude of sources, normally into a data warehouse. It is not untypical for such a warehouse to feature a couple of dozen sources and literally hundreds of data feeds. The resulting problems in understanding the quality of data obtained or reported are numerous:

- *Data lineage:* the derivation rules and origins of measures and risk indicators, including the source systems from where the data was obtained, are unclear. It becomes difficult to understand the scope of the data, as well as the impact of quality deficits in applications sourced from.
- *Semantics:* the business meaning of the data is unclear. More specifically, it becomes difficult to understand the significance for the task at hand, making the interpretation of reported figures more guesswork.

These are static problems in the sense that they will be the same as long as the sources feeding into the warehouse stay the same. Obviously, they are sometimes subject to change in that new feeders may be added or existing ones replaced or decommissioned.

In all this, metadata management can help. Take a look at Figure 5.3. Changing something about the feeds for, and derivation paths of, data in a warehouse is part of maintenance; that is designing, developing, and deploying an IT solution. It is at this last point where metadata about the meaning and provenance of data needs be finally captured. Consequently process controls need to be in place that ensure this actually happens. A sign-off, review, or other official hand-over will suffice.

Semantics is an obvious candidate; it has long been quoted as one of the strongholds of metadata management: data about (the meaning of) data. In its simplest forms, business

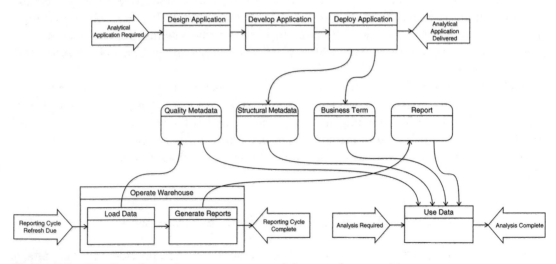

Figure 5.3: Coupling of metadata management and data warehouse maintenance

terminology is captured and linked to a particular data item, like an attribute or entity, to describe what it means to business. This, however, leaves some risk that terms are combined freely and, potentially, incorrectly. In more sophisticated forms of metadata management, therefore, business terms are structured separately and mapped to the IT solution, to ensure the same structure there, leading to integrity and consistency at the technical level as well.

As for data lineage, the provenance of computed measures can be modeled and captured in the repositories of modern design applications, which are now a normal part of ETL (extract, transform, load) tools. What essentially happens is that the computation formula is taken apart into measures, which form business terms and derivation rules with their operators which form structural relationships between the terms. The corresponding model is depicted in Figure 5.4.

Summing up, dealing with static data quality deficits requires risk mitigation at the point where solutions are bound, i.e. about to be introduced. The structured part of the problem is handled by metadata, while the unstructured part (insufficient skills, lack of will, etc.) is retained or must be mitigated otherwise.

However, there are also dynamic data quality deficits, and these are even more daunting. They stem from the dynamic nature of warehouses, which are often updated on a daily basis.

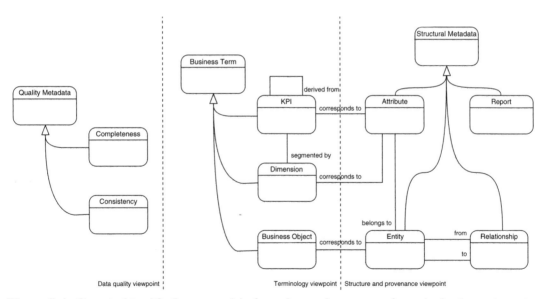

Figure 5.4: Generic (simplified) metamodel of warehouse data as seen from the business viewpoint. Note that the objects related to data quality may be modeled based on the terminology world, the structural world, or both. This is a design decision that affects which viewpoint is emphasized, but it does not change the general principle

These update processes have a tendency to sometimes fail, often for reasons not envisioned. Furthermore, they introduce an entirely new class of change dependencies: in any large corporation, regular events like calculating the day-end or month-end account balances, public holidays, etc. change the composition of data loaded substantially. These changes happen even more frequently than the more static ones above. All these factors have to be taken into account to interpret data appropriately, including:

- *Consistency:* when integrating data from many different sources, inconsistencies occur as a natural side effect. Many data warehouse designers scrap integrity checks in the interest of data completeness. However, this leaves wide-open the door to inconsistencies in the interpretation.
- *Correctness:* data in and by itself will not tell whether it actually reflects reality. It is important to take appropriate corresponding action. The main issue here is: how can one tell the data is factually correct?
- *Completeness:* the volume of data fluctuates by feeding source. Have all been loaded completely? If not, where are we missing data?
- *Actuality:* When a data feed fails, the data itself will not tell the business user about it. Somehow there must be a separate way of knowing: which segments of the data are now up-to-date?

As for the dynamic quality deficits, risk measurement and avoidance stands out as the practical issue during warehouse operation. Data has been loaded, so there is no point in trying to prevent things from happening. The main question is now *ex-ante use* (see Figure 5.3): can business work with the data? Does that apply across the board, or are there segments of the data where work is still possible? And what is the impact on computed measures?

Metadata can help guide this analysis. First of all, statistical information about the data loaded must be captured: what volume of data was loaded, where, and when? Are there alternative, perhaps more authoritative, sources against which the correctness of the data may be checked? With respect to what model is the data consistent, where, and where not? These pieces can support risk management as follows (see again Figure 5.4):

- *Measurement:* consistency of the data can be measured against the constraints envisioned by the data model, which is captured as metadata. Once data is loaded (i.e., bound), a second process registers the consistency violations and presents them, side-by-side with the actual data itself.

    As far as data originates within the company, correctness can be measured against a 'system of record;' that is, a system known to be the authoritative source for particular pieces of data. A simple comparison will bring to light data items that do not validate, which can again be marked.

Completeness and actuality can both be measured based on load statistics and job scheduling information. How does today's load volume compare against yesterday's? Last month's? Is it within a specified range? All this is based on metadata (yesterday, last month, range). Actuality can, based on the availability of data about job schedules, be computed with respect to the last load activities.

- *Avoidance:* based on the same principle, data can be marked as 'unfit for purpose.' This can take many forms, from traffic-light (red, green, amber) indicators based on simple thresholds to more sophisticated methods such as computations of risk figures that take the effects of lineage into account. Based on this, a business user can make an informed decision, or be blocked from usage altogether.

Note that some warehouse designers try to avoid (some of) the above problems through design: they do not allow for inconsistencies in the data and only obtain data from authoritative sources. Should data be incomplete or not actual, it is not used. However, at the extreme end of the spectrum this is risk management through risk avoidance, which entails risks of its own kind. And, in addition to that, they do not get around the issues of completeness and actuality.

What essentially happens, therefore, is measurement of risk (indicators) *ex-ante-use*, which nonetheless happens *ex-post-facto*. The risk posed by frequent change (i.e., data loads) is partially addressed by using the structural properties of data (model, job dependencies, statistics). The final unstructured assessment, however, is still left to the human.

5.5.3   Architectural alignment: measuring and mitigating operational risks

Chapter 3 described how metadata can be used to align business and IT systematically with architectural building blocks. The alignment of both viewpoints reduces the size or number of misunderstandings. What does that mean for risk? And, even more interestingly, can it be used systematically?

To answer, you have to get back to the operational risks. Whenever IT solutions replace humans, the following changes to the (intrinsic) risk landscape ensue:

- *Process:* Automatic execution of processes by applications reduces the frequency of them being performed inconsistently, incompletely, or otherwise wrongly.
- *People:* Due to the higher degree of automation, the impact of erroneous, fraudulent, or otherwise wrong use of applications increases.
- *Systems:* As the level of integration of IT solutions increases, so does the likelihood of systemic failure due to outages and the impact of design, configuration, or programming mistakes.
- *External:* Typically there is no significant change, other than a higher risk of systemic failure elsewhere, as above.

By providing architectural building blocks and ensuring their systematic reuse, we try to improve the alignment between business and IT and reduce cost. In return we get a higher systemic and people risk exposure.

Mitigating against the latter is mostly a concern of having the right skills and process-level controls like segregation of duties for some of the more difficult-to-handle risks like fraud or misappropriation. Here, metadata cannot do very much.

This is different for system risks. Systemic failure stems from the propagation of faults through many (or even all) IT solutions before humans can intervene. Here, IT can and must take mitigating action before the worst happens.

The first mitigating action is *complexity reduction*. More complexity means more risks gone unidentified. Complexity is a wide field, but one factor sticks out: the dependencies established through interfaces between applications – be they batch loads, synchronous or asynchronous calls, or data transfers and redundancies. Wherever there is a high number of outgoing dependencies from a system, we would like to either reduce that number (via bundling and reuse) or mitigate against the risk of outages or design, configuration, and programming errors (like monitoring and testing).

The second mitigating action is *impact isolation*. Should things still go south, we want them not to spread too quickly or too widely. We need to make sure that when ever there are long lines of dependencies, somewhere in between there is an artificial stop that increases the time a fault takes to spread or even requires explicit manual approval. Configuration management is an example where different versions of a solution are held in a repository, but only one is productive, leaving developers working on a draft version, isolated from the live environment. Or, introducing overnight or even weekly batch processing where online integration would be possible, theoretically increases the chances that there is enough time to discover a fault, or to prevent it from spreading by stopping the batch process temporarily.

The third mitigating action is *disaster recovery*. Core amenities like disk storage, middleware, the mainframe, and others are so central to the operation of IT (especially if they are tied to a physical piece of hardware) that they must be protected against catastrophic failure, which may still occur (fire, flood, earthquake, etc.). Storing backups of the most important data or providing for fail-over mechanisms are but some of the means to reduce the intrinsic risk.

IT solutions are not a big lump of code, but carefully crafted combinations of components that build on existing solutions. Today, no one thinks about programming a database or inventing a method for load balancing. This is left to reusable building blocks, to the realm of architecture. The process of ensuring this reuse happens as comprehensively as possible is that of architecture governance. Its major goal is to reduce complexity, less so the isolation of impact. Lastly, disaster recovery is a concern as well, but typically left to the infrastructure people to sort out.

How does this happen, and what role can metadata play in this? First off, architectural building blocks are *layered*, each building on other building blocks. An IT solution reuses them, aligning itself with the viewpoint behind the building block in a particular way. For example, by using the storage facilities of the company, the owner of a data warehouse buys into the backup schedule described in the service-level-agreement.

Different risks occur at different architectural layers. The risk of loss of data due to destruction of physical hardware is a concern to IT infrastructure. The risk of insufficient data quality due to failed data feeds is a concern of the data warehouse owner. Therefore, by reusing architectural building blocks, we achieve a twofold benefit with regards to risk management:

- **We can focus risk identification and control on the build and run process of architectural building blocks.**
- **The alignment metadata of solutions can be reused to assess the complexity of dependencies to the building blocks they use, and the impact of potential failures.**

As such, *system risk identification and control becomes part of architectural governance, supported by metadata*. The structured element here is easy to spot: the solutions and their dependencies establish a structure, which can be systematically assessed whenever anything changes. The impact assessment for such changes may be automated if the mode of alignment is described in a structured fashion as well, but typically this is an unstructured activity. Nevertheless, with metadata it becomes easier to make that step.

5.6   Case studies

5.6.1   *Data quality management in (risk) data warehousing*

In 1999, this globally active bank set out on a course to consolidate its analytical systems into one large data warehouse that provides a cost-efficient platform for the development and operation of data marts. Existing analytical systems had to be migrated, and new systems were to be developed for it from the start, once the platform became operational. The entire project took the good part of three years, finishing in early 2002. Today, after seven years, the platform is still growing and is home to the Group's Basel II risk calculation platform.

The application architecture, which is set out in Figure 5.5, followed the traditional model in which so-called subject area databases are separated from the data marts. The former held normalized, atomic, subject-area-specific, historized data, while the latter contained aggregated, business-oriented, query-optimized data. Data marts would only feed from subject area databases, while the operational systems would feed data only into the subject area databases. Knowing that this platform was entirely new, and envisioning the subject area databases right from the start as information buckets ready to be reused, the fathers of the project envisioned metadata management to be an integral part of the platform right from the start. The idea was

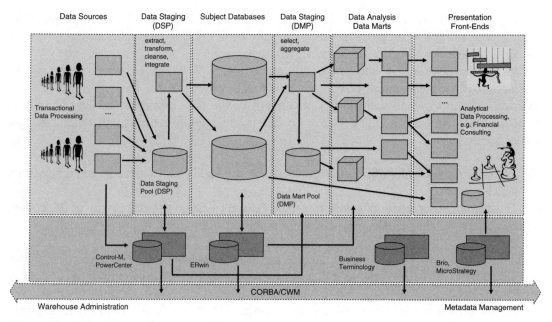

Figure 5.5: Warehouse (meta) data architecture

that, once the subject area databases are set up, you would merely pick and choose from them and put your data mart together, adding just a pinch of database queries and report structure.

5.6.1.1 Automated derivation of data quality measures

One other issue that was also foreseen was data quality. There were essentially three challenges that the project had to overcome:

1. Existing data marts had to migrate, and needed to have an understanding of the data quality on the new platform (particularly the subject area databases). In a way, this was just a mapping from old to new platform.
2. Newly built data marts needed to obtain an understanding of the entire platform's internal workings, including data quality. This was exacerbated by the fact that they, other than existing marts, had to identify their sources of data in the first place, which included the data quality deficit.
3. The data miners in the marketing department, who also had to migrate to the new platform, had a similar problem. Their additional issue was, however, that they were only working on the subject area databases, making the breadth of their challenge bigger.

These problems were compounded by the fact that, in order to keep operational costs low (and, actually, also because one data quality concern is actuality), the process of data staging, cleansing, integration, and aggregation is fully automated. Hundreds of load jobs execute every night, influencing the quality of the data warehouse's contents. In this maze of thousands of jobs, database tables, reports, and so on it becomes practically impossible, so it was thought, to assess data quality systematically.

The main challenges in this situation were the epitome of what metadata management is supposed to help with:

- many changes in the content and relationships of the data itself;
- complex data flow dependencies;
- platform mostly or completely new to users.

The viewpoint of users was typically their data-mart-specific perspective on data quality. They regarded the data warehouse platform as something secondary to their purpose. What was required was a mapping that helped them derive the former from the current (load) status of the latter.

Fortunately, in order to make all that automation possible, staging jobs, their data mappings, aggregation rules, and so on were modeled in the ETL tool, which was based on a metadata repository. This repository captured the sources and targets of data (feeder files, database tables). Furthermore, the tool also stored statistics about executed load jobs like number of database rows transferred and rejected, job execution status, and so forth. Hence, the idea was born to use the available metadata to derive, based on the data flow and load statistics, quality indicators for users of the warehouse and data marts. More specifically, the following quality aspects would be derived:

- *Actuality* was calculated from the timestamp of the most recently executed load jobs.
- *Completeness* was based on the data volume loaded.

The metadata of subject area databases and the data marts was grouped into so-called *projects*. This provided the entry point for warehouse users, from which they could drill down, up, and across. When the metadata browser was opened, the user could see a highly aggregated data quality status view of his or her project. It followed the usual traffic-light-logic:

- green: all (most recently executed) jobs completed successfully;
- yellow: at least one of them failed;
- red: all had failed;
- gray: some job is currently running (transition status).

Actuality was calculated as the day before the date when the last job belonging to the project had been executed successfully. This is a shorthand for the assumption that if a job had to be executed, it actually was. The lack of access to job scheduling metadata (which turned out to be a highly political issue) made this necessary.

This solution was a great success with users who were new to the platform. They loved the aggregated, single-page overview. Specifically, should there be a yellow 'light,' they could examine which load sessions had failed for their project. From there, using data flow metadata available in the ETL tool, they could perform an *impact assessment* by drilling across to the list of database tables that were (potentially) affected by the load session under investigation. However, three challenges remained:

1. Users of existing data marts and the data miners typically did not use the metadata browser.
2. The remaining users complained that the absolute numbers for loaded or rejected rows did not mean too much to them, since they did not have any prior experience to compare them to.
3. The data flow dependencies were captured at the physical level. This was deemed sufficient, since many consumers were power users and were mostly concerned with producing reports and writing queries, requiring access to the physical level. However, some difficulties were caused by loops in the data flow. This was due to technical necessities, sometimes leading to confusion.

The third challenge was not of major concern, more like a small nuisance that occasionally occurred. It was therefore not addressed further.

The second challenge was addressed with ingenuity. Many factors influence load volumes: normal fluctuations, banking activities like month-end or year-end processing, or public holidays. It would have been rather expensive to develop a metamodel that captured all these cases.

Hence, another route was taken to *complement machine processing with human tacit knowledge*: looking at the history of load volumes for a project's sessions, upper and lower expected bounds for the number of accepted rows were defined in cooperation with business. Once they were defined, the metadata browser displayed figures in red (instead of black) as soon as they left the confines of those bounds. This was an indication to the user that something *might* be unusual. It was the task of that person to find out, based on his or her own tacit knowledge (e.g., whether yesterday there had been unusually high activity) whether the highlighted session was indeed noteworthy or a false positive.

The first challenge turned out to be mostly of organizational nature: at that point, the data marts that already existed were migrated to the new platform as follows: build one subject area database and one data mart for each of the existing data marts. That in itself was not the issue, but the teams in charge of the technical implementation and business requirements remained the same. Therefore, to them the new platform merely had a different technical 'taste' to it, but from a business perspective nothing had changed. After having migrated their data to the new platform (and, as in the case of the credit data mart, thoroughly checking data quality once), the data quality in the marts was 'as before.' Hence the lack of need for metadata support. In the case of the data miners, it turned out that they required highly detailed information, which was not available from the metadata browser alone. Shying away from using different tools with different underlying models, they chose to pursue their own solution.

5.6.1.2 Critical success factors

The lessons from this showcase are clear: even with limited means, metadata can create a substantial amount of value for assessing data quality. The crucial contribution lies not in highly sophisticated computations based on dependency graphs, etc. The contribution arises from *reducing complexity for human beings to an extent that their tacit knowledge suffices to answer any remaining quality questions.*

Furthermore, organization and collaboration patterns matter. It turned out that existing teams were transferred 1:1 to the new platform, essentially eliminating any need for external, metadata-based support for managing complexity and volatility. In a way, tacit knowledge was enough to manage day-to-day operations.

Finally, this case study illustrates the value of systematic design and construction of applications: metadata about data flows was created almost for free as collateral of using the model-based design tools of the ETL product. This product also happened to record statistics, which could be easily combined with other metadata to create value. Had the teams each used their own design tool, implementation technology, and so on, it would have been very hard to capture all that data to the benefit of business.

5.6.2 Data quality management with role-based exception handling

Taking the previous case study a little further, consider this reinsurance company. To support business steering in Property & Casualty underwriting, key performance indicators (KPIs) about the various products were computed. These KPIs were stored in a data mart and provided to controllers for their perusal. They covered, among others:

- risk-adjusted capital (RAC);
- large losses;
- capacities;
- exposures.

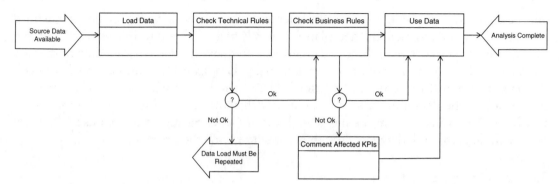

Figure 5.6: Process diagram for role-based exception handling

These KPIs were based on complex calculations, and therefore it was not always simple to understand their data quality. Furthermore, the way the data mart was structured, KPIs were segmented by more than a dozen analysis *dimensions*, spanning a data cube of pretty complex proportions. Not only was it rather difficult to spot (potential) data quality deficits in this cube, but it was also seriously challenging to assess their (real) impact. Not all deviations in the performance figures were alike. For example, year-on-year changes in overall performance could be considered more significant than drops in a particular country. Because the KPIs were segmented by so many dimensions, not all could be granted the same significance in terms of data quality management.

In this case, the solution was to introduce two additional steps in the data staging process (Figure 5.6). These steps were designed to help the ultimate recipients better understand the figures by way of *commenting* them. Instead of just loading the data into the mart and letting controllers use it, data quality was first checked based on rules. The rules tackled the issue from two angles: first, *technical rules* were designed to detect operational problems such as load job crashes, lack of data feed delivery, or unusual data volume variations. Second, *business rules* were designed to detect unexpected changes in the actual figures, such as unusual losses, or noteworthy performance lapses.

If a technical rule failed, which often happened because of missing source data, the load was repeated. This cycle was repeated until there were no more rule violations and the operators (who were actually business people with some IT savvy) could give a green light. Next, the business rules were checked. All violations were logged, and specially skilled business representatives took a look at them. This task, which came to be known as commenting, required profound knowledge of the business data, the goals of controlling, and the rule base.

Not all rules were equally important. It was possible to specify when the data that violates a rule must be commented and when it was merely to be brought to the attention of business (warnings versus errors). Violated rules could be marked to be commented:

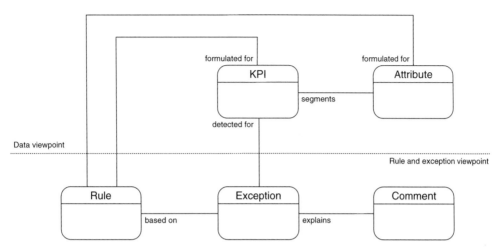

Figure 5.7: Data diagram for role-based exception handling

- in every case;
- only in case of certain (absolute or relative) deviations;
- when a limit had been passed

When a comment was added, the data was marked down as an *exception*, which meant that there was good reason for it to be there. These exceptions and their attached comments were made available to controllers, complementing the actual data itself.

The data model is depicted in Figure 5.7, and the data flow in Figure 5.8. As you can see, the interactions get quite complex. This is due to the multi-staged exception-handling process.

An observation about this solution: it turned out to be difficult for controllers to find the exceptions in their data cube, and sort them by importance. Typically exceptions in the data cube were distributed sparsely. To help users here, the solution provided a list of exception side-by-side with the actual data, which could be browsed and investigated more easily.

Another interesting observation: some people used the commenting mechanism to annotate the data *even where there were no exceptions*. They employed commenting to complement data with personal notes, highlighting certain things they thought important, or merely posted a message to other users. In such a way, commenting turns into documentation but nevertheless it was considered a helpful and welcome feature.

5.6.2.1 *Critical success factors*

The rule-engine ensures consistency with the rules *in general*, while still permitting staff to grant and comment *exceptions*. This is the central success factor. It is now possible to delegate,

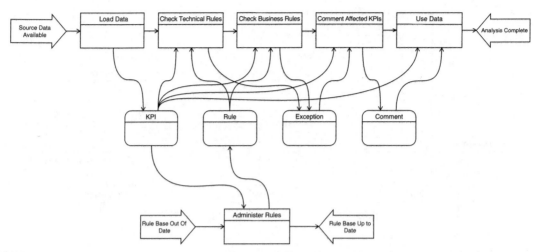

Figure 5.8: Data flow for role-based exception handling. The entity 'Attribute' has been omitted to reduce complexity. It exhibits exactly the same interactions with processes as 'KPI'

based on rules, the arduous task of checking data for unusual patterns to the machine. Those few cases that are found to be in violation can then be investigated manually. Furthermore, due to the fact that only a few select individuals are allowed to comment data, a certain degree of leverage and consistency is achieved as well.

A second factor of success is the simplicity of the rules. The constraint language allows for simple formulas (arithmetic like addition, multiplication, subtraction, division). This decouples business from IT: as long as the calculations are not too complex, business users are free to change them without having to involve IT. They do not need a lot of training. Similarly, IT can rest assured that inappropriate use of rules by business (which may impair performance) is unlikely, and checking the rules is computationally inexpensive, thereby ensuring stable operation.

5.6.3   Using architecture for operational risk control

The case of data language based on business terminology was mentioned in Section 3.5. We describe here how architectural standards and governance can work together to control operational risks.

As outlined in Figure 5.9, the data language framework is embedded within the company as an IT standard. When a master data source is established, an assessment of the candidate source is performed that tries to determine the merit with which it claims that title. For example, competing sources must be examined. The acceptance process also takes into account the various risk factors influencing the decision, and it is this part that deserves our attention.

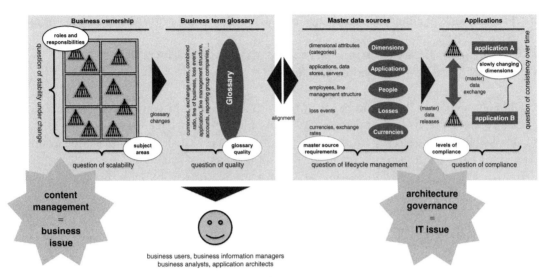

Figure 5.9: Essential design decisions of the data language framework

When a master data source is officially accepted, the architecture governance processes henceforth ensure that, within the usual tolerance margins, all applications are compliant with respect to (the attributes in) that master data source. However, this puts a great burden on the shoulders of architects: the operational risk of forcing applications to use a master data source must be assessed and where necessary, mitigated.

For reasons of simplicity, let us assume that there are three viewpoints from which the integration of an application with its master data source(s) can be seen:

1. *Business architecture:* concerns itself with business processes and the data used therein.
2. *Application architecture:* focuses on applications and their interactions, specifically exchange.
3. *Technical architecture:* ensures the secure, stable, and scalable operation of IT solutions.

Master source acceptance touches on business architecture in the form of the change process behind the attributes served out of the master source. It touches on application architecture in that it asserts from what other application a given application must obtain its master data. And finally, it touches on technical architecture in that a master data source must ensure uninterrupted service to the applications it serves. Bearing all this in mind, the use of a master data source incurs the following risks (examples only):

- People: use of monthly average instead of end-of-month exchange rate; accidental deletion of data.

- Process: lack of adherence to change process; stakeholder notified too late; communications glitches.
- System: unavailability of master data source; data loss; security breach.
- External: breakdown of market data feed.

Different operational risks can be mitigated with different architectural measures in different places. For example, the risk of privacy violations due to theft of backup tapes can be mitigated against by physically securing the premises. Theft or loss in transit can be mitigated against by encrypting the backup tapes. You can see that summarized in Table 5.1.

In the setting discussed here, master data sources provide reusable data and assorted maintenance processes for the benefit of applications. From the perspective of the organization it must be ensured that applications do actually use them, which lies within the realm of architectural governance.

In this case there are two checkpoints a project must go through, the so-called 'Information & Process Check' and the 'Information Technology Check' (Figure 5.10). To obtain architectural sign-off, the designers of an application must present the proposed architecture to a gremium of experts who take a look at it.

In the case of master data, the application files a *compliance statement*, which is essentially a declaration about the sources from which master data is obtained and how. It permits assessment of the operational risk associated with the proposed architecture (Figure 5.11). (This is, in effect, a risk self-assessment.) The Information & Process Check looks at these

Table 5.1: Different architectural viewpoints, their associated inherent operational risks, and controlling process activities

Viewpoint	Inherent Risk(s)	Risk Control as Part Of
Business Architecture	People, Process	Master Source Acceptance
Application Architecture	System, External	Master Source Acceptance Information & Process Check
Technical Architecture	System, External	Master Source Acceptance Information Technology Check

Figure 5.10: The solution design process features two checkpoints, one technical and the other related to business

risks, and by extension the Information Technology Check as well. Consequently, there are two different, yet coupled processes: one for building solutions (i.e., applications), one for standardizing building blocks (i.e., master sources) (see Figure 5.12). Both checks work together to reduce the operational risks.

Based on the available experience since 2004 it can be said that the operational risks to care most about are, in descending order of importance, process, people, and system risks. External risks play a minor role at this firm and, in this case at least, are mitigated at the application level. Typically system risks are effectively mitigated. Specifically the expectations of stakeholders sometimes lead to communication problems. Data owners assume that 'the data

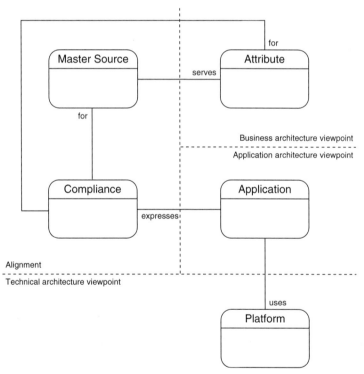

Figure 5.11: This data diagram illustrates how the different architectural viewpoints are connected via compliance and master sources. In this structure, master sources provide the bridge between building blocks in the business-architectural and the application-architectural viewpoint. The similar structural relationships on to the technology-architecural viewpoint have been omitted for clarity

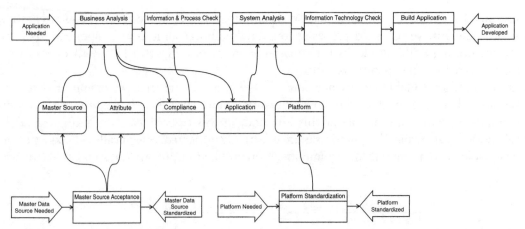

Figure 5.12: Data flow diagram for the data language framework. Standardization of building blocks is the activity that provides abstractions to build solutions on. Alignment with these is checked as part of the architectural checkpoint (s). The flows to and from the Information Technology Check have been omitted for clarity

language framework guarantees me the right to say how to do things,' while data consumers assume that 'the framework guarantees me a voice in the change process.' This can become tricky when applications obtain their master data not directly from the master source itself, but via hubs that consolidate and integrate it for a dedicated area of concern (e.g., Life & Health). Finally, people need training to understand the sometimes complex interrelationships of data so they take appropriate care before using or, even more importantly, change master source content. A typical case in point would be the application owner who does not think about the differences between the monthly average and end-of-month currency exchange rate.

5.6.3.1 Critical success factors

There are three major success factors. First, the framework came to life through a bit of a protracted story. What made it ultimately successful was the embedding of the compliance check with the architecture governance processes (riding piggy-back, so to speak). By doing so, the gremiums, the network of people, and the discipline if you wish, did not have to be invented, giving the data language a jump-start. Before the framework, the effort was dispersed across the company, whereas now a central point has been found where such issues are brought to the table.

Second, compliance is defined very precisely in the framework. Although there remains a lot to do in terms of standardization of master data sources, it is possible to check candidate applications quickly. This makes life easier for the governing organizations *and* the projects delivering the solution: it can be decided relatively quickly whether compliance is achieved (and at what level) or whether an exception is required. This strikes the desired balance between *effectiveness* and *intelligibility*.

Third, as a kind of a collateral benefit the *transparency* and *consistency* of data is increased: since the business terms underlying the data are documented in the company glossary, their semantics are accessible to all users in the company. Furthermore, consistency is defined in relation to the master data source. That makes all applications responsible for keeping up to date with changes there. However, even if they should fall behind it is at least possible to define a mapping. That way, consistency is still maintained (the usual challenges of data mapping notwithstanding).

5.6.4 *Managing operational risk with platforms*

For a more sophisticated case study of architecture management, consider this bank, which established a comprehensive method for managing IT architecture to reduce operational risk.

The main consideration that led to the the build-up of this approach was to ensure the IT organization's 'ability to change.' This ability proved a bit elusive to define, and for this reason it was broken down to a set of 21 *architectural goals*. The goals in turn are supported by 21 corresponding *architectural properties*, including:

- reusabilty;
- performance;
- security;
- maintainability.

These properties are intended to support – and ideally ultimately lead to – the desired ability to change. However, how can they be ensured when an envisioned solution – an application – comes along?

The trick lies in the use of *platforms*. These are (technical) building blocks, that is solution fragments that have known architectural properties, thus ensuring the achievement of certain architectural goals. For example, using the platform for Intranet applications ensures (through single-sign-on) security, using the database platform ensures (a certain amount of) scalability.

Each envisioned solution is checked as part of the architectural project review (project review board, see Figure 5.13) with respect to the platforms, the principles, and the goals. Alignment with the properties is measured and documented in the form of a 3-value-logic ('compliant,' 'not compliant,' and 'not applicable'). The latter proved to be necessary as an

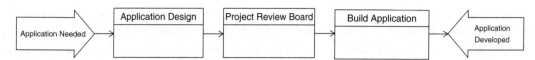

Figure 5.13: Process diagram for architectural alignment. A solution (in this case an application) is aligned as part of a project checkpoint *ex-ante*

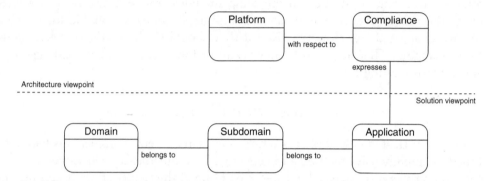

Figure 5.14: In this bank, solutions (applications) are assigned to a domain and subdomain to determine how alignment is to be assessed. Platforms are offered to implement a solution, and the compliance status recorded. This is then later used to determine the compliance index of a specific solution, or the entire portfolio

exception-mechanism for applications that turned out to be not subject to the alignment with a particular platform.

Using the 21 properties, the architecture team computes a *conformance index*, which acts as a *risk indicator* for the application's ability to change. Compliant use of platforms obviously gains higher conformance than non-compliance or the claim to be subject to the provisions of a particular platform. Based on this conformance index, a decision is taken as to whether to take it forward.

In this sense, this bank acts as described in the previous section: the building blocks (platforms) are provided ready-to-use, with known architectural properties. If an application uses such a building block, risk assessment is a matter of assessing the specific way the platform is used by the application (how it aligns itself) (see Figures 5.14 and 5.15 for details).

Alignment with given platforms is subject to many considerations. The company decided to delegate responsibility to domain architects, who assess compliance in a context-specific fashion. This ensures that domain-specific concerns are given more consideration, while increasing the risk of inconsistencies across the entire company. However, given the much stronger coherence of applications within a domain, this is a reasonable approach.

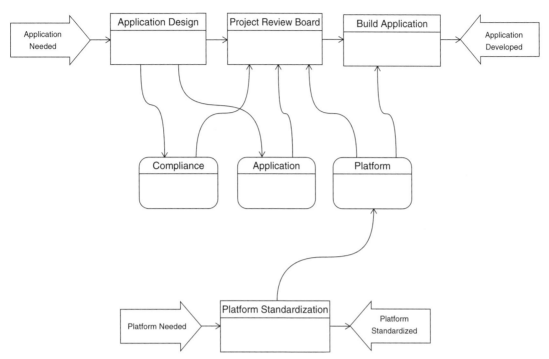

Figure 5.15: The data flow corresponds to previous case studies. As part of standardization, architectural building blocks (platforms) are provided and then checked as part of project reviews. Metadata about compliance levels is later used by architects

5.6.4.1 Critical success factors

In the beginning, the quality of the alignment metadata about envisioned solutions required improvement. Particularly, completeness and actuality did not reach the desired level. The central architecture team responded by *decentralizing* responsibility for its maintenance. They introduced the notion of a *subdomain*, essentially carving up the overall cake of domains even further. Subsequently, the *domain architect* worked together with the *solution architect* to align a solution with the overall architecture, being responsible for the quality of the alignment metadata.

As an aside, using project financials, the alignment metadata were ultimately used by the architecture team to prove to business and sponsors that using the provided architecture platforms led to substantial cost savings. This proved to be a reputational boost for the team, which thus 'proved' to management that they are worth their salt.

5.6.5   Terminology-based data quality management

This is a case study of a large private and commercial insurer in the United States and Canada, operating a data warehouse and assorted analytical applications to manage its financial positions and understand the performance of the business. As part of this, business terminology is actively managed to *reduce the inherent (indirect) risk* of losses due to incomplete, inconsistent, or otherwise deficient reports produced by the analytical systems. As such, it plays an important role in the management of their data quality.

5.6.5.1   Managing metadata: information and processes

The unit, which forms part of the company's IT, is responsible for maintaining common enterprise definitions, describing data elements such as:

- key performance indicators (KPIs);
- segmentation attributes (dimensions);
- business objects (entities).

In addition to this, business rules can be captured, describing how KPIs are calculated and derived from each other. Both definitions and rules are captured from a business perspective. IT are responsible for mapping them to their solutions models. The model is similar to the one depicted in Figure 5.4.

The business terms are published in an online data dictionary that is made available to all employees of the corporation. Users, both from the IT and business side, can browse the definitions, formats, and relationships of terms and thus obtain a better understanding. However, this dictionary has other uses as well, namely in systematically managing change and reducing the risk of data quality deficits.

5.6.5.2   Managing change

The definition of a business term may change over time. When that happens, a group of experts, the *business data network,* sit together to agree and specify the change in detail. At this point, changes are managed on a case-by-case basis. Not all can be systematically bundled, though an effort is made to achieve that aim.

This process takes into account business and IT needs, and assesses the impact on existing solutions. Metadata about which solutions use which business terms in their models is not captured, and therefore emphasis is laid on the (data exchange) interfaces. This is for a variety of reasons, not least the fact that a number of solutions are purchased third party packages, which do not expose their inner workings. Hence, they cannot be inspected, which is why it is difficult to know (terminological) dependencies.

However, what is known, is the total portfolio of solutions. Instead of specifically telling (in the style of an oracle) who will be affected by a given change, owners of all solutions in the portfolio are notified and called upon to react to the request for comments. Although some residual risk remains, this has proven to work well, since stakeholders are typically knowledgeable in the field and understand the impact reasonably well for this process to work reliably.

Once binding agreement has been found on a change, IT goes on to implement it. The terminological definitions are used to make the required technical changes, but how they are mapped to the technical world is up to the individual team. This again leaves some level of residual risk, but, for the same reasons as above, that level can be accepted and has been proven to be so.

Thus, the business terms describe the business view of the problem at hand, while the technical solutions are constructed based on their own view of the world. The mapping between business and technical world is specified by way of the term definitions, which is unstructured or loosely structured for the most part. Therefore, mapping activity is mostly manual, but *structured and guided* by metadata about the solutions portfolio.

The obvious disadvantage of this model (some risk of human error) is countered by an obvious advantage, namely that more complex terms and nuances in meaning can be captured without making the process overly bureaucratic or the metamodel too complex, which would incur risks of its own kind.

Take the case of the 'customer,' a concept that may mean many things to many stakeholders. (Actually, one is tempted to think it has an innate tendency to do so.) To people in regulatory affairs, regulators may be considered customers, whereas to the guy in marketing customers are the people and companies buying policies. Both viewpoints are valid, but how to reconcile them in the dictionary?

By allowing for differences in the meaning of a term, that is homonyms, change management becomes easier because only a single term needs be examined. The list of potentially impacted stakeholders may be bigger, but that is balanced by the knowledge of the domain experts, business people, and developers involved. In a way, we substitute concept reification with human tacit knowledge. It works, because the number of involved parties is comparatively low.

5.6.5.3 *Managing data quality*

How is data quality managed, and at what point in time? At this company, business terminology helps managing the completeness and consistency of data. Other dimensions of data quality like actuality or correctness are not affected.

Completeness of the data is achieved by using the business term definitions to *establish a joint understanding*. People are often quite good at telling what is missing in a definition. Given a reasonably good definition of a business concept, the term is used to discuss with stakeholders what must be changed. This may be during a regular change management round, or when taking up a new customer or plugging in a new data provider.

Consistency is established by using business terms as the basis for implementing solutions. Specifically using the reified business rules one can systematically check the derivation formula of KPI implementations to ensure that all required data has been obtained and taken into account in calculations. But also interfaces with third party tools can be treated more homogeneously, because mappings are constructed based on a joint agreement of the underlying semantics.

Hence, two sorts of metadata are used in reducing their risk: one, the portfolio of solutions helps to assess systematically the impact of changes in technical solutions, and to align those solutions with the business viewpoint where needed; two, the terminology itself is the vehicle for establishing what alignment means in terms of the business and reduces the risk of inconsistencies and incompleteness.

5.6.5.4   *Critical success factors*

Establishing the total portfolio of technical solutions and systematically managing changes to business terms is not overly difficult. On the contrary, the critical success factors are related to establishing business terminology in the first place. Based on experience, two factors stick out:

- Having the business agree on definitions to start with is difficult enough. Different viewpoints and traditions sometimes make it hard to find a common ground.
- Obtaining complete and accurate definitions is yet another problem. Here the challenge lies not with finding agreement but in making sure that all relevant viewpoints have been taken into account *before* agreement is sought.

As for the first challenge, introducing homonyms is always an easy way out, but it has the mentioned disadvantages. Therefore, establishing an organizational responsibility in the business is used as a technique to tackle the challenge. Obtaining buy-in and, more importantly, operational support from senior business management gives the effort clout and legitimacy.

As for the second challenge, the issue is not to decide disputed topics. Instead, one needs to make sure that all relevant parties have been brought to the table. This is even more difficult, since these parties are by their very nature often unknown. The only way out here is to use as much human tacit knowledge as possible. Domain experts are involved to cross-check assumptions and involve stakeholders previously left aside, where necessary.

6

Ensuring Compliance

I mistrust all systematics and avoid them. The will to a system is a lack of integrity.

Friedrich Nietzsche

6.1   Overview

- Regulation can be externally or internally driven.
- External regulation often tries to improve and stabilize markets (fairness, transparency, competition, risk) and balance the protection of interests between individuals and the public (fraud, crime, privacy).
- Internal compliance rules typically aim at reducing risks and improving the efficiency and effectiveness of the organization. Industry standards play a role as drivers for internal regulations.
- Organizationally, regulatory compliance requires general oversight, governance execution, and independent audit (both internal and external).
- Internal controls aim to achieve reasonable assurance that the objectives of governance are met and compliance is ensured. They can be detective and preventive in nature.
- Frameworks like COSO and COBIT provide guidance in the implementation of internal control systems. They help to plan, assess, and test the implementation.
- Reference models like ITIL offer best-practice templates for concrete conduct in going about compliance. They complement internal control systems by guiding implementors towards 'good citizenship.'

Aligning Business and IT with Metadata   Hans Wegener
© 2007 John Wiley & Sons, Ltd.

- In financial services, regulation is very diverse. From an IT perspective, requirements revolving around financial reporting, the Sarbanes-Oxley Act in the United States, privacy and crime prevention, and European efforts (SEPA, MiFID) play a big role.
- Important IT compliance issues include data quality, security, change management, and business-alignment.
- Metadata management supports IT compliance in systematic alignment, but also provides techniques for mapping models, managing variability, or shielding complexity from business.

6.2   The goals and means of compliance

6.2.1   External versus internal regulation, and industry standards

A lot of regulation is imposed by authorities exerting oversight over the operation of a firm. In some cases it is directly enshrined in legislation, in others it is based on the judgement of an office commissioned with the task. Such regulation defines minimal standards where there is an overwhelming interest (of the state, federation, or union) in ensuring compliance. These standards pursue a wide range of goals, the most important of which are the following:

- *Fairness:* this mostly relates to ensuring that markets cannot, by design, put participants at a substantial information (dis)advantage, which helps make them more efficient. For example, chinese walls between analysts and investment advisors help prevent moral hazard; disclosure rules for insurance brokers try to prevent bid rigging; disclosure rules for employees aim to avoid insider trading.
- *Transparency:* this also aims at improving market efficiency, by instilling discipline through enabling investor scrutiny. When information is made available to outsiders based on the same (reporting) standard, it makes a company's performance comparable to that of others. For example, publicly held (financial service) firms must disclose their accounts in a particular way by adhering to generally accepted accounting principles.
- *Taxes:* this is an obvious one. The scope, complexity, and number of rules governing taxation is legion and can easily intimidate the unprepared.
- *Competition:* some regulation is aimed at improving the competitiveness of particular industries or markets by providing a level playing field for all participant institutions. For example, the European Union's Financial Services Action Plan tries to improve the single market in financial services. It strives for a number of strategic objectives in retail and wholesale markets, prudential rules and supervision, and wider conditions for an optimal single financial market.
- *(Consumer) protection:* tries to protect consumers from exploitation by opaque and better informed financial institutions. It does so by setting (minimal) standards that ensure

consumers are on the 'safe side' when buying insurance coverage, signing annuity plans, or making investments. For example, risky investments may typically only be sold to well-off customers because they can (a) afford to lose money and (b) hopefully know what they are doing.

- *Fraud prevention:* this is related to fairness, but applies to other illicit forms of making money as well. It aims at making it easier to detect fraudulent activity. For example, by institutionalizing a four-eye-principle for all forms of asset transfer, a company can raise the bar for possible rogue behavior. By requiring the CEO and CFO to sign a company's financial statements, the stakes are made higher (and the responsibilities clearer) when fraud is involved, hopefully reducing the likelihood this really happens.
- *Systemic stability:* attempts to prevent catastrophic failures of the financial system at large by limiting the exposure to certain risks. For example, leveraged finance techniques that involve taking up huge amounts of debt in expectation of certain market movements makes regulators uneasy. This applies almost exclusively to banking, even though the systemic risk posed by increased reinsurance concentration has recently received some scrutiny.
- *Privacy:* whenever individuals give sensitive information about themselves into the hands of institutions like banks and insurance companies, it must be ensured that the firms take good care of protecting their customers' privacy. For example, the health status of a person should only be disclosed to people who need to know. Likewise, many countries regulate which part of a person's wealth status may be passed around and to whom.
- *Fighting crime:* to combat crimes like drug trafficking, terrorism, or other serious felonies, banks in particular need to support authorities in their investigation and prosecution of suspects. For example, detection of money-laundering is often high on the list.

However, not all regulation needs be external. There is good reason for a company to govern itself internally, such as for the following:

- *Professional and ethical behavior:* to counter the risk of legal action or a tainted reputation, companies often establish value systems and principles to guide the behavior of employees in day-to-day work life. This is often about making sure the corporation acts responsibly in society and industry. For example, many firms have chosen to keep a distance from business partners with a reputation for engaging in child labor, showing environmental disregard, criminal wrongdoing, and other acts unacceptable to the public.
- *Efficiency and effectiveness:* in order to make good use of the resources at its disposal, a company may establish oversight over the said resources and attempt to control access to them, or enforce their use. For example, all forms of reuse require governance to actively manage it, like the project portfolio, software components, or more elusively, skills.

Finally, there is compliance with industry standards, which can come in many shapes and sizes. These do not carry the same weight as internal or, even less so, external regulations. However, as a matter of good management it is important to consider these as well, since they bring with them financial benefits (cost savings, risk reduction). Sometimes they are even promoted to official status when chosen by legislators to serve as reference points for implementing certain requirements.

6.2.2 Oversight, governance, control, and audit

The Germans say that 'paper is patient.' Putting out regulations alone does not change (employee) behavior at a company. Checks and balances are required to ensure compliance really does work.

First off, someone needs to be charged with general *oversight* of compliance activity, that is someone with the responsibility to make sure stuff happens. Oversight normally implies some form of legal accountability of a person or gremium, which in the case of publicly held companies is typically the board of directors, and has the general responsibility for the *approval* and *implementation* of regulations, as well as for *setting policies*.

Industry standards are typically out of scope for this gremium, though it may indeed happen, for example when it concerns overall company policy, or when the financial impact is big.

For example, setting policies for reserves, investments, the risk management framework, or approving the migration from one accounting standard to another is normally a task for the board of directors.

Once regulations have been formulated, company activity is subject to *governance*, which is exerted by designated units charged with executing the implementation of regulations. Governance ensures the proper application of regulations. Of particular interest in this context are *controls*, which are vehicles designed to provide *reasonable assurance* regarding the achievement of the governance objectives. As in risk management, controls can be of a *preventive* (*ex-ante*) or *detective* (*ex-post*) nature. The governing body has the responsibility to perform the controls as specified.

For example, before an online banking application goes live, security experts check it to make sure that no (potentially sensitive) data can leak outside and no one can intrude the company network by hacking the system. The governing body is the security team, and the activity is the deployment of the application into the productive operating environment. As another example, an insurance product must integrate well with existing products to fit with the envisioned product portfolio of the company. Product responsibles check it for redundancies with other products before it is offered in the market. The activity is product development, and the governing body is product management.

Finally, to prevent moral hazard, independent *audit* of the *fulfillment of compliance objectives*, as well as of the *adequacy of compliance controls*, is needed. Within a company this function is fulfilled by the internal audit. External audits are designed to extend this beyond the confines of the company for cases of particular interest. Furthermore, in the case of regulatory authorities, extraordinary activity (audits or investigations) that focues on a specific topic can be imposed if there is good reason. For example, the financial statements of a publicly traded company are checked by external auditors. If money-laundering is suspected, investigation is a normal banking activity, where a request is made by the authorities to provide detailed information about individuals.

6.2.3   From goals to controls by using frameworks and reference models: COSO, COBIT, and ITIL

Breaking down the sometimes ambiguous, high-level principles stipulated by regulation to concrete internal controls is not straightforward. Since not everything is different between companies (let alone between companies in an industry), a time-honored principle is to provide guidance in the form of a *framework*, a construct of ideas that helps structure, assess, and measure concrete control systems. It does so by mapping the concepts of the (partially, at least) amorphous, fluid real world onto structured, well-defined, stable ones. This mapping enables a company to embed its own thought system into the construct provided by the framework. Hopefully this goes without great pain, which ultimately saves money and reduces the risk of running into legal problems because something has been forgotten.

An important framework when it comes to IT compliance is COSO. It was developed by the Committee of Sponsoring Organizations (hence the name) of the Treadway Commission, an initiative of the private sector that helps companies design, assess, and execute compliance controls. COSO features five components:

- *Control environment*, which can be paraphrased as the 'tone from the top,' relates to such issues as integrity, ethical values, operating style, and delegation of authority systems, as well as the processes for managing and developing people in the organization.
- *Risk assessment*, which is a systematic identification and assessment of all risks to compliance.
- *Control activities*, which entail the policies and procedures giving (reasonable) assurance that management directives are carried out.
- *Information and communication*, which ensure that internal as well as external parties exhibit not only awareness, but a thorough understanding of the goals of, risks to, and controls around compliance.
- *Monitoring*, which tries to detect control deficiencies and take corrective action for continuous improvement of the overall approach.

The COSO framework has gained widespread acceptance, not least because it is agreed to be a sound basis for achieving compliance with the Sarbanes-Oxley Act (SOX). Still, frameworks like COSO offer only a generic view on achieving compliance, because they do not often refer to a particular industry, let alone company. Fleshing out the details is therefore left to the implementor . . . unless you find a standard for that as well.

Complementing COSO, the Control Objectives for Information and related Technology (COBIT) is, as the name suggests, a set of objectives to ensure diligent control of the use of IT. COBIT was created by the Information Systems Audit and Control Association (ISACA) and the IT Governance Institute (ITGI). It is organized around four areas that are applied to IT activities:

- *planning and organization*;
- *acquisition and implementation*;
- *delivery and support*;
- *monitoring and evaluation*.

When it comes to IT and SOX, COBIT is a good start for establishing controls (another one being ISO 17799, which mostly concentrates on security). It guides management in its implementation of sound controls for all IT activity.

Finally, ITIL (Information Technology Infrastructure Library) is a set of best practices facilitating the delivery of IT services. It was developed by the British Office of Government Commerce (OGC). The ITIL, in a way, offers ready-to-go process templates, performance indicators, etc. ranging from service support to service delivery, asset management, financial planning, and many other sorts of IT activity. ITIL is a good start for laying out the IT activities subject to internal control, and gives reasonable assurance that, by design, the risk of following these activities is low compared to a home-grown approach.

ITIL is an example of a *reference model*, which can be defined as an instantiation or implementation of the concepts that a framework requires. Note the important difference between construct and content: whereas a framework like COSO or COBIT only provides a *thought structure*, a reference model like ITIL is about *concrete stuff*. A framework defines concepts and establishes rules that govern their use so it can be assumed (or even proven) that certain objectives are achieved. Once that lies behind you, you can use the framework (or *map* it) by describing your setting in the terms of that framework. This enables you to use its thought structure to ensure compliance. A reference model is a *high-level, best-practice view of an implementation to be governed*. It guides the concrete design steps and operates at a different abstraction level. It is concerned with how to make sure that internal controls are no longer necessary (or at least that one knows rather quickly where to place them), not how to control compliance.

For example, a particular control objective like 'avoid breach of privacy' may lead to an internal control like 'penetration test' to ensure that the security systems really work. There may, however, already be procedures suggested by a reference model that make sure that, by design, certain security characteristics can be ensured. This may not remove the need for internal controls, yet shift them from penetration tests towards testing compliance with the reference model.

One company I worked for models its processes at a very high level from the business viewpoint. That is, the reference model includes activities, roles, and responsibilities, but excludes applications or other IT-related concepts. When an application is developed, it is possible to *align IT and business*, for example by relating the application to the processes it supports. Alignment is achieved when no other application supports the same (parts of) processes – otherwise you would have found a redundancy. However, you can also use the reference model for aligning business and business: if there are specific requirements in a particular location or for a particular line of business, these can be embedded as long as they match with the high-level process. For example, a detailed process may not exhibit more triggers or results than the high-level process.

You may already have guessed that the thought structures of frameworks act as models, and company activities can be aligned with regulatory rules by supporting the mapping of the models of concrete framework implementations (that is, content) to the thought structure. Thereby you can separate alignment activity into structured and unstructured parts. But first, let us take a look at what regulations are of greatest value to financial services firms.

6.3   The regulatory landscape

Regulations abound in financial services. There is a plethora of rules with which firms must comply. Obviously, not all of them can be covered here, so I shall restrict myself to a few representatives and common themes.

6.3.1   Financial reporting

For obvious reasons, financial reporting plays a significant role for publicly held companies. Financial service companies are no different from companies in other industries in this regard. However, because many more of their operational processes revolve around financial management, reporting is much closer to home than elsewhere. For example, making reserves is such an integral part of the operation of an insurer that it cannot really be separated out as reporting alone anymore. Value-based management, which is a more recent trend that provides a forward-looking embedded value perspective on the finances of a company, only serves to increase this effect.

In any event, reporting on the financial accounts of a company is subject to different rules in different countries. In the United States, the US-GAAP sets the overall framework, which is maintained by the Financial Accounting Standards Board, an organization commissioned by the US Securities and Exchange Commission to establish financial accounting and reporting standards for publicly held companies. Specific issues are treated in so-called Financial Accounting Standards (FAS), which refine the rules of the overall framework. In the European Union, the International Financial Reporting Standard (IFRS) is used as the framework, complemented by International Accounting Standards (IAS), which correspond to FAS. Switzerland has its own regulations under the umbrella of CH-GAAP. Japan has a similar organization as the United States, the Financial Accounting Standards Foundation (FASF). Regulatory authority remains with the Financial Services Agency (FSA). Japan attempts to align itself with IFRS/IAS by allowing foreign and domestic issuers to prepare IFRS-based financial statements, but whether and how that will become possible remains open. Currently, the Japanese Securities and Exchange Law (SEL) provides the framework under which accounting must be performed.

6.3.2   United States: Sarbanes-Oxley Act

Particularly for share issuers listed in the United States, the Sarbanes-Oxley Act (SOX) has been one of the most important pieces of regulation issued in decades. At its core, it tries to improve the quality of financial statements of publicly listed companies. It does, however, concern itself less with particular accounting methods and more with regulating how the responsibilities around corporate governance are to be handled, such as:

- oversight over auditors, which led to the creation of the Public Corporation Accounting Oversight Board (PCAOB);
- corporate responsibility;
- whistle-blowing rules;
- auditor independence.

SOX is not immediately actionable. Interestingly, it does not directly mention IT (though the PCAOB does). For this reason, as has been mentioned above, frameworks like COSO and COBIT have entered the stage and become de-facto standards.

SOX-compliance is sought by an increasing number of companies that are not strictly required to do so. Analysts looking at financial statements are more likely to grant a company the benefit of the doubt if it can prove it is SOX-compliant. Some countries, notably Japan, are thinking about issuing a similar law themselves or have already instituted them, e.g. Australia with the Corporate Law Economic Reform Program Act.

Of particular interest in our context is, some say the notorious, Section 404 of SOX. It requires a company to evaluate and disclose the effectiveness of their internal controls. External auditors must confirm the company's findings. IT has a duty to ensure effective controls relating to change management procedures, documentation, testing, incident and problem management, and more. IT General Controls, as they are known, are controls that cut across all IT systems and ensure the integrity, reliability, and quality of the systems *in general*.

Application controls, which are specific to particular applications (producing financial reports or influencing them materially), focus on ensuring *particular* integrity, reliability, and quality goals are achieved. This includes control activities such as authorization, input validation, automated calculation, or reconciliation.

6.3.3   *Privacy versus crime prevention*

Banks and insurance companies store very sensitive data about individuals. Therefore, beyond the 'normal' data protection guidelines, specific requirements have been made to ensure that data gets disclosed on an even stricter basis than does your telephone number or home address.

The European Union has enacted its Data Protection Directive to protect the interests of individuals when personalized data is stored. Ironically, the same directive has made it easier for companies to pass data across borders within the EU, assuming the same level of protection is guaranteed in the other country as well ('safe harbor' principle). Switzerland has a law that is similar in spirit and letter. The United States so far has no comparable legislation in effect, but Japan has its Personal Information Protection Law.

However, privacy can sometimes conflict with public interest. To fight money laundering and, more recently, terrorism, authorities need the support of banks. In Switzerland, banks must support authorities in investigating suspected crimes. In the United States, the US Patriot Act (or more correctly, the Financial Anti-Terrorism Act) lays out various rules to aid the prevention of financial support for terrorist acts. Section 208 requires financial institutions to keep records about certain transactions, their volume, beneficial ownership, etc.

In health insurance, the interests of the individual need to be balanced with the interests of the public health system. For example, in the United States, the Health Insurance Portability and Accountability Act (HIPAA) regulates the protection *and* disclosure of health information. For example, incidents of highly contagious diseases are of public interest, as are cases of neglect, violence, or abuse. On the other hand, an individual's authorization is required to pass on data for marketing purposes or, interestingly, disclose psychotherapy notes. As always, there are a host of exceptions, most notably state law preemption, with the HIPAA being a federal law.

On the less harmful (though, in many people's eyes, no less illicit) side, tax evasion is a concern to some countries, and some tax havens, notably Switzerland, Luxembourg, Channel Islands, and Austria, have agreed to withhold taxes and pass them on to the country of residence of account holders. This helps balance the (privacy) interests of some countries against the (tax) interests of others. The European Union has issued a directive on that issue, but even that directive allows for varying amounts of data being passed around, specifically whether the account holders remain anonymous.

6.3.4   European Union and the Euro area

Europe is special in that it makes an enormous effort to harmonize the financial services market in the various countries belonging to the European Union and the Euro area, respectively. Two of these efforts are of major proportions and are described in this section.

The European Union has long pursued ambitious goals with its Financial Services Action Plan (FSAP), which aims to harmonize markets and make them more competitive. Among other goals, the European Union tries to complete a single wholesale market, establish an open and secure market for retail services, and ensure the stability of the financial system in its realm. In this context, the Markets in Financial Instruments Directive (MiFID) was issued. It is a regime for investment services and tries to establish a single market in investment services. It regulates, among other things:

- client classification (e.g., professional or retail);
- order handling;
- (pre- and post-) trade transparency;
- execution quality.

MiFID makes organizational and conduct-of-business requirements and attempts to harmonize the operation of regulated financial markets. It goes well beyond the provisions of the Investment Services Directive (ISD), which it supersedes.

Single Euro Payments Area (SEPA) is an Euro area effort to enable customers to make payments throughout the whole Euro area just as efficiently as domestically. Its scope covers

- credit transfer;
- direct debit;
- card payments;
- retail payment, clearing, and settlement infrastructure.

Especially with regard to the latter, the European Payments Council (EPC), which governs the SEPA effort, has decided to adopt the ISO 20022 standard (the Universal Financial Industry (UNIFI) message standard) as the basis for implementing a payment, clearing, and settlement infrastructure. The standard still needs to be fleshed out, which is likely to be done under the lead of SWIFT.

6.4 IT and regulatory compliance

In financial services, many process flows, validation rules, and data standards are deeply ingrained in the IT systems. It is therefore not surprising that IT faces major challenges in achieving, testing, and maintaining compliance with regulation. It is a sign of the times that the EPC mentions rather technical details of standards such as UNIFI (e.g., that it is XML-based) in its official reports, which hints at the significant role IT plays in operating the financial system.

From a business perspective, all transaction-intensive areas like payments, clearing, settlement, or trading are inconceivable without the heavy use of IT. This mostly affects banking, but insurance companies have caught up as well. Data-intensive areas like financial accounting, risk management, pricing, or asset management depend mostly on IT as well. These trends will continue.

When it comes to compliance, IT suffers from the fact that on the one hand the technical complexity is substantial, whereas the other regulations are rarely ever very concrete. (They are not meant to be, anyway.) This brings about the problem of *mapping* principles and rules to concrete implementations. This process is often ill-structured, and hence painful, riddled with problems, and just generally fraught with risk.

For example, imagine a large corporate data warehouse in a multinational bank. Data from around the world is integrated, consolidated, and analyzed. There is not only the run-of-the-mill bank clerk, who gets the weekly customer birthday report for her branch, but also data miners who work on identifying opportunities for selling investments to high-net-worth individuals, cutting across the entire warehouse. Operators and developers need access to all data to identify, assess, and correct production errors. Each of these IT employees uses one or two handfuls of tools, each gaining access to the data through different access control mechanisms. Data warehouses traditionally push the envelope of the available computing power, so performance considerations come into the picture and constrain the range of technologies permitted for implementation of access control. How will all this be reconciled with banking privacy law? Some technologies will have to be used for legal or other compliance reasons, making implementation more difficult or costly. Maintaining this mapping can become a herculean task.

On the other hand, IT can help to reduce significantly the number or magnitude of compliance issues. No insurance company worth its salt does not maintain its accounts in applications; no investment bank operates without the help of trading systems. By automating the activity flow of business processes, enacting rule-based data validation, or leaving the computation of risk figures to machines, we can ensure that certain characteristics relating to compliance are met.

The problem is the same as in risk management, namely that because of this leverage effect, diligent control of automated systems before their deployment becomes highly important.

Hence, the peculiarities of IT in financial services make the following issues of particular concern for compliance:

- *Alignment:* with a higher degree of automation, it becomes more difficult to map requirements stipulated by regulation to the IT implementation, while upholding systematic alignment with the business. For example, for SOX-compliance a company typically maps its business processes to the chart of accounts in the general ledger and identifies those processes that have significant impact on the latter. Which of the processes are implemented in applications, and do they align with the business?
- *Impact analysis:* with increasing integration and a higher degree of 'straight-through processing,' it becomes more difficult to assess the impact of requested changes, both in terms of IT and the business.
- *Security:* the multitude of tools, applications, rules, and flow paths is detrimental to ensuring compliant use of people's data. Systematic mapping and verification of access privileges using business concepts and implementing them in a variety of tools is key.
- *Data quality:* The importance of data quality for risk management has already been mentioned. Transparency in reporting is another case where it matters. Correctness is key to crime prevention, such as in the identification of individuals whose activities are indicative of, say, money-laundering.

Of lesser concern are compliance issues such as fairness, competition, fraud prevention, consumer protection, and professional and ethical behavior. These do play a role here and there in IT (e.g., through system-based double-checks when assets are transferred), but they can be tackled through other means like the control environment or information and communication.

As has almost become good custom to point out by now, architectural alignment helps in achieving IT compliance. Systematic governance is key to ensuring the compliance of applications. In IT, standards play a significant role. There are perhaps hundreds that any IT person can choose from, and a normal project will not be surprised to have to comply with dozens. Of particular interest are:

- *Alignment:* reuse of particular data items or services implementing process activities that align (directly) with the model of the business. This has a direct effect on alignment.
- *Impact analysis:* isolation of change effects, again by reuse of components, data, or rules. This has direct effects on impact magnitude.
- *Security:* ensuring cross-tool and cross-application mapping of authorization rules, which has a direct, *ex-ante* effect. Validating existing privileges against assumedly compliant ones is another direct, yet *ex-post*, effect.
- *Data quality:* direct and indirect effects are the same as in risk. In addition, centralizing the identification of individuals poses another direct effect.

As before the interesting question here is: *where can metadata management support the systematic alignment, use of standards, and impact assessments?* Read on to find out.

6.5 The role of metadata management in ensuring compliance

The role of metadata management in ensuring architectural compliance has already been described. Insofar as building blocks can be identified and provided, the general 'how-to' should be clear. I would instead like to focus on some issues that have so far not been emphasized, but which are practical problems.

Managing access control has been mentioned. Role-based access is a way of providing building blocks to be used in reducing complexity. However, there are only so many roles you can design without repeating yourself. For example, it does not make sense to create two different roles for clerks in two different bank branches. Obviously, you would create one configurable role with one parameter (the branch). It would perhaps only be a little more difficult to ensure consistent access privileges between clerks of the two branches. But what if an employee works in many branches? How about all the (hundreds, maybe thousands of) other roles in your company? Which branches are there, anyway? How about access to different customer segments, detail data, or data from other legal entities? And, to top it all off, each role maps to a number of applications, tools, and technologies in particular ways. Ensuring compliance in such a setting quickly becomes a daunting task.

Two metadata management techniques can come to the rescue: model generation and metadata extraction. Roles as they are seen from the business viewpoint are mapped to privileges as permitted in the technical viewpoint. Administration of roles takes place based on the business viewpoint, and metadata-based generation takes care to create, update, or delete privileges in all the tools and systems required. Metadata describes which these are.

For example, the access control models of some tools have limited expressive powers. It becomes necessary to map complex role privileges to the simple means of the technical layer. Think of the branch-specific role from before and imagine that the third party tool bought only allows you to restrict access to individual database tables, but not individual entries (row-level security). Should you wish for entry-level access control, and assuming it was possible technically, an appropriate mapping would be to generate for each variant of the role (that is, for each available branch) a different variant of the validation rules in the software, adding an access control step.

On the other hand, it is often necessary to live with existing legacy systems. These may have been built a long time ago and there is no money to improve their implementation. There may also be no interfaces to generate access privileges from the outside (which raises big security issues of its own, by the way). One way of dealing with this situation is to take existing authorizations at the technical level and attempt to map them back to the business viewpoint. Once that has been done, compliance can be checked *ex-post* by comparing the 'as is' with the 'to be' state, taking corrective action as required.

As an aside: the mentioned problems with limited expressive power and lack of interfaces in access control systems (especially of third party tools) are somewhat notorious. Sometimes the limitations are so grave that the business viewpoint must be changed (you may say 'dumbed down') to cater to the abilities of technology. Managing such architectural exceptions, specifically in security, is an important issue that has implications for metadata quality (see Chapter 8 for more about systematically managing that aspect).

The automatic execution of process activities, the evaluation and validation of business rules, and the mapping of data from/to external parties are important problems in trading. The FIX (Financial Instruments eXchange) protocol, which is widely used in securities trading, is a specification for passing trade-related messages between trading platforms. Each platform is responsible for complying with the provisions of the protocol, for example by executing trades at a certain point in time, on a specific market, or at a certain price. Not all details are specified, but the numerous business rules must be mapped to existing IT systems. Whether this happens by systematically aligning them with the provisions of FIX at the software code level, or by reifying the business rules in a rule engine and the data mappings in a mapping engine, is the bank's matter. Either way, for the same reasons as above, metadata can play a constructive role in solving these problems. FIX is but one representative of a line of standards where such problems of this complexity occur. There are numerous others where similar metadata techniques help you master the challenge.

In financial accounting and reporting, there is not just one financial statement, but different reports: the annual report, the half-year report, the reserves report, and so on. Each has a different level of detail, omitting some accounts and emphasizing others. By the same token as above, the number of variants occurring in this setting is phenomenal. Furthermore, what do you do when two companies merge? How are the accounts of both reconciled? Again, metadata about the structure (and meaning) of the general ledger, its composition, the rules governing data, and so on, can be used to manage this complexity. I would particularly like to point you to 'feature modeling,' which is good at managing variants where there is an underlying common theme (model, I should say) but many variations.

In combating money-laundering and terrorism, the said problem is appropriate identification of individuals. This is a situation where a bank has no control over what is factually correct (people move freely, and particularly criminals show no propensity to divulge their real identity), but does have an obligation to be diligent in getting to appropriately, factually correct, identification of individuals. Therefore, a real issue is the disambiguation of records, that is to match secondary information (name, address, date of birth, etc.) and attempt to reconstruct factually correct data. Furthermore, because quite a few criminals use shadow firms to conceal their intentions, combining data about individuals with the ownership structure of firms is necessary as well. The core process here is investigation and detection of suspicious activity. The support process is integration of data from various sources, supported itself by mapping and matching machinery that uses metadata such as:

- ownership structures; or
- name mappings (particularly for individuals whose name has to be transliterated to a different alphabet).

Finally, shielding the complexity of IT from business users is an important precondition for making change management work. Technically at least, business is responsible for signing off on requested changes based on an assessment of the impact of that change. This implies that the risks are properly identified, assessed, and perhaps already mitigated. I say technically because, realistically, IT plays a big part in assessing the impact because business cannot be expected to understand all the technical details, which leads to a cross-bleeding of responsibilities. A typical phenomenon to observe is that business de-facto delegates decisions to IT, thereby letting IT shoulder a responsibility that belongs elsewhere. So the choice seems to be between exposing business to the full complexity of IT, or living with the risk of unclear responsibilities, right?

From a compliance perspective this is lamentable, but there is a way out. All you have to do is explicitly segregate business and IT viewpoints and integrate them through metadata. Business formulates change requests (to IT systems) based on an aggregated picture of the world, e.g. one where there is only 'applications' and 'dependencies.' For a large organization, this is perhaps a list of 200 and 1000 objects, respectively. IT, on the other side, deals with the full complexity, i.e. the hundreds of thousands of tables, interfaces, applications, services, software packages, and so on. The mapping between the two viewpoints, which guides IT in its implementation of changes, is metadata. It is captured as part of building and operating systems, but managed separately. In ITIL-speak: change and release management are supported by configuration management.

6.6   Case studies

6.6.1   Ensuring US-GAAP compliance with business terminology

The US-GAAP regulations, as opposed to IFRS, are rule-based. This means that the accounting principles are not broadly formulated and interpreted 'in spirit,' but require specific clarification for particular cases not covered by existing rules. A side effect of this is that companies using US-GAAP for financial accounting are forced to update their accounting requirements regularly.

This is case study of an insurance group that uses a business terminology glossary to model and manage its chart of accounts, specify the data to be reported therein, and document the specific requirements of US-GAAP. The glossary is used for financial accounting at the group level, which is performed separately from (or, if you wish, in addition to) local regulatory reporting.

The particular beauty of this solution stems from the high level of integration (both data and processes), the flexible management of numerous different reports, and the high level of process maturity reached over the years. The history of this solution dates back to 1991, when a Microsoft Word document first captured the accounting requirements for the group in standardized form. The technical platform of the glossary evolved (Microsoft Access followed, today it is based on DB2), and with it the level of sophistication.

6.6.1.1 Managing and disseminating US-GAAP versus local GAAP requirements

The volume of paper required to document accounting requirements properly is astonishing: thousands of pages are filled with ease. For obvious reasons, disseminating that much paper is a drag. For some time, PDF (Portable Document Format) files were distributed over the company Intranet, but that left searching for specific terms or accounting rules tedious. Along came the idea to create an online glossary that could be searched but, where required, still printed out. Furthermore, especially mass-changes to the chart of accounts had to be managed in a structured fashion, both to support IT in its subsequent efforts to implement changes in the reporting applications and also to reduce the risk of human error. In addition, two different accounting schemes have to be supported.

The team came up with a very simple model of a general ledger and the data in it. All important accounting concepts are explained as business terms (all have a name and definition), that is accountants use their lingo to search for requirements and investigate details. From their perspective, the following types of terms are provided (Figure 6.1):

- *Accounts:* make up the general ledger. They are structured hierarchically. For example, the chart of accounts starts with 'Assets' and 'Liabilities' and trickles down from there, with 'Derivative financial instruments on foreign exchange, qualifying for hedge accounting' and others somewhere down below.
- *Attributes:* segment accounts along various dimensions. For example, the legal entity reporting, the line of business covered, the currency in which it is reported, and so on may be required to describe figures reported for an account.
- *Values:* document the permitted range of values to be reported for a given attribute. For example, only United States Dollar, Euro, British Pound, Chinese Yuan Renminbi, and other investment-grade currencies may be used.

Each account has a proper definition that describes in general what it is all about. You can then add a number of *comments*, which are used to refine or interpret the general definition for a specific type of GAAP. Comments have types, which is how the notion of jurisdiction is *reified*. It is thus possible to determine clearly which rules to use for which GAAP.

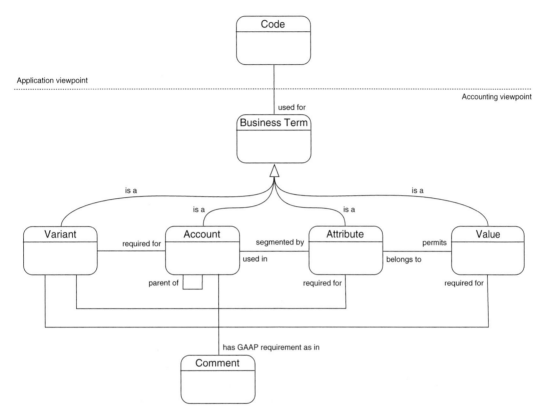

Figure 6.1: Data diagram for documenting accounting requirements based on business terminology

So far, the glossary merely plays the role of a documentation platform. However, in addition to the business term definitions, the glossary also stores the application *codes* used to represent the accounts, attributes, and values in the IT systems. For example, United States Dollar, Euro, British Pound, and Chinese Yuan Renminbi are reported using the ISO codes (USD, EUR, GBP, CYN). This establishes a direct link to the implementation viewpoint, because accountants obviously prefer to type in 'USD' instead of 'United States Dollar.' The applications in turn use codes to optimize query performance, especially for the account hierarchy (e.g., the account represented as '11025' is parent of the account represented as '110251').

From the change management perspective, four steps are necessary to retain US-GAAP compliance, once a change comes along (Figure 6.2). First, a team within the company records requirements as they occur, monitoring the bulletins of external research service providers. Second, at regular intervals, these external requirements are turned into company *policy* by a change management gremium that decides how accounting is to be performed internally.

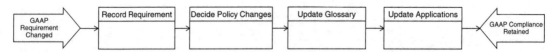

Figure 6.2: The process of maintaining the US-GAAP requirements is straightforward

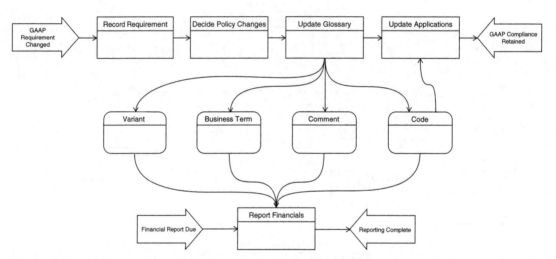

Figure 6.3: The interaction between the process of maintaining US-GAAP-compliant (internal) regulations and the actual financial reporting process is supported by metadata. The business terms describing accounts document the requirements, which are then used as reports are filed

Third, based on the decisions made there, the business terms in the glossary (accounts, comments, attributes, values) are updated. Fourth, the reporting applications are updated as well, making the circle complete. Note the use of comments, which effectively describe the *alignment* of the company with external compliance requirements by reifying policies.

Taking the reporting process into the picture, we arrive at Figure 6.3: the glossary with its business terms, comments, and codes acts as a communications hub between the central accounting team, accountants across the world, and IT, thereby integrating the different viewpoints and ensuring proper alignment with regulatory rules.

6.6.1.2   Using feature modeling to manage financial report variants

One major reason for structuring the chart of accounts was that different variants of the group financial report have to be produced. About two dozen of them are needed to satisfy the demands of:

- external parties (investors, analysts, authorities);
- loss reserving;
- investments.

The unpleasant fact is that for each of these a different variant is needed that sports a different level of required detail. With the general ledger featuring around 800 accounts, each segmented by a dozen attributes, and each of these with dozens of values, the combinatorial complexity is enormous.

The glossary therefore reifies variants as an abstraction of its own in the glossary model and supports administrators with *feature modeling* to manage complexity (see Figure 6.1). The full level of detail is required only for the annual report, the variant that is used to model all others. Administrators then strip detail off accounts for other variants, essentially describing the delta between the full-blown chart of accounts and the one under work.

Since the differences between variants are tolerable, it is cheaper and less risky to model the differences rather than each variant afresh on its own. And, best of all, since all variants are built based on one chart of accounts, it is possible to ensure consistency across reports when aggregating figures.

6.6.1.3 Critical success factors

What carried the effort was the support from high-level company executives, most importantly the group's Chief Financial Officer (CFO). Today, the gremium deciding on change requests sees representatives from across the company, covering accounting, controlling, taxes, reserves, the regions, and more. With these high-caliber managers, the change process carries authority.

Another success factor is tight integration with reporting applications. The data documented is also the data to be reported, which reinforces the importance of the glossary. Even applications outside financial accounting use the business terms there, furthering its reach, authority, and leverage.

An interesting side-topic is task support: only a handful of administrators maintain the business terms and their relationships. They have privileged access to the glossary. However, sometimes it is necessary for a run-of-the-mill accountant to perform a systematic search of the term base to investigate cross-cutting topics. For example, occasionally particular changes in accounting practice require a review of the documentation for key phrases, such as 'FAS 52' or others. One smash-hit (you may really call it so) was the introduction of full-text search to the glossary, enabling non-administrators to prepare material for change requests or investigate their impact.

On a lighter note, ad-hoc requests can be delegated quite easily, easing the workload of the administration team. For example, external auditors regularly request documentation about this or that account or some particular piece of regulation. Printing it on paper would both be inefficient time-wise and also a waste of resources. The team has therefore come to refer the auditors to the online glossary, which is well-received.

6.6.2   Ensuring SOX 404 compliance in IT

The insurance group from Section 6.6.1 set out to become SOX-compliant. For Section 404, internal controls had to be established in various areas to ensure the accuracy of financial statements. Among them were entity-level controls (ELCs), process-level controls (PLCs), and IT general controls (ITGCs), the latter of which will interest us most. The company decided to choose COSO as its internal control framework, and so the way the company handled Section 404 quite naturally evolved from there.

To start with, the company scoped its effort, identifying the relevant legal entities. This list is subject to change, obviously. At the time, it was already managed as business terms in the company glossary (see Section 6.6.1), and so a change management process was in place. However, the candidate lists for SOX must be extracted from there, which happens on a slightly different schedule. Therefore, a mapping is needed to keep both in sync as they change independently. The lifecycle of the business terms (representing the legal entities) drives this mapping to the model in the tool used to manage control assessments and issues. The same takes place for the relevant accounts in the general ledger. These are maintained in the business term glossary as well, and a similar process keeps the list in sync with the SOX list. What is different in the case of accounts is that their hierarchical structure is also obtained from the glossary. It later drives aggregation activities, such as in the case of issues (those affecting accounts at 'higher' levels matter more than ones affecting accounts at 'lower' levels).

Once scope was set, PLCs had to be set up. Some of these are performed by applications. Since applications perform these controls on an automated basis, they must be commissioned, tested, and documented properly. This is the realm of ITGCs. However, at this company the situation was a little more complex. At the same time as the SOX project ran, the IT operations department also ran a project to embrace ITIL. Hence, since both work towards similar goals, they were united under the umbrella of an end-to-end change management project. The goal was to establish both SOX ITGCs and ITIL change, release, and configuration management. Here is how.

6.6.2.1   Using COBIT and ITIL to implement IT general controls

Within the SOX effort, COBIT came to be used as a framework for establishing internal controls. As part of that, controls in 'application development and change management' had to be installed, for example to:

- **ensure appropriate management approval of application development and acquisition activities;**

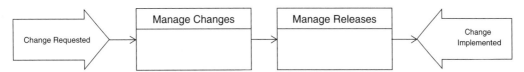

Figure 6.4: The ITIL standard requires this process: changes go first through the change, then through the release management process, after which the change is implemented

- migrate and convert data accurately;
- ensure deployment of tested applications only, and through personnel separate from the programming team (segregation of duties);
- ensure changes to applications are authorized appropriately.

ITIL came to the rescue. In ITIL, considerable conceptual work has been done to ensure exactly the above – yet, at a high level. More specifically, three processes including roles and responsibilities have been described in the standard (Figure 6.4), namely:

- *Change management:* minimize the impact of change-related incidents upon service quality. This concerns itself mostly with the question: what should be done, and what not?
- *Release management:* deliver new application releases into the operational environment using the controlling processes of configuration management and change management. This concerns itself mostly with the question: when and how should it be done?
- *Configuration management:* provide accurate information on configurations and their documentation to support change and release management. This is mostly about keeping stock of what is around.

The idea was to embed ITGCs in the change and release management processes. Approval and authorization would be taken care of within change management, and issues related to data migration, testing, and deployment would be found under release management. All this would be seamlessly supported by a configuration management database (CMDB), integrated with all necessary data sources in IT. For example, a request for change (RfC) would be filed for a particular application, as would a request for deployment (RfD). RfCs and RfDs would compile the necessary sign-offs from the required gremiums or individuals, thereby documenting that the process has been followed by the book.

It so happened that years before the company had established a central application inventory, which held a list of all applications in use. The only task left to the team, so it seemed, was to lump stuff together and let it work. However, that turned out to be too optimistic.

As can be seen in Figure 6.5, the situation was much more complex than initially thought. There were three viewpoints on the topic of 'application:'

- *IT cost accounting:* the existing application inventory had been built to charge costs to owners for processing time, disk space, and the like.
- *ITIL compliance:* the CMDB emphasizes the change management process, that is managing units of change for minimizing negative impact.
- *SOX compliance:* this emphasizes those applications that implement automated PLCs.

This situation led to different levels of granularity. For example, since applications in the inventory are chosen based on assigning costs to the parties causing them, there were location-specific entries in it (e.g., 'Oracle Financials Americas' or 'Oracle Financials Italy'). Others were more monolithic: there was a single entry for a very large life and health application whose scope spanned continents. From the SOX perspective, however, only the underwriting component of that application was listed as relevant, and only the part of it that was dedicated to North American business. Finally, since the CMDB and the ITIL change process focused on organizing sign-offs for units of change, elements that were managed together in the same process were subsumed under the same abstraction, which here came to be known as a *component*. So, what was the team to do?

Surrender was not an option. One critical aspect of proving SOX compliance is the mentioned ability to provide a *trace* from the deployed application back to the RfCs that originally caused it to be the way it is. This requirement made it absolutely essential that there be an integrated, seamless path from the SOX list of applications to the deployed products, including all compliance collateral such as RfCs, RfDs, test results, migration scripts, software code, and so on.

The different viewpoints were accepted and metadata employed to map between them. The CMDB, for reasons that will be explained in more depth below, was chosen as the centerpiece of integrating these different viewpoints (see again Figure 6.5).

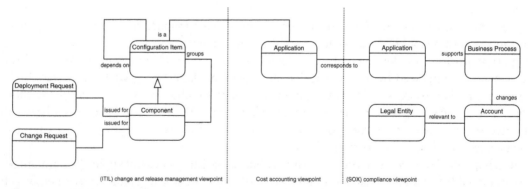

Figure 6.5: Different viewpoints dominated the modeling of data. As part of SOX compliance, all three had to be integrated. The cross-sectional relationships (application to configuration item, application to application) represent the, albeit simple, metamodel

- The application used for SOX compliance stored the legal entities, accounts, business processes, and applications. This was left untouched.
- From there, a SOX-relevant application would map to one or many technical applications from the cost accounting point of view or vice versa (m:n mapping).
- In turn, the technical application would map n:1 to components, which was the CMDB term. As a matter of fact, a component groups configuration items (an ITIL term), of which such applications are but one example.

Currently, the SOX-compliance and cost accounting viewpoints are being consolidated as far as the abstraction 'application' is concerned. This effectively integrates both models and eliminates the need for some mappings and metadata.

In this way, viewpoints could be integrated and existing inventories be reused. However, this does not yet provide a full trace from RfC to deployed product, including links to SOX. Read on to find out how that worked out.

6.6.2.2 *Automated capture and integration of metadata*

ITIL emphasizes the notion of a configuration item (CI), which is a unit of configuration that can be individually managed and versioned (that is, be stored in a CMDB). Typically, this will be an item such as hardware, software packages, middleware, database management systems, and so on. Anything that goes through the change and release management process must be a CI.

The first problem with this is that CIs in a large organization can easily number in the millions. Since the 'size' of CIs is your own choice, you have a certain leeway in reducing that number by making the CIs more coarse-grained. Yet, in this particular situation, this was not an option. In application construction, test, and deployment (that is, in the release management process), a large number of CIs occurs. Artificially reducing that number would not fit reality. There were basically two options:

1. Explicitly separate the change management from the release management viewpoint, and keep the two sets of CIs consistent on a manual basis.
2. Devise a scheme to integrate both viewpoints, ensuring mutual consistency. There is one single set of CIs.

The risk of the first option is that quality suffers and, ultimately, you will be incapable of proving causal relationships between changes to CIs from inception (change management) to production (release management). The risk of the second option is that people who administer and authorize RfCs and RfDs (who are typically business representatives) get overwhelmed by the sheer number of CIs, leading to other quality deficits.

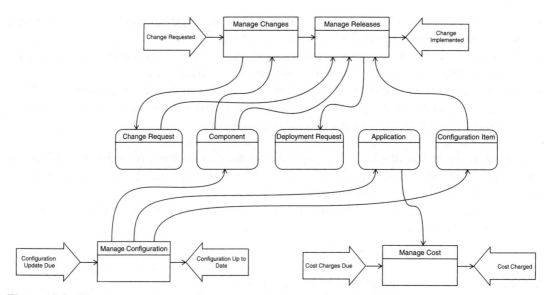

Figure 6.6: Three viewpoints can be integrated via metadata: configuration management provides the basis for change and release management. However, it also provides (part of) the data for cost accounting and SOX controls (not shown). Taken together, they allow a complete audit trail from the formulation of a change request to the deployed product. The process sequencing ensures that the respective data is maintained accordingly

The solution was built on two principles: first, separate the two viewpoints explicitly and integrate them via metadata. Second, automate the capture of CIs as far as possible. This works as follows (Figure 6.6).

Change management works on logical-level CIs, the *components*. These are coarse-granular placeholders for large units of change. For example, (the relational database management systems) Oracle or DB2 may be chosen to act as components. Consequently, a security update or an increase in patch level would be treated as changes to but one component, even though, say, DB2 consists of many different parts. However, not only technical constructs like DB2, but also artifacts more relevant to business, like the partner system or the non-life data warehouse, may be chosen to act as components. Yet, contrary to CIs, there will only be dozens, maybe a few hundred components, but not millions. They exhibit dependencies, which subsume all sorts of component interactions. The main point of these dependencies is that they be used to *identify the set of possibly impacted stakeholders*, should a change in any such component occur. Impact analysis, which is a normal part of any change management, is performed manually. The main purpose of component dependencies is to ensure no one gets forgotten. Here, the main use of metadata about these components is to *reduce complexity and let human tacit knowledge do the rest*.

Release management works on the physical-level CIs. They are fine-grained and expose the entire complexity of IT infrastructure to the user, such as tables, jobs, processes, transactions, and so on. They number in the millions and exhibit all sorts of dependencies, like 'runs in,' 'is composed of', or 'calls.' For example, the above non-life data warehouse uses PowerCenter to transfer reference data from the reference data store into its own database. At the logical level, this is but one dependency. At the physical level, however, there is a host of dependencies, like 'PowerCenter mapping loads from the DB2 tables of the reference data store' and 'PowerCenter mapping stores into the Oracle tables of the non-life data warehouse'. The main use of metadata here is *process automation*, for example by automatically deploying software packages into production. The rate of change and number of CIs to be dealt with is just too big for this to work safely in a manual fashion.

Both the physical and the logical level are held together by metadata extraction. The physical level CIs and dependencies are established by a specialized tool that scans the *entire* IT infrastructure and puts it together in a consistent, integrated, and consolidated form. This is a fully automated process. As opposed to that, the logical level is administered manually. Through metadata extraction, however, the quality of the (component) metadata held there is quality-checked by comparing it to the (CI) metadata at the physical level.

For example, an inventory exists in the company called the data store directory, which holds ownership metadata. It tells you which database table belongs to which application (in the sense of the established application inventory). This way it is possible to tell that the non-life data warehouse has a logical-level dependency to Oracle, and through other mechanisms, to DB2, the partner system, and the reference data system as well. If these logical-level dependencies have not been created before, a consistency violation is logged and, after a while, manually corrected as part of the quality management process. There are other quality checks at both levels of abstraction, such as CIs dangling in the air (not connected to hardware through a series of dependencies).

6.6.2.3 *Critical success factors*

Through an intelligent combination of model integration, complexity reduction, manual activities, and process automation, the solution is able to appeal to many stakeholders at once:

- SOX people can trace change effects seamlessly from an RfC to the deployed product, because the models are completely integrated.
- Business users can continue to formulate RfCs based on the coarse-grained abstractions they are used to, because of the separation between logical and physical level.
- IT staff can work in the physical-level world to which they are accustomed, while being certain that their work is compliant with regulations. Most importantly, their need for automation is fulfilled.

- The people in cost accounting need not worry, because their platform for charging application owners remains almost untouched.

This comes at a higher cost and complexity, though, incurring the risk of (meta)data quality deficits. The management of cross-level consistency is an important task to sustain this solution's utility. Chapter 8 will return to this topic.

6.6.3 *Terrorism and money-laundering: supporting the customer investigation process by automating data mappings*

This case study concerns a globally operating bank that wished to streamline its customer investigation process. Customer investigations are carried out in connection with prosecutions, administration of estates, or other legal actions. This bank has to handle about 5000 individual investigation requests per year plus an increasing number of special embargo requests, such as the various terror–related search lists. The reasons for such investigation requests can vary widely, so I would like to focus on two particular aims, namely combating terrorism and preventing money-laundering.

In the recent past, many countries have issued anti-terrorism bills, most notably the United States with its 'Patriot Act' in 2001. These bills impose the requirement on the part of banks to cooperate with authorities by providing reports upon request. Furthermore, banks monitor client transactions on a continuous basis to detect suspicious activity hinting at money-laundering.

There is a (rising) number of blacklists, such as terrorist lists, the United States' 'Office of Foreign Assets Control' list, the 'FBI Control lists', and so on. Furthermore, a bank strives to avoid having so-called *politically exposed persons* (dictators, shady types, etc.) as customers, obviously all to comply with regulatory requirements and avoid reputational and legal risks.

The original investigation process was *distributed*: in the investigation *request phase*, a number of internal departments would become involved, possibly using several applications or archives to compile the requested data and send it back to where the request came from. There, during the *reply phase*, results were consolidated and forwarded. This process had several shortcomings:

- It led to redundant processing of requests, in terms of people as well as applications involved.
- Some investigation activities performed were simply unnecessary, such as reporting data from sources irrelevant to the request.
- There was a risk of inconsistent handling of requests decentrally, particularly where names of individuals had to be transliterated to the Latin alphabet.

- Ambiguities ensued when results were consolidated centrally, leading to data being considered that described the same person or company by mistake, or when relations that did exist between persons and companies were not detected.

A decision was taken to revise the process, *centralize* it completely and *automate* it partially. The revised process (Figure 6.7) now works like this: upon request, an employee in the central organization uses the application to generate a list of *potential positives* with respect to a given investigation. This list is passed to a compliance officer who decides, based on further investigation, which should be the *true positive/negatives*. That list is then passed on to relationship managers to take further action.

The specific problem to solve here was the integration of data from various sources. The internally used customer file provides data such as name, date of birth, or (correspondence) address. This has to be matched with externally provided data, most importantly search lists related to terrorism, politically exposed persons, and so on. The personal details (name, date of birth) of individuals are at the center of the matching process, since this is often the only thing known about them. In addition, criminals often obscure their identities by forging their address details. Hence the problem was *metadata extraction* (Figure 6.8): establishing relationships

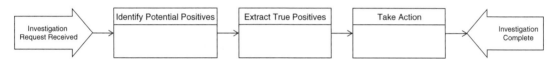

Figure 6.7: Process diagram of the customer investigation process

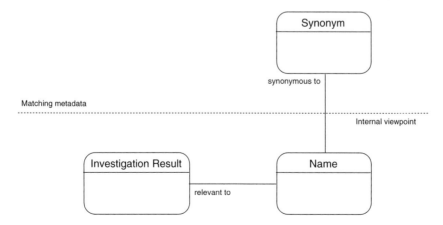

Figure 6.8: Data diagram of the customer investigation process

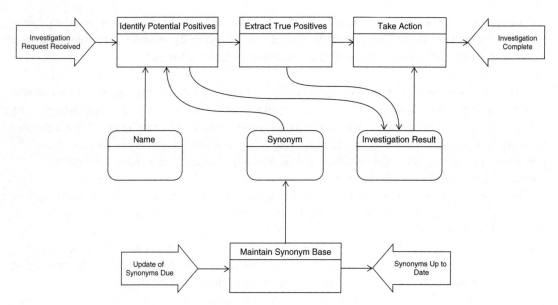

Figure 6.9: Data diagram of the customer investigation process

between persons (names) based on knowledge about similar-sounding or equivalent names (synonyms). The synonyms are the metadata that link names used in the internal viewpoint. The relationships express the potential positives, that is the matches between individuals. The next step is to identify the true positives/negatives, thus completing the difficult part of the investigation request.

The bank decided to purchase a product on the market that supports these steps. It comes with a synonym database and a rule engine that generates candidate matches. Taking a look at the data flow (Figure 6.9), you can see how this couples the processes: the synonym base is maintained outside the compliance team, in fact outside the company altogether. This semi-complete metadata (synonyms plus rules) is deployed at the bank and combined with customer data there, ultimately to yield a candidate list for the compliance officers' perusal.

6.6.3.1   Critical success factors

The critical piece that made this solution a success was outsourcing the provisioning of synonym data, as well as the matching engine and rules. The bank stands little chance of keeping track of all the potential ways names may match or not, irrespective of the cost incurred. Apart from that, it is not its core business to do so.

Another notable success factor for the process itself was the semi-automatic handling of mappings. There were various cases where the machine claimed a match between individuals that in fact were not the same person. In one particular case there was a man who was born in the same year, had once lived in the same house, and had the same name as another man who had caught the authorities' attention. Only because the birth dates were known exactly did this not lead to identification of both men as 'identical.' Another example (irrelevant from a compliance viewpoint, but relevant from a reputational perspective) is people who have several correspondence addresses for their several bank accounts. Automatic matching may lead the bank to write a letter to the home address, only for the account owner's wife to find out about her husband's secret second bank account.

6.6.4 *Ensuring tax compliance ex-post-facto: another case of metadata extraction*

Sometimes, compliance rules become effective retroactively, requiring financial service companies to produce historic (meta)data that had not been previously captured. The activities that might have captured that data have long been completed. In this case, a creative reconstruction of what was most likely is inevitable.

This is the case study of a German service provider to banks in the securities business, offering clearing and settlement processing services, among others. As part of their services, the company produces tax records for customers to be presented to authorities. One challenge concerned a change in Section 23 of the German tax code (EStG) that affected the handling of *capital gains tax* in cases of so-called *speculative investment activity*. The other challenge was a change to Section 17 of the code concerning *corporate actions* such as mergers, acquisitions, stock splits, etc. The gist of the matter is that the state wants to know when an investment was made, when it was sold, and under what conditions.

For example, when an individual subject to German income tax purchases stock and then resells it, the duration of possession determines whether the activity is considered a speculative investment and is therefore taxable. The duration is generally held to be one year. Taxes are also to be paid after a corporate action becomes effective, but not in all cases. In one case, the old investments are considered to have been sold *and* purchased at the original acquisition price, in the other they are considered to have been sold and reacquired at the respective current market value. The question of whether the one or the other case applies is determined by the legal conditions and statutes under which the corporate action took place.

As such, the company had to provide tax records to customers that take into account the historic activities leading to the current status in a customer's deposit. To that end, historic (meta)data about transactions had to be established from the company's own records, and additional data provided by external data providers, where applicable. Yet, the situation was complicated by the fact that quite a few customer activities could have made that history and its handling ambiguous.

For example, if a couple put together their investments in a single deposit, a disambiguation of the securities jointly held is required. Who owned what before the fact must be known to do that. Also, gains from currency exchange fluctuations are not taxable if the underlying activity is renting out an apartment to someone else. If the rent for the apartment is paid to an account in, say United States Dollar denomination, then the exchange rate gains on that account are not considered as taxable under the law.

All the metadata about the transactions was only partially, if at all, available in the 50 or so applications that the company operated. In this situation, two tasks had to be mastered, both subject to the above compliance considerations: first, the historic data had to be made available; second, the applications had to be subsequently migrated to hold the historic data, and capture future data henceforth.

6.6.4.1 Utility-focused extraction of history

At the formal level, this amounts to extracting metadata from available (historic) transaction data. The main issue here was that exactly that history was not available. In this situation, the company resorted to a *utility-based* approach: the metadata related to the taxation viewpoint did not have to be 100 % correct, since customers would usually contact their tax advisor after reception of the bank's records to provide additional information before filing the official return. For example, the company may not know that a foreign currency account is used for renting out an apartment, but the customer surely knows and can add that missing piece of evidence for the tax authorities.

As such, the company could just have assumed the worst case and declared all transactions taxable (bar those that are known not to be). However, that would have put off quite a few customers, since the burden of figuring out what is really taxable and what is not would rest exclusively on their shoulders. By the same token, ceasing the effort and declaring all transactions not taxable would have been considered equally unacceptable. Instead, the focus was put on maximizing the quality of the tax-related reports from the perspective of the process within which they were used, that is their utility for the customer.

Hence, in a first step, the history of transactions was scanned to extract *automatically* tax-related metadata where possible. This step focused on the true positives/negatives, that is cases where it was known that the transaction was taxable. The rules and business logic used in this step were purely based on the available data history. The transactions of about 90 % of all customers fell into this category, which is already a good achievement.

In the second step, the company tried to identify false negatives, that is transactions of customers that were ambiguous from the tax perspective, as far as could be told from existing data. This step was driven purely by the impact on the customer base: about 10 corporate actions were identified that created ambiguity for a lot of customers. For these, the metadata was *manually* compiled. The company directly contacted the firms involved in said corporate actions and enquired about the nature of the change. This metadata was then added to the rule base, and metadata extraction run once again. This post-processing step increased the customer coverage rate from 90 % to 96 % (true positives/negatives).

At this point, the company ceased its efforts. With the remaining 4 % covering only unusual or uncertain cases costly to reconstruct, the reports sent to customers always contained a remark that the tax-related data should always be double-checked by an advisor.

6.6.4.2 *Critical success factors*

The main success factor was that metadata quality was defined from the customer's perspective: optimizing the *utility* of the metadata provided about the transactions. Demanding complete coverage of all possible cases would have been a herculean task which, given the time constraints of the project at hand, would not have been feasible.

This case study also shows that a relatively simple approach can achieve a substantial coverage of cases. The combination of rule-based metadata extraction, case-based metadata extraction, and human tacit (tax code) knowledge was straightforward, yet it ensured that compliance was given the attention it deserved.

6.6.5 *Metadata-based reuse of rules in money-laundering detection*

This is the story of a small software startup specializing in rule-based tools for detecting and handling money-laundering. But, in a way, this is also the story of a shared 'market' for detection rules that rests on reification and metadata. It is particularly illustrative in the light of Chapter 3, as it demonstrates the power of metadata in supporting the formation of building blocks and fostering reuse.

The startup, which was founded in 2000, developed a platform for designing, managing, and executing business rules to detect statistically relevant behavior in their data. The peculiar thing about this platform is that, from the start, it was built for reuse and composition of rules. Out of the box, the platform provides about 50 rules that, taken together, give a bank confidence that it is doing enough to satisfy regulators. More specifically, these rules had been checked by lawyers for compliance with the regulations in various jurisdictions, offering a 'no worries' package. With that, the startup intends to answer the question of many compliance officers: 'What do I have to do to be compliant?'

The rules go quite far. They demand a certain set of data to check against, which is something that not all banks can provide. Also, some of them use sophisticated algorithms (full second order predicate logic, that is) and statistical methods that are not easy to understand. For that reason, and also in order to accommodate the following, not all of the rules provided out of the box were used by banks:

- checks addressing reputational in addition to purely legal risks;
- peculiarities of the available data;
- organizational learning, training, and execution process.

Hence, the shrink-wrapped package had to be customized to local needs and requirements. This had been foreseen.

6.6.5.1 *Architecture, tools, and processes*

The architecture of the management platform features three distinctive tools that work together to support three distinctive processes. These address the different needs of an organization when it accustoms itself with such technology. Mostly, such an architecture is designed with the assumption that this process is long (in the order of months to years) and riddled with changes (due to new or improved understanding of the data or the rules themselves).

First off, after the solution has been installed, it enters the *setup and training phase*, which is supported by the *rule builder*. The available rules, which are stored as metadata, can be changed, composed to build new rules, or discarded in favor of entirely new ones. In this first step, the rules are adapted to the environment. For example, some data may not be available, making some checks unworkable. Others may have to be put in their stead. Or, for legal or reputational reasons, some checks are abandoned and others added. In any event, the rule builder is used to model these rules. As collateral to the modeling process, metadata about the rules is produced:

- Documentation of the semantics: what does this rule mean in business terms?
- Rule structure: what data do I have to provide to such a rule, and what data is passed on?

This metadata is used in a different process, the *detection phase*, to read transactional data and check it against the rules formulated. The *aggregation builder* does this job. More specifically, it uses the rule structure on the original transactional (or pre-computed, aggregated) data to detect suspicious behavior. The result of this phase is a list of candidate cases, requiring further handling by humans to filter out the true positives.

This leads to the last step, the *handling phase*. The list of candidate cases is passed to the respective staff for further investigation. Again, a tool permits banks to configure to whom cases get routed, depending on certain limits, and who may close cases, forward them to other staff (higher or lower in the hierarchy), or return them.

Figures 6.10, 6.11, and 6.12 illustrate the workings of this platform: there are three different processes, each using different data and metadata, supported by three different tools.

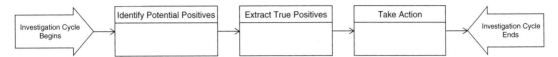

Figure 6.10: The process is similar to the one in Figure 6.7

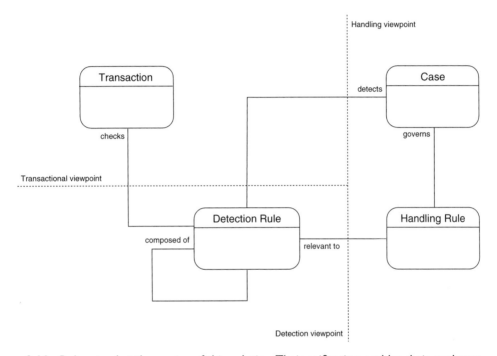

Figure 6.11: Rules stand at the center of this solution Their reification enables their exchange

6.6.5.2 *Supporting the emergence of detection and handling rules*

As can be imagined, setting up, configuring, and training such a complex solution is a learning process. It works in cycles where previous decisions are revisited, reviewed, and sometimes also revised. This means that the rules previously captured can be altered, for example:

- Some customers worked *top-down*, beginning with many detection rules and progressively taking them away as too many false positives/negatives were detected. Others worked *bottom-up*, starting with few rules and slowly increasing on their target rule set. Interestingly, most customers ultimately arrived at about 25–30 detection rules.

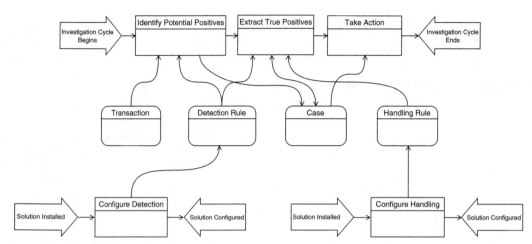

Figure 6.12: This solution requires three steps to run: first, detection rules are formulated; second, handling rules are set up; finally, both are run. Further adjustments are made as experience grows

- After the training phase, customers often decided to *reverse handling flow*. First, many cases were sent to a high-level compliance officer who subsequently delegates work to lower-level staff. After a certain time, when confidence in the rules and processes has grown, most cases were assigned to the lower-level staff and only occasionally escalated to higher levels.

This cyclical learning process was supported by the alteration of the metadata reifying all these rules. The platform was ideally suited to support that process, because it offered all the flexibility needed to deal with this form of change. More pronounced perhaps, any platform that is not just installed but adapted to an environment in a continuous-learning fashion, will benefit from such an architecture.

After a while banks began to approach the startup to ask what rules other banks were using. This was understandable, since the rules were reified in metadata and could thus be extracted from (and reimported into) the platform. As such, they were accessible to review. The company decided to hook up banks with each other to exchange, discuss, and reuse rules. This met with enthusiasm, and subsequently meetings started to do just that. This is an instance of an emerging market, supported, if not fostered, by reification. Some banks indeed decided to reuse rules and could readily export and import them.

6.6.5.3 Critical success factors

The main success factor is the reification of rules, their structure, and the data required for them. Without a joint metamodel there would have been a much lower chance that the banks could have compared (read: mapped) their rules (read: models) successfully. At the very least it can be assumed that the process would have taken much longer, be riddled with more semantic problems, and generally be trickier.

This case study also shows that establishing a rule-based software system is not for the faint-of-heart: only 15–20 % of banks built rules, completely left to their own devices. All others used the consulting services offered by the startup or its technical partners. The conceptual tasks required as part of setup, training, learning, revision, and correction can demand in-depth knowledge. Quite often, this knowledge is not available in compliance departments. From their perspective as a user, it is crucial to have continued access to in-house IT or consulting services.

Learning was typically characterized by three problems. First, banks had to identify and understand their own data, gather its semantics, and learn to trust it. This is mostly a data quality challenge. Second, banks had to understand the detection rules provided out of the box and select those that suited them. Third, and this is the challenging part, bank staff began to optimize rules for results, question them, and adapt the platform configuration to their exact needs. This normally took a matter of months, not days, giving an impression of the duration of such activities.

6.6.6 Access control between legal entities in data warehousing

The data warehouse discussed in Section 5.6.1 is a platform of substantial proportions. Today, an estimated 11 000 users have access to reports, can issue database queries, and construct analytical applications. These people serve many different parts of the organization, spanning a multitude of business units and legal entities.

Sharing data between business units is merely, you may say, a political issue. There are various reasons why employees do not want others to see 'their' data, and there was strong opposition to make the warehouse platform as open as possible. However, the buck stops with legal requirements. Sharing data between legal entities, particularly data about customers, is subject to extremely strict rules. Generally speaking, unless there is a clearly identifiable operational need, or the customer has explicitly consented, sharing data is prohibited. The penalties for violations are quite drastic, and so access control became one of the core concerns of platform management.

Consider the number of people accessing the data warehouse today; then, also consider that access is typically not only granted in a single place like the reporting tool, but also cuts across a whole line of places: database, data staging tool, server operating system, and more (Figure 6.13). Furthermore, consider that there were already existing systems that had to be migrated to the new platform. Here, the access privileges had to be maintained where possible. All in all, the complexity occurring in this area was substantial; and, perhaps more

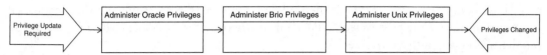

Figure 6.13: A manual process execution would mean that administrators have to repeat the same steps for each target technology (Unix, Oracle, Brio), very likely creating inconsistencies over time

importantly, the rate of change in access rights was even trickier to handle. In a word, this was an ideal playing field for metadata management. Here is the full story.

6.6.6.1 Role-mapping across the tool and application landscape

The data warehouse typically features five types of users that access the data held in it, and the tools that make up the technical platform. They differ substantially in number, needs, and, perhaps decisively, the tools used:

- *Developers:* design and implement analytical applications, using the platform tools and data. They need full access to tools and data to do so, but only up until the test environment.
- *Support users:* in the productive environment, access to data is restricted to trouble-shooting (e.g., failed loads) and maintenance activities (e.g., data quality analysis). Access to platform tools in production is prohibited. Today, the number of support users (many of which are not developers) in this case ranges around 150 people.
- *Standard reporting users:* retrieve standardized, perhaps parameterizable reports to perform their daily work. They number well beyond 10 000.
- *Ad-hoc reporting users:* design and execute reports to fulfill unforeseen data analysis requirements. They have limited access to the platform tools, most specifically databases (for query construction) and reporting tools (for report design). They total to about 200 people.
- *Data miners:* highly educated specialists who perform complex statistical analyses, e.g., for marketing purposes. Require direct access to all data in the databases. Only a handful of employees belong in this category.

Today, about 700 different such roles have been defined for the warehouse. It should also be noted that there is a host of technical users that run the platform processes like loading and transforming data, although they are not of interest here.

The main approach to managing this maze was looking at the numbers and the data flows. If you look at the number of people, standard reporting users are clearly the group that requires most attention. They typically 'see' only a tiny slice of the overall data cake; they mostly use data marts; and they usually only access them via the reporting tools and database. This means that, using the products used in this platform, 10 000 users must be created on Brio (the reporting tool), several hundred on Unix (the operating system), and 10 000 on Oracle (the relational database). Furthermore, roles must be created in each, and the granted privileges (i.e., assignment of a user to a role) kept consistent.

Hence, three different viewpoints had to be kept in-sync: first, the logical viewpoint, where roles like 'Clerk' or 'Report Designer' are modeled; second, the Oracle viewpoint, where corresponding users and roles are administered; third, the same for Brio and Unix. Over time, the assignment of Oracle roles, as well as of Unix and Brio groups to logical roles, may change. For example, for performance reasons a specific implementation in Oracle may be chosen in the new data mart release, requiring changes to the Brio groups as well, and so forth.

The compliance challenge was solved as follows: first, the three different viewpoints were reified, each featuring a model element for users and roles (Figure 6.14). Then, a generation mechanism was devised that maps the roles at the logical level to those at the physical level (Oracle, Brio, Unix). Each time a new logical role is added, changed, or removed (in other words, makes a step in its lifecycle), the mapping metadata is bound. This enables the tool that the bank uses to create automatically corresponding privileges in Oracle, Unix, and Brio, once the administrator has created them at the logical level.

The administrator only concerns itself with roles like 'Clerk' or 'Report Designer,' and users like 'Frank' and 'Sally.' Unbeknownst to the administrator, however, in the background these may be mapped to 'RCLRK' or 'A0431391.' This design effectively ensures *ex-ante* the

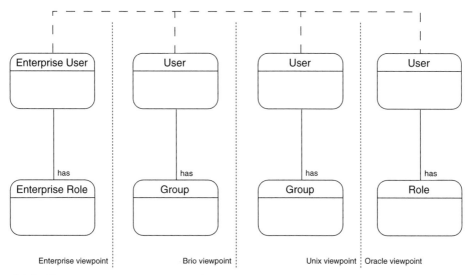

Figure 6.14: The mapping between the different viewpoints is relatively simple. Users map to users, and roles to roles/groups. At the model level, complexity cannot be seen

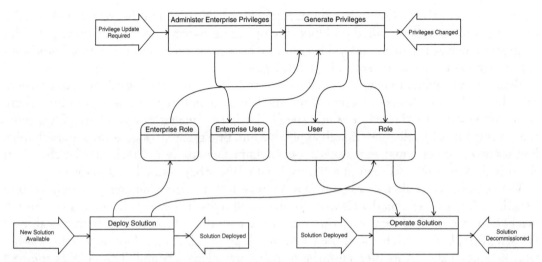

Figure 6.15: The (revised) process flow comes about with a different data flow. As part of solution deployment, an enterprise role and a number of roles for Oracle, Brio, or Unix are created. Furthermore, the mapping mechanism is made known to the generation process, which takes care of mapping an enterprise user and role to the appropriate tool user and role/group. Note that the operational process for the solution only relates to the latter

compliance of access privileges across the tool landscape. Besides, this design also improves performance, as many manual steps have been eliminated.

The only step that has to be added to ensure compliance is to check the mapping logic for compliance. (That is, to make sure that, for example, no database administrator roles are assigned to a user obtaining an innocent-seeming logical role.) This step comes at the end of the development process, where *architects and business representatives* take a look at the proposed mapping (Figure 6.15). Architects ensure compliance from an operational perspective (e.g., that row-level security in the database is used on a need-to-have basis, thereby ensuring appropriate performance). Business representatives, or more precisely; the data owners sign off the role from the perspective of (internal and external) regulations.

Yet, so far only one out of four groups of users has been addressed. What about the others? It so happens that their number is relatively limited. There is not so much fluctuation, and substantial costs are associated with automation. For example, the data staging tool does not allow creation or administration of users from the outside. Tool integration would require expensive customization. The construction cost would go up substantially, without significantly reducing friction or extraction cost. Therefore, in this case the bank decided not to reify any mappings for the complex roles, but to administer them manually and pursue *ex-post* compliance checks.

6.6.6.2 *Extraction of role models with data mining techniques*

As was mentioned before, the existing data mart applications had to be migrated to the new platform. This posed a challenge: four out of the five applications had a clearly defined user community that exhibited a strong correlation between membership in particular organization and role memberships (e.g., people in the credit department had all 'Credit Manager' privileges). However, one application stuck out. It had users distributed all across the bank. This data pool provided raw, but consolidated operational data like personnel records, account information, reference data, and others. Most of its users were authorized individually, i.e., there was no identifiable role structure in the user community. The only hint was the 630 database views assigned to about as many users.

Due to the fact that the user community was spread so widely, it was not possible to ask people personally. This could have meant the analysis having to cover large parts of the bank, which was considered impossible, given the existing time constraints.

Another part of the task was to find a good tradeoff between the number of abstractions (roles) and their size. Theoretically, each user could be assigned one role, authorizing him or her individually. However, this would compromise intelligibility. Too coarse a role set might have led to security gaps, compromising confidentiality. According to the principal architectural decisions the task was to extract roles and associated mapping metadata. This had to happen in a way so that the result would be very stable, yet intelligible, and at the same time faithfully reproduce the existing authorizations.

In concrete terms, the database views had to be taken and an analysis run of which of the users were granted which views, and then generate an assumption from that as to which roles there should be. This assumption was then validated with the end users. Since there were data miners available in-house, the team asked them for a favor: use data mining as a method to extract roles from the existing authorizations like views and database grants. It turned out to be an excellent idea.

Three scenarios of possible association between existing access rights, users' organizational unit, and the roles stood at the beginning of the data mining process:

1. An association exists between the organizational unit of users and the views to which they are typically granted access. In these units tasks are related to the hierarchical division of labor (vertical dependencies).
2. Users exist without association between the views to which they are typically granted access and the organization in which they work. These are tasks that are related to work spread across the organization (horizontal dependencies).
3. A certain range of untypical cases (no association) exists.

Using an association rule induction algorithm (*a priori*), 32 patterns were identified, from out of which nine role candidates were extracted. All of these were checked with business representatives to confirm assumptions. 354 users could be covered, which made up 90 % of the community targeted in the first step. Only four out of 32 patterns remained unused, which was mostly due to time restrictions, rather than because they did not yield useful candidates. During no interview with the business side were assumptions revised substantially. Data mining proved to be an excellent technique for extracting metadata.

6.6.6.3 Critical success factors

The separation of simple, common cases from complex, rarely occurring cases was the dominant cause of success in the above setting. By handling rare cases manually, and by pursuing *ex-post* instead of *ex-ante* compliance, helped make access control management feasible, cost-effective, and reliable. Furthermore, it eliminated some of the more tricky technical issues such as automatically administering users in the data staging tool.

One more, as yet unmentioned success factor, was the integration with the existing user administration organization and process. For obvious reasons, establishing a new user administration organization and process would have been a herculean task, and again, not possible within the timeframe set by project milestones. However, the team commissioned with user administration (and some of the governance tasks around it) did not want to learn the administration of half a dozen tools. This is where the generation mechanisms did wonders. The team only had to master one tool, while a number of them were administered in the background. As such, complexity was effectively shielded from them.

One more tiny detail: it became apparent during the project that some logical-level roles had to be combined. For example, customer advisors are typically permitted to see only the data of customers they personally advise, or perhaps are advised from out of their branch. This required reifying the likes of branches, business units, and locations in the logical viewpoint model. Accordingly, the generation mechanism had to be updated, and so on. It was important for the success of the solution to balance the number of roles (as low as possible) against their intelligibility (not over-generalized). As stated in Section 4.2.2, roles had still to be a commodity that needs only to be parameterized instead of being highly customized, exposing the whole complexity to administrators.

6.6.7 Documenting the Opening of Relationships

In 2000, an internationally operating bank wanted to improve its relationship opening process for its retail and private banking customers. During relationship opening, the bank compiles documentation about the customer and the nature of the relationship. The necessary forms must be filled out and signed. In most cases, the forms are designed to document facts about the *beneficial owner*, i.e. the person who ultimately owns and controls the assets managed as part of the relationship. For example, the bank must understand whether:

- the person opening the account acts as an intermediary for the beneficial owner or not;
- the customer is a politically exposed person, requiring special handling;
- the customer is someone who the bank does not want to do business with, known to engage in fraud schemes, or suspected to be a terrorist;
- appearing in person is required;
- withholding tax must be applied because of the beneficial owner's domicile.

Until 2000, the relationship opening process was conducted jointly by the customer advisor and compliance officers. A relationship was opened by the customer advisor, forms handed out and signed, and then passed on to compliance for double-checks. Occasionally, customer advisors would hand out the wrong forms, forget to ask certain questions, or omit to fill out required form entries (Figure 6.16). Although the double-checks caught many of these errors at a later stage, the bank was exposed to reputational risk, had to perform costly corrections, catch up with their customers, and also risk running foul of local compliance requirements.

The bank decided to improve the internal, process-level controls for relationship opening by automating them. An application was designed that:

- actively guides customer advisors through the various steps of the process;
- compiles forms and wordings;
- checks forms for completeness.

A total of 120 (PDF) building blocks for compiling and printing the necessary paperwork are in use today, with translations into five languages, resulting in 600 building blocks. Many of the

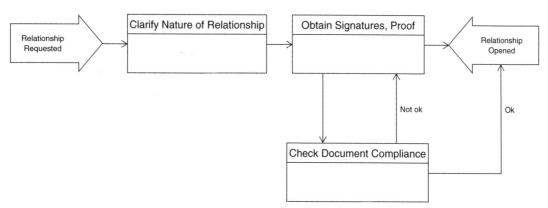

Figure 6.16: The original relationship opening process involved *ex-post* compliance checks of documents captured earlier. This occasionally required the bank to get back to the customer for clarifications and rework

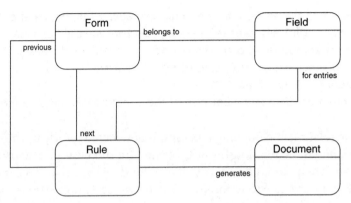

Figure 6.17: The process of relationship opening, before and after changing the internal controls from *ex-post* to *ex-ante*

rules governing this process are determined by regulatory authorities. However, beyond these requirements the banking industry has developed further rules. They establish common practice that is not strictly enforceable, but will be considered before court if not followed. Therefore, to be a good corporate citizen, the bank must consider both sets of rules to be regulating its conduct.

The application was based on a business rule engine that worked in the form of a question-and-answer game, controlling the activity flow of the customer advisor. The engine works in the style of a state-transition machine, deciding after each question how to proceed based on the answer, and whether to produce collateral by printing out forms to be signed (Figure 6.17). The total number of business rules rose quickly to about 10 000, giving an idea of the combinatorial complexity (and operational risks) of this task.

Metadata management plays a crucial role in making this possible. A total of three processes are involved and play together to ensure compliance (Figure 6.18). First, managing regulatory compliance requires the bank to monitor the latest developments in industry practice and regulatory requirements. This step particularly strives to ensure that all relevant changes are tracked. Second, once new rules come out or existing ones are updated, they are maintained in the business rule database as metadata. This step embeds the required changes with the existing rule set, possibly making adjustments to how they are composed to achieve greater simplicity or reuse existing rules. Third, the relationship opening process is coupled with the business rule maintenance process, thereby implicitly ensuring regulatory compliance.

6.6.7.1 Collateral benefit: improved performance

In 2003, when the rule base had grown to a substantial size and the benefits had become evident, the bank took another step to exploit it further. It realized that, once the customer

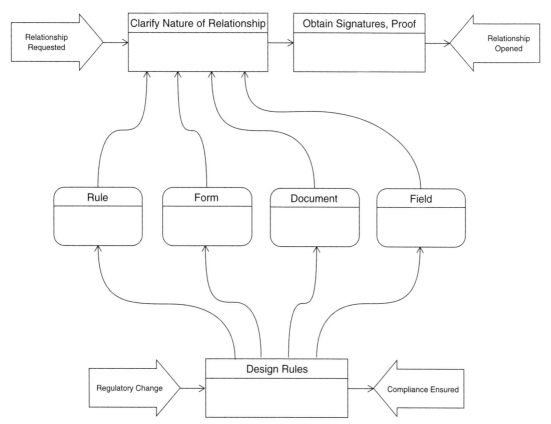

Figure 6.18: The relationship opening process and compliance management: two processes coupled to work together. Note that relationship opening and regulatory compliance have been decoupled and the interaction between the two reified in the form of metadata

advisor had arrived at the end point of the opening process (that is, the rules were evaluated and no further data needed to be gathered), all that remained was to create a customer file and assign products to it like deposit accounts, investments, etc.

This was a piece of cake, given that the rule engine stored the state of interaction in its memory, including all relevant data about the relationship. It was hence only a matter of simple model generation to create the mentioned data in the bank's systems. In fact, this is one of those cases where a rule engine, which operates a support process based on metadata, hands off data to the core process for further use.

One little problem for the solution designers surfaced pretty early and was exacerbated by model generation: people make mistakes. Hence, for usability and user acceptance purposes it was crucial to provide an 'undo' facility. It had to be possible to revisit previous entries and, optionally, correct them. Yet, now that the rule engine made stuff persistent in the bank's databases, just reverting the engine's memory was not enough. Compensatory transactions were required, making the whole solution even more complex than the 'undo' mechanism already did.

While increasing the rule base, the bank also decided to increase the number of employees maintaining it. So far, only one person had accumulated the wealth of rules in structured form. This person was now 'helped' by three other employees, a total of four. This helped to scale substantially the number of rules, but led to an unwelcome side effect: redundancy and inconsistency. The employees found out that some of them created rules twice, making rework in the case of changes to the rule base more tricky. In a word, the quality of the metadata deteriorated.

6.6.7.2 *Critical success factors*

The single most important success factor in this project was the incremental growth of the rule base, and the simplicity of the solution, that is the metamodel. Slowly increasing the size of the rule base helped the organization get used to this way of working. More specifically, the operational risk of using such an approach was limited, since the change over previous increments (with less or simpler rules) was manageable.

The case study also shows that from a certain rule base size on, systematic management and, most importantly, *reuse* becomes necessary. To some extent this can be replaced by introducing *idiomatic* solutions, that is tacitly agreeing how rules should be modeled (e.g., naming, structuring) without technically enforcing it. But at 10 000 rules, and particularly if more than just one person administers the rule base, more systematic forms of organizing metadata become indispensable.

This is a reconfirmation of what was said in Chapter 3, and reinforces the point that 'meta' is purely a relative property: this rule-based solution requires a more sophisticated architecture to foster reuse. An imagined *rule architecture* may take different forms, such as higher-level abstractions in the shape of groupings, iterations, and so forth. In order to support the establishment of such an architecture, metadata *about* the business rules is needed, effectively 'demoting' the rules themselves to the status of mere data.

Part III

Practical Problems and their Resolution

7

Evolution: A Practical Guide

Rules are for the obedience of fools and the guidance of wise men.

Douglas Bader

7.1   Overview

- Managing metadata is like managing data, expect that metadata is used in a very specific way.
- The supportive nature of metadata requires you to emphasize its (context-specific) processes utility rather than its (context-insensitive) product quality.
- If you design a metamodel, you are in the business of organizing other people's work. Therefore, the single most important optimization problem in metamodeling is getting the granularity right.
- Three means of optimization are domain-orientation, task-flow liberalization, and stepwise refinement.
- The activities of structured transformation are, in this order, deciding what to change, impact analysis, and change propagation.
- Division of labor sometimes requires intermediation of change requests. Direct modeling of changes by requesters is typically an exception.
- Legacy (data, applications, etc.) often constrains change adoption. The situation can be eased by changing the flow of metadata and managing quality during transitions.
- Grouping changes helps manage the tradeoff between risk and return, for example by product, location, or in temporally equidistant blocks.

- Different responsibility models (provider–consumer, peer-collaboration, semi-automation) make the impact analysis phase more efficient, while keeping bureaucracy at bay.
- Reducing the risks in change propagation requires, apart from architectural means to limit the impact of mistakes, central stakeholder management and good communication.

7.2   The 'management' in metadata management

From the perspective of trade practice, metadata management is characterized by an odd absence of methodology (that is, a systematic way of doing things) and, in my opinion, a suspicious emphasis on technology. It might be that it is such an abstract topic that it does not lend itself easily to generalization. Or may be there is no reason at all for this.

I think the latter is the case. There is no real reason why metadata management should not be done with a methodology in mind. On the contrary, in terms of the general challenges to tackle, I think that metadata management; is exactly like data management; only the decisions to take are different. This chapter outlines the foundations of such a methodology.

Metadata is data, except that it is used in a very specific way. This very specific way should influence your view on it. Other than that, you should care about the same activities as in data management, and that is:

- *Scoping:* more than anywhere else it is important to find a sweet spot between bureaucracy and anarchy that really helps the organization achieve its goals. For that, understanding the scope of the metadata management effort is crucial. Scoping is here to guide all your subsequent decisions at the metamodel and the metadata level.
- *Modeling:* lays out and partitions the universe of all metadata within your scope of concern. Since it relates to data used in the processes supported by metadata, the granularity (level of detail) of the metamodel and the constraints governing it will be your main concern.
- *Quality:* as everywhere else, not all metadata can be perfectly complete, consistent, and so on. You must understand the leverage effects that it has and how to manage quality adequately in the light of these effects.
- *Evolution:* even metamodels change. This should happen rarely, but if it does you should know how to handle it. Metamodel evolution is an expensive endeavor, and you should be really careful when trying it.
- *Usage:* finally, metadata gets used in other processes. This activity cannot be regarded as separate from the above, because the processes using metadata are intricately entwined with the processes managing it, via the metadata itself.

I would like to take a little detour at this point. In the above you may have stumbled over my repeatedly mentioning the link between the support and core process, and the role metadata plays in it. Ultimately, we are interested in optimizing the *quality* of metadata, not in and by itself, but with reference to something else: a process. We want to optimize the *utility* of metadata. This is different insofar as we assume a particular context of use and look at quality from the perspective of that context.

It is here, in my view, where many publications on metadata management fall short of what is needed. They look at metadata management from the data viewpoint only. *This prevents the reader from seeing the importance of the process utility of metadata, by focusing merely on its product quality.* As you will see in what is to follow, taking utility into account enriches the picture noticeably.

However before we get to that, let me revisit the above in Figures 7.1, 7.2, and 7.3: managing metadata requires a cyclical scope review. Once that is accomplished, the metamodel and processes are redrawn where required, and the quality management approach adapted as needed. Assuming that the metamodel has changed, metadata needs to be migrated. This leads to a re-binding of existing metadata. However, this re-binding is part of the scope review (and, naturally, the modeling effort), not of regular activity due to changes in the business objects

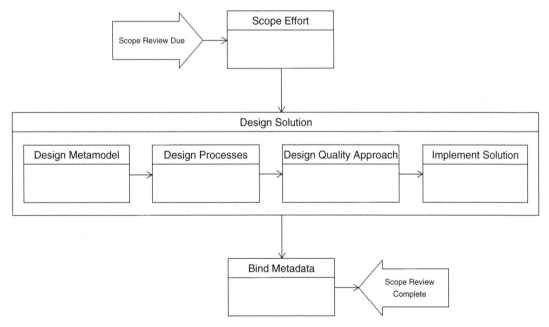

Figure 7.1: In order to design metadata management properly, the scope must be set. The scope determines which change the metamodel needs to support. The processes to capture the metadata are then designed, followed by the quality management approach, which complements the metamodel and processes. After implementation of the solution you are ready to begin binding and using metadata

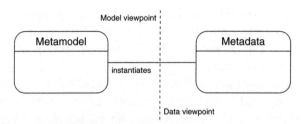

Figure 7.2: Metadata is, in principle, trivial. However, the concrete uses and processes for its support and, above all, its coupling with other processes, now make it less trivial

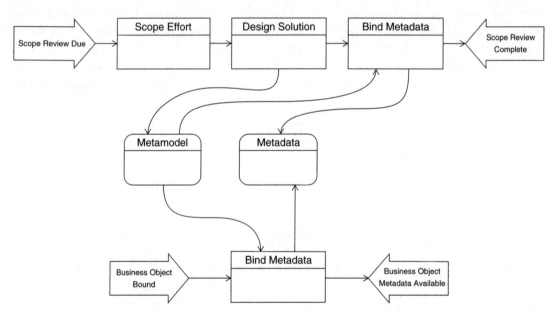

Figure 7.3: The metamodel is designed and then used in binding metadata. The bracket around both is scoping. Once the scope changes, the steps need to be taken again. Typically this is done on a regular schedule, or when evidence suggests that the metamodel is no longer adequate for the change problem(s) at hand

themselves. The costs are to be kept in mind, and you should avoid changing your metamodel too often or risk not creating value.

If the metamodel gets redrawn, the processes providing and using it must also be redesigned and redeployed. In this situation, metadata is like data. However, we know more about how the processes must be redesigned. How the metamodel design affects the processes, and vice versa, shall be the subject of the next sections.

7.3   Metamodeling

Metamodeling is intended to maintain the ability of an organization to react quickly to anticipated change. In that vein, our interest is to improve performance, manage risk, and ensure compliance. As was stated in earlier chapters, a metamodel is used to define mappings between different viewpoints and automate change adoption, it reifies how compliance can be achieved, and it can indirectly help manage risk by providing structural and terminological data. Given these premises, how should you design a metamodel?

Modeling metadata is like modeling data, except that the *granularity of the metamodel* determines a large part of its utility. Granularity in a rough sense describes the amount of (structural) detail expressed in a model. From this perspective, therefore, a finer granularity of the metamodel means that more detail about the relationship between different models is expressed.

Models in turn are used in the core processes which are supported by metadata management. These processes are built upon solutions (such as applications) that use a particular architecture, upon which the metamodel is based. The metamodel reifies (some of) the architecture's concepts and building blocks. Hence, and this is extremely important to understand, *the more fine-granular a metamodel is, the less liberty it leaves to the solution designers as to how they may design their own model(s)*. And, that is, across the *entire* portfolio. I would like to stress this point yet again: when you design a metamodel, *you are in the business of organizing other people's work.* You should be mindful of that fact.

For example, imagine the risk manager who wants accurate, consistent, and timely data on market and credit risk. Data is reported from a data mart, and data quality assessments are supported by metadata. The risk manager wants all the metadata he or she can get, leading to a fine-granular metamodel. However, the designers and developers of the data mart, their colleagues from the source systems delivering data feeds, and perhaps a few others as well, must all produce the metadata reifying its model. The metadata must be collected before the application gets deployed (bind time of the solution), and after data has been loaded (bind time of the data). And so on. Apart from the question of value creation, this approach creates a substantial burden for the IT teams. In fact, they may not even be able to deliver the metadata at all because it is not available or inaccessible. And there is still the issue of legacy.

Furthermore, the more detail you gather, the more likely it is that some event is regarded as a change (since it affects the metadata about some object). This in turn means more work on the systematic change adoption front, slowly drifting you into the realm of bureaucracy. In its terminal form, metadata capture and use is nothing but a pointless exercise.

Hence, you should let yourself be guided by some basic techniques from task organization that help you strike a balance between anarchy and bureaucracy while still reaching your goals. They all trade metadata quality for task flexibility, yet in different ways. In return, you obtain the ability to scale to a very large organization, tease your people less (and later), and progressively migrate towards more refined metamodels.

7.3.1   Domain-orientation and quality management decentralization

A large financial service company that is distributed globally and has specialists working here and there, is difficult to control or understand centrally. However, metadata and reification try to do exactly that. There are numerous reasons why, beyond a certain scale, this idea brakes down:

- Knowledge about the domain at hand is not available or cannot be provided at a tolerable cost. For example, local regulatory requirements are often, well, only applicable to a certain location. Financial accounting know-how is available in that department only, not elsewhere.
- Even the best designers will despair at metamodeling the entire company, and the bureaucracy will be of epic proportions. Enterprise data modeling failed a few decades ago. For the same reason, company-wide metadata modeling will fail.
- There is often no economic reason for integrating metamodels, as was shown in Chapter 3 and 4.

However, you are trying to ensure compliance with consistent handling of certain matters across the company, right? Model generation requires exact specifications (to an extent), does it not? Exactly. But fear not: it may not matter as much as you might believe.

For example, what you can observe is that corporate functions like IT, HR, or Logistics are pretty well isolated from processes like investment or underwriting. A change in, say, the recruiting process will usually not trigger a change in the underwriting process for the non-life branches. Consequently, a metamodel spanning reified abstractions from underwriting and HR would make little sense and be of limited value.

On the other hand, functions like risk management or financial accounting are often entangled with the central products and core processes of a financial service firm. Here you will need more good judgement to decide if and where to separate viewpoints, because changes do indeed often have far-reaching consequences in other areas. Hence, a metamodel can create value and help you along.

Domain-orientation deliberately sacrifices consistency for efficiency based on the hope that this will not exactly wreak havoc. It works like this: the overall cake of company metadata is carved into slices, each of which is managed and owned separately. There is no central control, giving domain owners full liberty in managing 'their' metadata. This liberty is acquired at the expense of different quality levels. Since quality is now handled decentrally:

- Consistency *between* domains will drop, because ownership of overall consistency is waived.
- Completeness *within* the domain will increase, as there are fewer metadata items to keep track of and manage.
- Correctness *within* the domain will increase, since the purpose for which the metadata is used becomes clearer.
- Actuality *within* the domain will likely increase, because people close to the problem take ownership.

You should note that, since consistency is a quality feature of high importance to automation, you should be careful about using such metadata liberally for performance improvement across domains purposes. Also, impact analysis can suffer from the lack of relationships (again across domains), potentially ignoring existing dependencies. However, it is often less of an issue for compliance with metadata, because these two activities depend more on, for example, actuality and completeness, depending on circumstances.

For example, the latter two aspects are illustrated by the case study in Section 5.6.4. After the maintenance of domain-specific architectural alignment metadata was decentralized, correctness and actuality increased. The business terminology management framework mentioned in Section 3.5 is based on decentral organisation. Business terms are managed in around 20 different domains, each with their own quality management approach. They are divided by product (e.g., 'Traditional Life & Health,' 'Traditional Property & Casualty'), function (e.g., 'IT,' 'HR,' 'Risk Management') and domains with external change drivers ('Loss Events,' or 'Geography').

From an organizational perspective, the task of metadata quality management is taken on by a domain-specific role rather than a particular company-wide organization. From the model perspective, fewer elements are managed by that role, and they exhibit no more cross-domain relationships.

7.3.2   Task flow liberalization and late-term quality management

When people start to see that they have quality deficits in their data, the knee-jerk reaction is often to organize and constrain the way others can deliver that data. For example, if you assume that most of the data an insurance contract requires is determined by the line of business, you would like to organize your capture around exactly that. Consequently, the very first thing you would require your underwriters to enter is the line of business. The benefit is that you can address consistency at the root: once you have that data available, all other data can be cross-checked.

This is a natural, understandable reaction. And, in some cases, it is actually the right thing to do. However, many a situation in metamodeling is not that clear-cut. Quite often you find yourself in a situation where it is far from clear where to begin, because many different viewpoints need be supported. You will find yourself in a bind, because people are used to all sorts of different styles of working, and agreeing on one particular way will prove difficult.

For example, consider a typical development project. You need a data model, perhaps an object-relational mapping, a user interface, tests, and then there is the business logic. For all these viewpoints you may need metadata to do certain things. Where do you start? With the user interface? That will make the database guys squirm. But the other way around may just as likely be the wrong approach.

Especially in complex settings with iterative working styles, the command-and-control vision of metadata management (clear task flow, stepwise quality management, incremental freezing, that is, binding of metadata as in Figure 7.4) breaks down for the following reasons:

- People make mistakes and learn, which makes rework of previous assumptions a normal part of work, not the exception.
- People like to approach a challenge from different angles, sometimes in parallel.
- The domain is so complex that a 'one best-way' cannot be conceived of.

And yet, somehow, people manage to deliver running software at the end, and so there must be some way to capture metadata at some point. The trick is to abandon the idea of a clockwork organization and think of *metadata not as the driver of people's work, but as their guardian angel*.

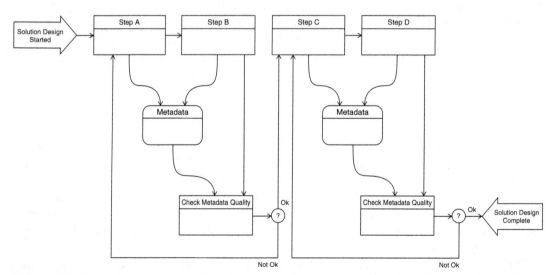

Figure 7.4: An early metadata quality check stage limits the work undone if intolerable quality is detected. On the other hand, it prescribes a certain sequence of activities

This approach is based on the assumption that intelligent people not only have a general interest in doing good work, but also have the capacity. This means that organizing their work from the outside, with whatever good intentions, is to a great extent superfluous. On the other hand, intelligent people are normally interested in improving their work. If they can obtain information about say, how compliant they are with a particular piece of regulation, they will actually use it. The magic lies in telling them what to do without forcing them to. Many a modeling effort meanders in its early stages (when the learning process is in full swing) and then eventually closes in on an agreed state (as understanding matures and the desired solution model emerges). Metadata can support this crystallization processes by providing *complementary* guidance to designers.

Think of it as the IT equivalent of what instrument landing systems or traffic collision avoidance systems do for airline pilots. They offer guidance, but do not ultimately force pilots to follow. They are appreciated as minders, but very often respected so deeply that they attain the status of drivers nevertheless. In like mind, you will want to guide designers slowly towards your goals, without prescribing the exact path. With metadata, these are the steps you need to be taking (Figure 7.5):

1. Take the quality rules of your metamodel. Classify all of them as optional.
2. Check your metadata as you find it delivered against these rules. Provide the list of quality violations to the model designers as complementary *warnings*.

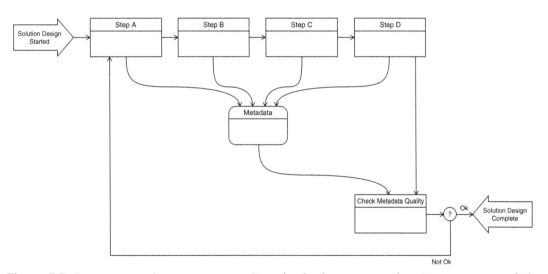

Figure 7.5: Late-term quality management discards checks at more than just one stage of the production process in return for more flexibility in task performance. The disadvantage is that deficits discovered at a very late stage may be costly to fix or, perhaps, never fixed at all

3. As you approach the point where metadata must be bound, progressively make the rules mandatory. Provide the list of violations to model designers as *errors*, which prevents them from moving further in the process.

With this approach, model designers have all the liberty they need at early stages of the design process, and yet are put on notice that they may have to correct this and that. As time passes, the checks become increasingly restrictive, fencing in deviant behavior. And, surprisingly, the nature of these violation reports changes over time: whereas they are first used as collateral, they increasingly move to the center of attention.

For example, consider again the case study in Section 3.5: temporal aspects play a great role in the design of the glossary. Business terms have validity periods, as do groups of business terms such as attributes (enumeration types like currencies, countries, or lines of business). Obviously, it makes no sense to put a business term into an attribute where the validity period of the term ends before the validity period of the attribute (undefined state). Hence, the repository checks whether the validity period of an attribute covers all the validity periods of its values completely. Now imagine an administrator who must shorten that attribute's validity period. Forcing this person to first update the validity periods of all terms before changing that of the attribute could become pretty unnerving. What the repository does, however, is to only issue a warning. Then, as the modeling process comes to an end and the entire attribute with its values is submitted for publication, the restrictions are tightened and some warnings actually become errors, preventing further steps before correction.

There are some challenges with this approach. First off, and this is more of a technical limitation (though a major one), the distinction between warnings and errors and the slow evolution of warnings into errors, is not well supported by tools. For example, compilers for programming languages, constraint languages, and query languages often only distinguish 'correct' from 'incorrect' input; they sometimes allow for 'possibly correct' input, but never support 'possibly correct later.' As a consequence, you are often forced to abandon the use of the tool-internal mechanisms, and build some of your own externally.

Then, allowing model designers to roam freely before raising the flag, exposes you to the risk of rogue behavior nevertheless. Time pressures in projects can lead to the phenomenon in which metadata capture is perceived as a (if not the only) stumbling block, preventing delivery of a solution. An often observed reaction is to sideline the metadata guys politically and plough on regardless.

Finally, this approach dwells on a well-defined, fine-granular metamodel, especially for consistency checks. This kind of metamodel is not always possible to come up with in the first place. Furthermore, you need well-delineated phases in the design process, to segregate the different stages of quality rule classification. If you have a coarse-granular metamodel, or if you cannot delineate production process phases well, you should resort to other means.

7.3.3   Top-down stepwise refinement

As always, *stepwise refinement* is an option at your disposal when the learning process concerning how to design the metamodel is still on. Sometimes you may feel unsure about which elements to include in a metamodel, or you may have run into issues that need to pan out well first. Hence, you engage in that old tradition of *divide et impera, trading short-term metadata quality for long-term modeling flexibility*.

In a way, this metamodeling alternative sees you design your metamodel, data, and the supported processes progressively differently. In an early stage, the metamodel is coarse-granular. The processes using metadata are characterized by manual, unstructured change adoption. Likewise, the processes capturing metadata are characterized by more manual work. Then, as the metamodel is refined, change adoption becomes more structured, making the supported processes more efficient in adopting change. The capture of metadata is more and more automatic and efficient as well.

This sequence of events describes a maturation process in which the organization moves progressively towards an optimized change adoption process: based on a thorough understanding of the quality deficits at play, the liberties people can take in the *design* process are tightened, which corresponds to a clearer and stricter definition of the architecture upon which the design is based. As this happens, the *supported* processes become increasingly more efficient at adopting changes. This can go both ways. As a matter of fact, stepwise composition (where you start bottom-up) is the mirror-image sibling of stepwise refinement. The maturation works just the opposite way: where in one situation (top-down) you refine the metamodel, making the supported process more efficient, in the other (bottom-up) they become more effective, being embedded in an increasingly bigger context.

The big disadvantage with stepwise refinement (and, by extension, stepwise composition) is that it requires you to update the metadata each time you change your model. That may substantially raise costs. As such, you should be hesitant to perform this too frequently because of the risk of alienating your metadata providers. Furthermore, as always, such a protracted, drawn-out exercise can be stopped short because of political pressures. On the other hand, its incremental nature makes this technique a low-risk affair from a project perspective. It is thus very well-suited for long-term efforts in which you have a manager's buy-in to go on the long-haul.

So, now you are set. Change can come your way! Read the next sections to understand what happens when it does.

7.4   The activities of structured transformation

Supporting the systematic evolution of an organization, that is its *structured transformation*, is a process that involves numerous steps. From the logging of change requests to the deployment of a solution, various parties must be involved and collaborate. Some of these steps stick out, however. They are not straightforward tasks, often requiring a thorough understanding of the company and the problem at hand, and are not easily generalized.

This is where solution templates can help you draw closer to a concrete approach. They contain all the crucial elements of the problem and solution, but leave out some of the details to make them applicable to a broader range of contexts. These templates are divided into three groups:

- *Deciding what to change:* this group concerns itself with the question of how, given a change in the real world, it should be reflected in the model on which solutions are based.
- *Impact analysis:* based on a given model change, this group identifies the affected stakeholders and establishes the impact on them as well as the applications they might use or own.
- *Change propagation:* given a separation of responsibilities in the overall IT architecture, this group plans the steps necessary to propagate a model change through the corporation and executes them.

These steps require some explanation. Although they are presented here in succession (suggesting a waterfall-style approach), this is not how it happens in reality. Very often, the steps are performed iteratively to permit revisions and corrections. As such, please keep in mind that you are likely to be concurrently busy with all of them as far as planning and taking decisions is concerned. Once you have started propagating the model change, however, all planning and modeling should have come to a halt.

Deciding what to change is first and foremost a creative process. Since much of what happens in the external world lies beyond your control, each situation will bring new challenges and constraints to take into account when mapping it to your own model.

Here, your organization matters: large organizations are characterized by a strong division of labor. Not everyone who *requests* a change will also be the person to *model* its implementation. A typical case in point is the manager who says: 'I want this function in that application' without further considering whether that is possible, cost-effective, and so forth. However, sometimes that manager is capable of making very specific provisions as to how to implement that function.

To the extent that this translation process takes place, an organization also exposes itself to the operational risk that the change will be implemented correctly, cost-effectively, in time, etc. There are different responsibility models to cater to different levels of staff sophistication and the ability to tolerate risk.

Also, there are variations in how creative you can or must be when formulating changes. Obviously you will not abandon everything you previously had and start with a clean slate. There are limitations as to where you can ignore precedent. For example, databases often store a long history of business transactions and performance figures. This data cannot be done away with easily, and there are sometimes regulatory requirements (in financial accounting, for example) as to how long history must be kept.

Another consideration of yours will be if and how to *group changes*. Generally speaking, lumping changes together that have an impact in the same place or similar places will make them simpler to control for consistency, but more difficult to propagate through the organization. Smaller changes are easier to propagate, but may lead to inconsistent handling with respect to others.

As such, deciding what to change is subject to the question what *would* be an appropriate corresponding model change. After that, all sorts of constraints need to be catered to, watering down the purity of the original idea. How to limit some of the 'impurity' shall therefore also be the subject of discussion.

7.5   Dealing with division of labor: intermediation versus direct modeling of change requests

The saying goes that 'the devil is in the details.' Not everyone is suited to taking on every task, because rarely does anyone know everything there is to know about the details. This applies to change requests as well, where the person requesting one is not necessarily the person modeling the request itself. This brings about risk: the more a company structures its transformation processes using metadata, the more it needs to make sure that what it does is the right thing to do. Because, if it does not, it will make systematic mistakes.

Generally speaking, there are two extremes: let the originator of a change model the request, or have an intermediary model it for the originator. As you may imagine, the choice between the two depends on the originator's level of knowledge in the realm of the model elements to be changed (the metadata). This obviously has to do with skills, but it also has to do with the granularity of the metamodel. Coarse-grained metamodels that reify few concepts and/or relationships are typically better-suited to be used appropriately than fine-grained metamodels. Hence, here are two options for you to consider when deciding what to change.

7.5.1   Direct modeling of change requests

The direct translation of business requirements into the models used for designing IT solutions has always been a lofty goal. In its imagined ideal form, business people not only formulate required changes themselves but also, by designing changes to models as well, directly affect the way applications process data, validate input, or report on the business.

The achievement goal is contingent on taking into account a number of factors. First, an in-depth understanding of both the business and IT requires either sophisticated training or a profound experience base in the same company, ideally both. If you cannot muster either, the (welcome) direct effects of your work carry an (unwelcome) risk of costly mistakes. Second, the level of granularity required to model changes with direct effect is typically much higher, requiring more metadata of better quality. Third, solutions are often not designed to deal with certain types of changes during the maintenance phase, thereby limiting the range of change effects. Fourth, the change process, particularly impact analysis, lies in the hands of a few people or even a single person. This requires risk mitigation through architectural measures such as *impact isolation*.

The direct modeling of change requests assumes that an individual or group takes direct responsibility for the modeling of a change to metadata, thereby effecting direct changes to solutions (often via model generation). These people must be well-trained and embedded into a risk-aware environment. Furthermore, this model does not work well if there are many IT solutions requiring the involvement of IT specialists to effect the change, which causes friction (unstructured change/impact).

The huge advantage of this model is that business is in control of what really happens in the IT systems. The potential drawback is that it is left to its own devices and *really* is responsible for what happens. For this reason, this model is often only chosen when the metamodel allows for simple parametrization, maybe feature modeling. It rarely occurs that full-blown meta-programming is put into the hands of business.

For example, investment portfolio managers are typically very adept at understanding financial instruments and modeling the composition of a portfolio. The trading process is then controlled by the delta between actual and desired portfolio composition. In this, portfolio managers are on their own, but simulations help find the optimal composition, thereby reducing the company's exposure not to operational, but market risk.

The master data management platform presented in Section 5.6.3 is used in the product management division to model (metadata about) products. This data is obtained directly from dedicated master sources, most of which the product management team administers. The operational risk of mistakes spreading throughout the company unchecked is mitigated by a two-pronged approach: first, metadata must be administered and published, that is visible to applications, by two different employees (4-eye-principle). Second, the configuration management intrinsic to the repository ensures that even if a mistake makes it through, it can be rolled back quickly.

The credit product modeling study mentioned in Section 4.7.3 is a case of parametrization: the person in charge of administering credit product metadata *directly* influences the way the applications work (that is, which rates, limits, and so on they offer). However, given that the impact of changes can be overlooked relatively easily, and assuming that the typical mistakes will not threaten the existence of the company, this is a tolerable operational risk.

The case study of Section 4.7.2 is an example where IT's trust in business broke down because the operational risk was assumed to be too high. Theoretically, business was capable of modeling an executable specification of the tools they needed, but the development team thought this too tricky. Here, a period of exploration may have increased that trust so that direct modeling would be deemed acceptable by IT.

7.5.2   Intermediation of change requests

As opposed to the previous model, *intermediation of change requests* assigns responsibility for modeling changes to a different person than the one requesting them.

Quite often, business does not have the skills, knowledge, or nerve to get into the details of what exactly a change is all about. Sometimes this is for a good reason. The intricacies of IT solutions, their limitations, and capabilities may not be known to the requester. Or, even worse, the requirements are not perfectly clear yet and deserve further investigation. In such a situation, an intermediary can help to reduce uncertainty, translate, negotiate, and then ultimately model the change commensurate to the request at hand.

The intermediary is responsible for capturing, collecting, and consolidating change requests. Furthermore, this person is responsible for modeling the changes so they can be implemented properly. For this, the intermediary must have similar (decent, not only cursory) knowledge about both viewpoints.

This responsibility model works best in situations where division of labor has resulted in a big(ish) knowledge gap between the different modeling viewpoints, such as between business and IT. It also helps when there are many stakeholders whose interests have to be balanced out. Finally, with this model, mistakes can be caught through double-checks, which naturally occur as part of collection and interpretation. *An intermediary contributes value by reducing friction cost.* The intermediary sometimes enables an organization to engage in full-fledged meta-programming, though this is still rare.

The disadvantage of this responsibility model is that intermediaries are often themselves specialized, covering only a small range of the overall problem landscape. They also increase latency between formulation of a request and its ultimate implementation.

For example, in the case study outlined in Section 6.6.1.1, a team of specialists collects change requests from around the globe, consolidates them and translates them into changes to the general ledger. In this case, the team also administers the business term glossary, which informs accountants how to report figures, and drives (to a certain extent) the way that applications use them.

The case study mentioned in Section 6.6.2 is another such example. Here, changes to components can be captured at a coarse-granular level. A change manager is responsible for checking these entries, adjusting them (e.g., by amending the component to which a change request was erroneously assigned), and driving the remaining process forward.

Another example I know of is a large European stock exchange that used a rule-based modeling tool to check valor data delivered from external providers. The original idea that business would model the rules themselves proved illusionary, as too many problems occurred in the exploration phase. Consequently, trained IT staff were put in place of business to translate requested changes into rule base changes.

7.6   Dealing with impedance: embracing versus overcoming precedent

Impedance is an effect that occurs in physical systems subject to change. For example, a coil resists the flow of an alternating current. Impedance is a nice metaphor for what happens when change occurs. First, forces in the organization build up that resist a proposed change. Over time, they subside and change takes its course. Sometimes the case for a change is overwhelming, though. For example, regulatory requirements pose such a strong force in favor of change that it will be hard to resist. You are perhaps at liberty to interpret them creatively, but that will generally be about it.

So, as far as this discussion is concerned let us focus on those cases where you (or others, for that matter) possess a certain freedom of choice. This is especially the case for changes triggered from within the company, such as reorganizations, product evolution, or location-specific developments.

One of the strongest forces resisting (radical) change is legacy. The investments into so-called 'old' applications are often substantial, and it is extremely difficult to demand their complete overhaul. As such, they typically must be accepted for what they are: the main driver of your decision what to change. You have to *embrace precedent*.

That is not to say you should become a fatalist. However, given that you may not have time eternal to adopt the change at hand, for the duration of that process a legacy application can be assumed as inert. That is also not to say that legacy is always resistant to change. I have seen very well-designed applications that were pretty static from one viewpoint, but quite dynamic from another. However, they do limit your freedom of choice, because of their dominant position in the company.

At the other extreme end of the spectrum, you may find yourself in a situation where there is no precedent at all; that is, the solutions you could work with are not uniform and thus cannot be treated in the same way. This, in its own odd way, is a precedent in itself. Here it is important to establish a viewpoint that mimics uniformity to the outside, while catering to the variability on the inside.

Then again, sometimes you actually must *overcome precedent*, because it is too costly or risky to maintain the state of matters. The typical case in point is data migration due to company-internal viewpoint changes. Once a company reorganizes its profit center structure, many (if not all) of the transactions associated with that structure must be mapped. This is because over time there are so many changes to the profit centers that the amount of data generated by a copy-paste policy would bog down the IT department.

Overcoming precedent means that you look for opportunities to migrate in a controlled fashion from one (state of) viewpoint to another. You assume that all solution models migrate, not just a few. In this, you try to minimize the risk of operational disruptions while maximizing the speed with which migration can take place. This requires different modeling techniques than in the case of embracing precedent, mostly in the area of mapping and transition support.

7.6.1   Embracing precedent

So, you have decided to embrace the existing precedent. What next? Since you continue to strive for improving performance, managing risk, and ensuring compliance, some of these activities become more difficult than others.

As far as *performance improvement* is concerned, legacy is an architectural building block. Model generation does not work for you, since legacy is usually neither be disaggregated nor reintegrated. Although this road is effectively blocked, you can take some solace from the thought that the legacy application is likely to be reused, which hopefully improves performance as well.

Managing risk is affected as well. Since introspection of the data lineage into and within the building block is not possible, and cannot be derived with metadata extraction, assessing data quality becomes difficult. The semantics, however, are provided as is. Semantics cannot be derived, which is why there is a manual activity in the first place.

With respect to *ensuring alignment*, more manual work is required. If you lack access to the internals of legacy, metadata extraction does not work. This also applies to assessing the operational risk of a suggested solution based on its alignment metadata.

Take the example of *third party software*. Purchased packages are often closed to the observer, which is why it is difficult to change anything about their inner workings. In one data warehouse project I was involved in, we used a tool to design data load jobs. It offered read-only access to its modeling repository (which, strangely enough, was declared a metadata repository), but no write access. The issue was that the design and operational processes of the analytical applications in the data warehouse were organized in a particular way, which required a consistent internal structure. For example, access privileges for the developers were supposed to be segregated by application. They were supposed to be permissive in the development environment, but highly restrictive in the productive environment (to address operational and legal risks). The jobs were scheduled with a third party tool that had the same characteristics as the design tool. In this situation it was impossible to devise a metadata-based process that starts with the application list, associated developers, and generates access privileges from there, which are fed into the load job modeling and scheduling tools.

So, assuming that the metadata you need is more difficult to come by or use effectively, what should you do? Give up? No, there are two options at your disposal, both of which leave the ideal route but still get you where you want to be:

- *Mixed metadata flow:* obtain metadata manually at the time it should be bound while using automated techniques where possible, maintaining an outside image of seamlessness.
- *Metadata flow reversal:* use metadata extraction instead of model generation and compare desired and actual state, taking corrective action where necessary.

Both techniques require certain prerequisites and have a few drawbacks. Let us drill down into the details to see what they are.

7.6.1.1   *Mixed metadata flow*

Assume you are in a situation where you need to improve performance by generating models from metadata. Normally you would expect your process of binding metadata to obtain it in a semi-automated fashion where designers model the building blocks they require and then hand over the associated metadata to you. From there you can carry on, making it available for use.

However, some of your designers may not be able or willing to do that. There can be several reasons why this is the case, but whatever the reason, you are now challenged in your metadata management process: to the outside world, you are acting as a collector, consolidator, and integrator.

This is a typical situation in software production: some data modeling tools do not provide access to their metadata, yet you should provide it. Other such tools do provide the desired metadata, which you can (well, almost) just pipe through. Because they are all in active use, streamlining the suite of tools is not an option. Hence, the question is how to organize the provisioning of metadata.

One approach to this problem is to mix and match the flow characteristics. For all sources of metadata in which automation is possible, you do couple the processes together as discussed earlier, achieving a seamless flow of metadata. All other sources you do not integrate, but obtain the metadata manually, arriving at a different data flow. To the outside world, however, the image is that of an integrated metadata management solution.

The good part about this technique is that you can slowly mature and scale your process, growing experience over time. The downside is that manual collection obviously increases the likelihood of quality deficits. For that reason, it is generally advisable to use a more coarse-granular metamodel. Yet, that may conflict with your other interests of seamless model generation. I have only seen this work in select areas, for example when the area of responsibility of the managers of said metadata increased over a longer time (years, not months).

7.6.1.2   *Metadata flow reversal*

Assume you have a building block (like an application) that cannot be disaggregated any further, and is not accessible to other automatic forms of manipulation. Extracting metadata about

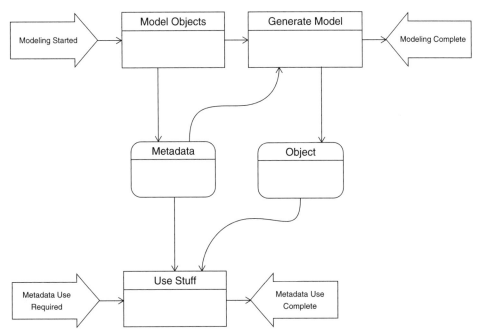

Figure 7.6: This is the ideal way of using metadata to generate models. It assumes that write access to objects is possible. However, this condition is sometimes not met

the building block's internal structure is possible, however, the traditional form of model generation (Figure 7.6) assumes that write access to the (model) objects to be generated is possible, posing an obstacle. You are interested in supporting a model generation process with metadata. The metamodel reifies concepts representing the building block's structure that lie below the level of granularity that can be manipulated, but are accessible via metadata extraction.

You have the alternative of reversing the flow of metadata (Figure 7.7). The main idea is to separate out the desired ('to be') state, maintain it externally, and cross-check it with the actual ('as is') state by using metadata extraction. Steps include:

1. Manipulate the building block in the manner you used to, waiving your model generation ambitions. This modifies the 'as is' metadata of the building block, which is exposed to the outside world for (read-only) access.
2. Set up a metamodel that reifies the concepts required to control the 'to be' state in metadata. Capture that data separate from the 'as is.'
3. Once manipulation of the building block is considered complete, compare 'as is' and 'to be' state. Take corrective action when differences are detected and retry.

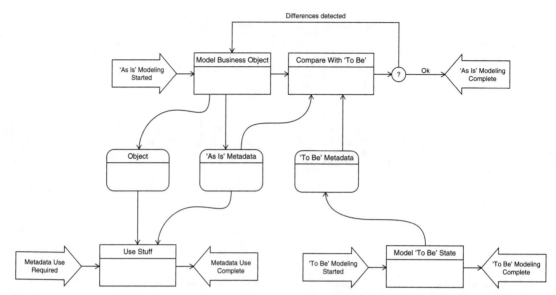

Figure 7.7: With metadata flow reversal, objects are created with other means than model generation. The consistency with metadata is checked by extracting 'as is' metadata about the objects and comparing it to the 'to be' metadata created separately. Due to the rework that will occasionally be required (top), this approach works best when differences are typically small

This solution works best when the 'to be' metamodel is comparatively simple. If it was as complex as the 'as is' model, you would not gain much from the comparison. First, setting up the 'to be' would practically double your cost. Second, more complex models mean that the chances of differences between 'as is' and 'to be' state rise, causing you additional cost for comparisons.

Furthermore, you may not want to perform the comparison steps too often. Taking corrective action can become quite labor-intensive, and it is an entirely manual activity.

As a result, you can continue to use the tools and processes offered to manipulate the building block, while ensuring alignment with the desired state. However, the separate, manual collection of that metadata increases the likelihood of quality deficits, which are a potential risk.

Whether you take corrective action *ex-post* or *ex-ante* is a matter of risk management. Some differences are minor in nature and can be corrected later. Furthermore, *ex-ante* correction disrupts the flow of activities of the supported process. This, by the way, is a common complaint by developers.

The data warehouse example mentioned above (Section 5.6.1) was solved exactly this way: there existed read-only interfaces to the repository, allowing for a cross-check with other 'to be' metadata. Thankfully, differences arose very rarely.

7.6.2   Overcoming precedent: retaining versus regaining consistency

Overcoming precedent requires the migration of solutions from one model to another, making sure that things go smoothly and you end up in state that is equally consistent as the one before the change. This is not as easy as it seems. Change often throws a company into (a limited form of) disarray. Not all activities occur in sync, and it is far from self-evident that you end up in the desired state.

For one, consistency is of crucial importance to all forms of *time-series:* risk-management techniques in most shapes and forms depend on them for trend analysis. Some of these time-series are years if not decades long, requiring many changes along the way. The model under which data was originally captured may have but a bleak resemblance to the model with which it is analyzed today. This problem even has a name, *slowly changing dimensions.*

Take the case of corporate actions: the performance of a stock at a defined moment in time should not be influenced by a stock split or a merger. Instead, assuming a split of 1:10 the performance should be exactly the same as when a split of 1:5 had happened. Or, if a company acquires another, the stock value may change, but the firm value changes as well. Hence, looking across time, consistent handling of such changes means to reinterpret the data in the light of an evolved model.

Or, take the case of the introduction of the Euro: for a certain number of years, banking applications had to be able to digest transactions in Euro just as well as in Deutsche Mark or Dutch Guilder. Switching directly overnight from the one to the other would have incurred huge risks for the financial system. Also, data had to be migrated, requiring both old and new to coexist.

Two main challenges occur when overcoming precedent: one, consistency across time (where required) must be *retained.* Two, while the transition is in progress, consistency may not be established across the solution portfolio, but must have been *regained* after completion. Read on to see how to handle these challenges.

7.6.3   Retaining consistency: disambiguating history

Any change involving more than one model element before or after the change has the potential to create ambiguity as to how the lifecycle of business concepts is to be handled. Yet, the lifecycle determines how history is handled, which has an impact on trends reported.

Think of the reunification of East and West Germany in 1990: should there be two old model elements and one new ('Germany')? Or should this be handled as if the old West Germany outlives the East, taking over the whole lot? In the former case, the historic data of both old are mapped to the new country, whereas in the latter the figures of but one are involved. Conceptually and technically these are very different evolution steps.

Or, vice versa, think of the split of Czechoslovakia into the Czech Republic and Slovakia: which of the new countries is assigned what recorded data? Does one continue to live under a different name, or do we see two entirely new model elements arise?

Disambiguation is the activity of deciding how to look at a change in order to *define what the company's view on reality is*. Once that step has been taken, all activity flows from there. This *canonical view* determines which *impact* is considered consistent with the view on the change at hand; that is, which adoption steps are assumed to be semantically correct from a certain viewpoint.

Only after a canonical view has been established, a mapping between old and new model can be created, and only then can migration commence in a consistent fashion. More specifically, migration can be automated, given that the mapping metadata is available. Without disambiguation, migration activity is at risk of being performed in different ways, under different assumptions, leading to inconsistent results.

Disambiguation is fraught with many uncertainties. First of all, by its very definition, people may view an ambiguous sitation in different ways. This creates potential for disagreement, but can at least be overcome. However, there are cases where a mapping cannot be found at all. A company reorganization typically changes the line management, cost, and profit center structure so profoundly that it makes no sense to attempt to disambiguate history. In such a situation it is sometimes required to start with a clean slate and forget about the past.

As an example, take again the study in Section 3.5: the repository of business terms allows for variants of hierarchical structures, e.g., where some terms are left out or added. This allows viewpoints at different levels of detail, cancelling-out irrelevant aspects, or even catering to jurisdictional requirements. When data is exchanged between applications, however, the superset of all variants is used for disambiguation. All variants are uniform from a structural perspective, that is: if one term is a more specific term than another, it is so in all variants. This permits the construction of mappings that can be used for all applications using this umbrella model.

As for the Euro conversion, the European Central Bank determined the official conversion rates between the various old Euro area currencies, thereby establishing the canonical view on history and ensuring a consistent mapping.

7.6.4   *Regaining consistency: managing transitory stages*

Retaining consistency is often more of an ideal: there are just too many change processes going on in a large company at any given time. Certain pockets may permit consistency throughout, but for a company at large this is practically impossible. A certain amount of inconsistency is inevitable. More specifically, when starting out with systematic change management you will often witness quite some degree of inconsistency. Therefore, the question is less how to avoid it, but how to keep it in check. Or, down the line of Don Quixote, how not to fight windmills.

From the architectural perspective, consistency is a problem of systematic *alignment*, permitting for a little deviation here and there, until consistency has been regained. You start out with the old model, which is your 'as is' state, always assuming that all the solutions in your portfolio are consistent with the model at this time. From there you design the new model, which represents your 'to be' state. Aligning one solution at a time, you slowly transition your way towards that goal.

The problem with such transition phases is that they permit inconsistencies. That in itself is not the problem (it is the very point of the whole exercise). The real issue is how to ensure, once you have established the new 'to be' baseline, that you ultimately reach that baseline with your entire solutions portfolio.

The challenge is not to convince the owner of an individual solution to migrate to the new baseline model, but to orchestrate a large group to do so. This is so because they are *interdependent*, for example because they exchange data (i.e., were designed using a joint data model) or because they support the same business process (i.e., were designed after a joint activity execution model). Hence, you must allow an individual solution to pretend to the outside world that it operates on the old *and* new model, while internally working on the new model. This is a little like fencing in a flock of sheep: once the shepherd has decided it is time to go home, he commences to drive the flock towards the open gate. The fence acts as boundary to the movement of sheep, which means that after a certain time all will have passed the gate. The sheep who have found their way home are in the desired state, while the ones still outside are in a transitory state. Both coexist, but some time later none will be outside anymore.

When changes to a model occur, the lifecycle of some model elements ends, some are created, and some are just updated. New model elements do not create any challenges, since there is no precedent to overcome. Updates to an existing element can be handled equally seamlessly, since the precedent is not touched (structurally, that is). However, the end of the lifecycle of an existing model element must be overcome in a structured fashion. At some point in the future, no one must use them anymore.

Take the currencies in the above Euro example: between January 1, 1999 and December 31, 2001 you would want your applications to migrate to using Euro internally, while allowing for Euro *and* Deutsche Mark, Belgian Franc, or Dutch Guilder. To customers, however, account balances are issued in Euro.

Managing transition this way means that the lifecycle of model elements features not just two states (alive, dead), but a third as well:

- *Active:* the model element can be used regularly. Its lifecycle has not ended yet.
- *Inactive:* the model element must not be used anymore, anywhere. Its lifecycle has ended.

- *Obsolete:* the model element should no longer be represented to the outside, although it may still be used inside a solution.

The magic of this lifecycle is that the baseline assumes only two states (active, inactive), but during a transition a third (obsolete) is permitted. However, once transition is complete, *all solutions can switch without risk* to the new baseline, since their internal model is consistent with the new baseline. Hence, by definition, they can also represent it to the outside world.

Take the example from Section 6.6.2: components must be consistent with (and connected to) the configuration items discovered through the scanning mechanism. However, that may not always be the case. For example, a component may have reached its end of lifecycle while the applications (which are also configuration items) that belong to it have not yet been decommissioned. This is an inconsistency between the 'to be' and 'as is' state, between the logical and the physical level. From the lifecycle point of view, applications are now considered 'obsolete,' of course assuming that they will not be assigned to yet another component. The inconsistency can now give rise to compensatory action, for example by first decommissioning the applications and then the component, ultimately reaching a consistent state again.

This example is also illustrative from another perspective: the more dependencies there are, which is to say the more relationships you find in the metamodel, the more likely it is that you will detect inconsistencies. This is a tradeoff you will always have to manage: a fine-granular metamodel gives you more headache with respect to alignment, because deviations from the 'to be' are likely to occur more often. On the other hand, a coarse-granular metamodel will be less able to ensure complete consistency, because the 'to be' is more ambiguously defined. What matters most in such a situation is what kind of mapping you have between the different viewpoints bridged by the metamodel.

Obviously, your situation can become a little foggy when you need to handle many changes occurring at the same time. What does consistency mean in this situation? How can complexity be kept in check? To do so, you must take a fresh look at your notion of consistency and start grouping changes.

7.7   Grouping changes: optimizing risk versus return

Grouping changes means identifying packages of changes that have some characteristics in common so that you reduce the risk of permitting inconsistencies. On the flip side of the coin, however, you will want to avoid the trap of over-engineered methodology or, worse even, formalism.

What you should be looking for is to find a balance between risk and return, between consistency and speed. You need heuristics to do things mostly right and, if wrong, be consoled that the impact of your mistake will not be grave. For obvious reasons, this means finding changes that 'belong together' in some shape or form, so that you can handle them in isolation without ignoring too many other changes that should theoretically belong with them as well. Here are but a few alternatives:

- *Packaging by product/process/function:* organizes changes along the traditional lines of business operation. Some companies emphasize their products (e.g., insurances, investments), others their processes (e.g., transactions, intermediation).
- *Grouping by location/market:* jurisdiction, which is a synonym for location, is a strong driver of regulatory changes. Although some regulations span jurisdictions, many do not. For cases like these it makes sense to group changes along jurisdictional borders. Also, some market practices like how business relations are handled, are still highly influenced by locality. Here the same rule applies.
- *Temporally equidistant:* many processes in financial services such as accounting, underwriting, or making reserves, work in cycles. That means that for a certain period the business works on a steady basis. For example, the chart of accounts stays the same until they have been closed, which is typically a quarter or a year. These cycles can be used to group changes from a temporal, that is a time-based, perspective.

Grouping changes by process, product, or corporate function is by far the most popular. There is precedent, people usually understand (and share) the motivation for it quickly, and it is also not very controversial. Exactly that, however, is also its drawback: some corporate functions lend themselves to this approach quite nicely (e.g., Logistics, IT, HR), but companies today are usually still quite bad at systematically organizing themselves in, say, a process-oriented fashion. For that reason you can see distributed ownership, lack of agreed understanding of the concepts at hand, and generally much less guidance as to what constitutes consistency. As such, successes are often not widespread.

The advantage of temporally equidistant change groups is that they galvanize the attention of owners and users alike. If you know that tomorrow is the deadline for filing the change requests, you will prioritize accordingly and perhaps not submit many of the low-urgency requests. Hence, you see less clutter piling up in the change logs, thus reducing the chance that people lose track and overlook an inconsistency in the details. Furthermore, it gently supports impact analysis (see next section), as not only deciding what to change, but also subsequent activities, will be working on that frequency. What you will observe is that stakeholders are more likely to attend meetings, thereby increasing the likelihood that a change is looked at from all necessary perspectives.

On the downside, some changes just simply do not occur temporally equidistant (think of external events). Also, especially when you really have to be sure that you have reached close-to-perfect consistency, forcing stakeholders on a schedule may not work for you.

The advantage of location-based grouping of changes is that it can deliver high value for a defined problem area, and that ownership of the problem is well-defined. That limited scope, however, is also its worst disadvantage: typically the beef is in places elsewhere. For larger efforts that profoundly transform a company, like Sarbanes-Oxley, that can be, and indeed is, different.

For example, in the case study of Section 3.5 you find a mixture of several approaches. In financial accounting, temporally equidistant change groups are the norm. Some product-related areas are using that scheme as well. Interestingly, it happens frequently that changing the terminology is hampered by the limited ability of applications to change (or adopt those changes, for that matter). On the other hand, there are also areas where changes are not grouped at all. These are relatively small and confined. Either inconsistencies are not possible or they do not have a material impact. Finally, there are areas where a function-oriented grouping of changes is used.

7.8   Organizing impact analysis

One of the central tasks of managing change is analyzing the impact of a proposed change. This activity can do a great deal to reduce the operational risk in the propagation phase of change management. If stakeholders are informed about an upcoming change, they can raise their concerns. If they are not informed, they will occasionally have an unwelcome surprise, leading to costly corrections, hiccups, and unnecessary friction.

If you have an organization in place that takes care of this, congratulations! You can consider yourself lucky. However, this is not the rule. Therefore, assuming you have not yet built an organization, what are your options? And how should you approach the task?

First, the main question you should answer yourself is what the scope of impact analysis should be. There are essentially two models. One tries to establish the impact of a change originating somewhere on the *immediate neighborhood*. This approach is relatively simple. If the impact leads to changes in the neighbor, that triggers another round of impact analysis and so on *ad nauseam*. The second approach tries to establish the impact on the entire portfolio, taking all knock-on effects into account. It requires an extremely fine-grained metamodel and very mature processes to work properly. Furthermore, after a certain number of indirections the cause-effect relation tends to break down, and it becomes difficult to see which change is genuine and which is just an effect of some other change. For this reason, I have only seen the simple model work at larger scale, and I highly recommend you follow that approach.

After this you should take stock of the precedent in and culture of your company: is the business heterogeneous or homogeneous? Do departments or locations have big or small autonomy? Have there been attempts before to establish systematic impact analysis, and how did they fare? These questions will give you an idea of how best to organize impact analysis.

Next, you must establish ownership. *Owners* are the individuals or gremiums responsible for signing off on changes to applications, process, and the like. Owners take part in impact analysis in that they receive requests for change and perform an analysis of what that change would mean for them. In this role, they act as *stakeholders*. I promise you, organizing ownership is the hardest task of them all. I know not a single company that did not have substantial or serious issues mastering this step. Expect no miracles to happen, but a long, protracted process that can take months, if not years. Chapter nine will talk about this at depth.

Finally, you must decide on the collaboration model. One change and another are often not alike, and neither are their impacts. Since the magnitude of impact corresponds quite well with the amount of political noise generated, you can save yourself a lot of headache by organizing it in such a way that:

- all stakeholders have a right to raise their concerns;
- as few stakeholders as possible will want to raise a concern;
- the cost of processing concerns is minimized.

What you should strive for is that, although always permitted to speak up, stakeholders usually remain mute when a change request comes along. But even if they do, their concerns can be accommodated quickly. Furthermore, consider again the earlier caveat that an impact analysis may lead to the conclusion that a proposed change is in fact too expensive, risky, or whatever. In that case you go back to square one and start all over. This situation should be avoided as far as possible.

This optimization problem is, obviously, a tricky one. It takes into account the characteristics of the domain, the changes, and the organization at large. Generally speaking, you can distinguish three different models of responsibility, two of them geared towards changes triggered internally, and one designed to accommodate external drivers. They resolve the forces influencing the organizational solution in their own way.

7.8.1 The provider – consumer responsibility model

The *provider–consumer responsibility model* expedites the decision-making process by giving one particular stakeholder privileges in the process of deciding what to change, thereby easing impact analysis. It is beneficial to single out a participant in the change process to lead the pack and have the others follow in situations where:

- complex dependencies make the decision difficult on what to change and what the impact will be;
- many changes need to be grouped into a consistent whole;
- a subject deserves to be taken forward by a 'torchbearer.'

The provider–consumer responsibility model is chosen when an owner acts as a factual *provider* to (many) other stakeholders, which are in a *consumer* position. The responsibilities of the provider are:

- take modeling leadership by setting the standard for the company (de–facto or assumed);
- offer a support organization (consultants, advisors) and learning material (documentation, cookbooks, manuals) helping consumers to follow;
- be responsive to legitimate proposals and requests, but also to criticism.

This model requires very strong ownership, if not leadership. It generally works best when the owner is an executive manager or a high-level gremium that exerts substantial clout within the organization. Specialist leadership sometimes works as well, though less often. Otherwise, criticism and politics creep in, and the whole atmosphere becomes difficult to control. However, this model should not be confused with a command-and-control dictator style. On the contrary, the job of a provider can be likened to that of a product manager.

For example, external regulations exert a strong force over how a company must change. The study in Section 6.6.1.1 is a case in point. Here it is the US-GAAP that drives the change process. However, an internal group takes care of translating the external requirements into an internal model (the business terms describing the general ledger). All else follows from there. The gremium that decides on what to change sees representatives from many corners of the company. But, once a decision has been taken, the impact is assessed by stakeholders, and rarely is a change revised. More interestingly, there is a central support organization knowledgeable in IT and financial accounting which helps other employees around the globe implement the change correctly.

Internal parties may exert just as much clout, though. For example, IT and HR departments normally decide on their own how to change, because they play merely a supporting role in the company processes. An IT department may decide on its own which operating system security patch to install on employees' machines, since it assumes (rightful or not) that the impact will not be big. Stakeholders may be impacted by that decision in that their purchased software product suddenly stops working. Requiring IT to test all possible combinations of patches and software products installed would quickly lead to gridlock and exploding costs. On the other hand, IT should be wise enough to offer support to those stakeholders that are adversely affected, so as not to alienate them.

The dominant position of the provider is not easily broken. The consequences of this model are hence that it is easier for (rightful) concerns of consumers to be overheard. Also, success depends quite a fair amount on the availability of complete, accurate, and intelligible documentation and training. There is only so much a support organization can do. If the number of questions raised by (potentially) impacted stakeholders rises, the supporters will be overwhelmed and the quality of stakeholders' impact analysis suffer. This is why a provider–consumer responsibility model is usually established only over a long time, which gives the provider enough opportunity to mature its own organization and processes.

7.8.2 The peer-collaboration responsibility model

The provider–consumer model demands a decent amount of maturity from the organization taking the lead. This maturity cannot always be assumed as given. On the contrary, quite often a company lacks a dominant force that could influence the handling of impact analysis. The *peer-collaboration responsibility model* on the other hand does not assume any such dominant force.

More often than is desirable, an organization has not yet assigned responsibilities as clearly as would be needed to attribute unambiguously ownership of a domain. Yet, sometimes this is not even needed. There are situations in which the impact is so readily understood and small that making a big fuss of the impact analysis is counterproductive. And finally, there are areas of a financial service company that overlap so strongly that it would be very hard to carve out clear responsibilities.

Therefore, the peer-collaboration responsibility model is used when more or less equally strong/empowered stakeholders have to work together to decide on and establish the impact of a proposed change. It works best when:

- the vested interests of stakeholders overlap notably;
- they stakeholders exhibit a willingness to collaborate on changes;
- the changes are typically simple or have a limited impact;
- the organization has not (yet) established clear ownership of the domain under consideration.

This model makes fewer and more lenient assumptions about stakeholder behavior. As a consequence, assessing impact and deciding what to do is riskier, fraught with more potential for political haggling, and generally the whole process a little more fragile.

For example, in financial services companies the corporate functions of risk management and financial accounting typically overlap quite substantially with the core business processes and products. Changes in either area often have an impact in the other. Such effects mean that complex changes are risky. The classic example in this case is changes to the corporate structures (profit or cost centers), which have reverberations in many corners of the company. Consequently, impact analysis often requires the close collaboration of stakeholders and a lot of front-loaded clarification.

On the other hand, take the case of financial service companies that need to maintain their lines of business across the applications of the entire firm. The line of business exerts a strong influence over how the business processes work and what data is required. As such, managing the lines centrally would be practically impossible, since the impact would often radiate very far. Therefore it is beneficial to grant some independence to the owners of those many individual lines and only collaborate on the things that matter, such as which lines of business are more specific than others. This is a model I have often seen succeed.

Although the provider consumer model is pretty stable but requires some time to establish, the peer-collaboration model is established easily but is inherently fragile. The order breaks down as soon as some stakeholders go their own way. From an impact analysis standpoint, these two are generally the organizational models at your disposal (your mileage may vary). Yet, there is another, third model that seeks not an organizational but a design solution to the problem of impact analysis.

7.8.3   The (semi-)automation model

As has been mentioned, impact analysis is often a creative process. Given a change, humans set out to assess the situation and return to the requester with a list of things that must also be changed as a consequence of that original change. However, this need not always be so.

In certain situations, so much is known about a change *in advance* that a solution can, by design, prepare for its occurrence and *automatically* adopt changes. Some change patterns permit devising an algorithm that, given the right metadata to drive it, will automatically transform the solution model. Hence, impact analysis becomes irrelevant.

When one company acquires another, the list of legal entities belonging to the former can easily be extended. Processes like the computation of regulatory capital can just extend their work to the new entity, given that enough is known about it. Similarly, a product that is being decommissioned may just require deletion of all records, and that is it. The split of Czechoslovakia into the Czech Republic and Slovakia can be handled in an automated fashion.

The steps required to manage the impact of such changes are a little different, because they address the *metamodel*: starting with the list of changes that exhibit the biggest likelihood to occur, their impact on the models of individual solutions is assessed. Next, assuming uniform treatment of these changes, an architecture is devised that allows taking changes to metadata and generating solution models, using that architecture. All other changes that cannot thus be adopted are handled manually.

For example, the terminology glossary presented in Section 3.5 is used to adopt automatically certain changes in applications. The membership of values in an attribute, and the values' taxonomy (that is, ordering of generic and specific values), is provided as metadata. An application reacts automatically to changes in that metadata. If, for example, a value is added, it can be readily offered to users for entering data. If, however, a value is removed, the existing data in that application can be mapped to a successor value, assuming that (mapping) metadata is available as well.

A thing to consider in (semi-)automated change adoption is, again, operational risk. The changes to metadata must be made with great caution, since any mistake will reverberate throughout the organization. And, as that is not always possible to avoid, mechanisms must be provided to deal with such errors. This is the realm of change propagation, which comes up next.

7.9   Change propagation

At last! All your decision processes lie behind you and you have the change modeled. Now it is time to actually adopt it. Change propagation is the process of changing the underlying models of our solutions portfolio. Were this an ideal world, we would simply generate everything from where we are and be done. However, this is usually not the case. Some of the reasons have been discussed above. The main concern at this stage is operational risk.

However much effort you put into metadata management, you will not achieve complete coverage, nor total consistency, nor other lofty goals. You must live with the very real possibility of events that thwart the show. And in good tradition, you should embrace *risk mitigation* techniques that reduce your exposure.

For starters, take a look at the *dependencies* between your solutions. Are there pockets exhibiting close proximity but loose coupling with other areas of your portfolio? There are typical candidates to look for, such as:

- jurisdictions;
- products;
- processes;
- markets.

All these exert some influence on the variability in solutions, thereby affecting their dependencies. For example, Life & Health insurance business is typically just loosely coupled with Property & Casualty business. As an effect, the applications (solutions) rarely maintain strong ties with each other. Consequently, starting with change adoption in Property & Casualty will not pose a risk to Life & Health.

This is, once again, an example of the interplay of architecture and change (and metadata, for that matter) management: isolating the effects of changes through architectural means or, as in this case, exploiting these naturally occurring effects helps to plan and control change propagation.

In this context, note that people are sometimes not attuned to the idea that dependencies can cross many stations and have an effect 'straight through' at the other end of the globe. For example, for technical reasons IT often builds reuse-oriented objects like operational data stores or services. These act as hubs and are therefore, from an end-user point of view, invisible. However, to the originator of the change and the metadata owner, they often act as a stakeholder, which leads to the odd (though understandable) confusion of who should communicate changes to the final recipients, the business.

For that reason *central, solid stakeholder management* is key: each and every stakeholder must be known to the people managing the change process. I have come to be convinced that staged communication via intermediaries often breaks down and messages get lost in transit.

However, there are exceptions: some of these hubs act as representatives of a community, bundling change management activities and providing a specific business service. They are capable of organizing the communication in a reliable fashion.

So, once risks are mitigated to tolerable levels you must control the process to ensure eventual alignment of all solutions. This can be achieved with run-of-the-mill 'to be' versus 'as is' comparisons. In my experience such propagation processes normally take months if not years. The line between what is and what is to be can become blurred. You should expect this not to be an exact science, therefore. Too much eagerness can get you bogged down in the details.

Another important task is *communication*. Please make an effort to inform your colleagues who are affected by the changes well in advance. And with this I mean, mostly, business. The tighter the coupling between your processes, the more people will become confused by sudden changes that were enacted in a remote unit whose name they do not even know how to spell. Therefore, communicate early and often. More specifically, what I have found to be essentially effective is to *communicate via simple examples:* due to the division of labor, abstraction is for a few, whereas effect is for the masses. People can rarely expend the time to understand thoroughly the motivations, tradeoffs, and decisions taken in order to arrive at a particular change. Hence, simplicity is a way to gain and keep their attention.

Communicating simply is a terribly difficult task: I remember one particular presentation slide that evolved over the course of about a year. It has come to represent the epitome of our team's efforts: everything that we do. This slide originated from four other slides that were gradually condensed to emphasize only the very essence of our conceptual world, and it took about ten people to evolve it. It is still accompanied by about a hundred other slides that explain the complete picture, but that information is rarely asked for.

In this chapter, you have seen that designing your metadata management processes and metamodel is an exercise in tradeoffs. You will also perhaps have noticed the frequent mention of metadata quality deficits. This is for a good reason. I have experienced that sound quality management is a key to success in metadata management. How you can address it is therefore the topic of the next chapter.

8

Quality: Achieving and Maintaining Valuable Metadata

There are two ways of constructing a software design: One way is to make it so simple that there are obviously no deficiencies, and the other way is to make it so complicated that there are no obvious deficiencies. The first method is far more difficult.

Charles Antony Richard Hoare

8.1 Overview

- You must prepare for the occurrence of metadata quality deficits. They can be avoided *ex-ante*, monitored *ex-post*, or their impact reduced.
- Quality deficits can affect completeness, intelligibility, correctness, consistency, actuality, and granularity.
- Many quality deficits are caused by human error, lack of ownership, or process deficiencies. They interact with metamodel granularity, which can have a large effect on metdata quality.
- Intelligibility is best maintained by managing homonyms and synonyms, and by ensuring concise yet comprehensive definitions. Typically the latter is the most difficult goal to achieve.
- Completeness has the biggest impact on compliance management. Quality assurance revolves around finding precise scope definitions, and cross-checking the metadata with other sources.
- The single biggest contributor to correctness and actuality of metadata is to establish straight-through processing.

- Consistency is improved by metadata reuse. Organizing such reuse follows the same alignment principles as presented in previous chapters.
- Granularity can be monitored by taking a close look at how metadata is being used. Other than that, skilled people are the best way to ensure granularity that is adequate to the problem.

8.2   Quality deficits: origins and impact

Quality deficits are the result of normal imperfections in people and processes. *They are to be expected.* As has been pointed out earlier, they occur because you are neither able, and nor should you want to erect a bureaucracy that rules out every possible mistake that can be made. The downside of this decision is that indeed not all will be perfect, and you must prepare yourself for that to happen. Settling for less than a total bureaucracy brings about the risk of quality deficits. *You must prepare for such deficits to occur.* You do not do so at the peril of losing the investments made in the metadata.

Since metadata has a leverage effect, caring for its quality is a sound investment. Building on the foundations laid in Chapter 5, there are different methods of dealing with risk, and this chapter looks at the following:

- *Avoidance:* prevents the occurrence of deficits through enacting *ex-ante* quality controls.
- *Loss control:* prepares metadata users for the occurrence of deficits by limiting their exposure.
- *Monitoring:* detects (and handles) deficits by means of *ex-post* quality controls.

But first we need to take stock of the risk landscape by identifying and measuring the extent of risk exposure we face. Since we are ultimately interested in aligning business and IT, we do so from the perspective of our three alignment goals: performance, risk, and compliance. And as always, the assessment will focus on the principal nature and qualitative extent.

8.2.1   Where deficits occur: quality and the lifecycle

There are six different types of deficits you should be interested in, namely *completeness, intelligibility, correctness, consistency, actuality,* and *granularity*. These deficits have different origins, most of which relate to the lifecycle of model elements. Metadata reify their properties from a particular viewpoint, and any change event occurring during their life time is where metadata quality deficits can potentially arise (Table 8.1).

Intelligibility is defined as the ability of metadata to communicate precisely and effectively what a model element is about from a particular viewpoint. The goal is to represent and evoke concepts without the need for further explanation, provided there is an agreed

Table 8.1: Causes of quality deficits as they occur over the lifecycle of a model element

Event Deficit	Create	Update	Delete
Intelligibility	Homonyms, synonyms go undetected (governance); definitions are neither concise nor based on a shared understanding (awareness).		Lack of ownership.
Correctness	Manual capture of metadata; incorrect disambiguation during reification in reverse engineering.		N/A
Consistency	Decentralized administration; coarse-granular design.		
Actuality	Lack of (binding) process adherence.		N/A
Completeness			Lack of ownership.

understanding of the concept. In most cases, intelligibility deficits are only of concern to terminology management and documentation: they provide metadata to humans to foster a joint understanding of meaning. For example, the term 'United States Dollar' readily conveys the meaning of 'official currency of the United States of America,' while 'premium' or 'customer' are terms that typically, and may I say ironically, do not enjoy a shared understanding in financial service companies.

Deficits in intelligibility often arise from a lack of concise definition of the business terms used in a company. Any concept used in modeling merits proper definition. Finding a definition that is understood in the same way by a large audience is a difficult task, because you often find yourself trading off semantic precision against public appeal. But intelligibility can also originate from deficits in the terminology itself, such as *homonyms* (terms of the same name but with different meanings) and *synonyms* (terms of the same meaning but with different names). Reasons include distributed administration of the glossary, as well as missing or deficient reuse policies. For example, 'customer' may be defined differently in marketing and underwriting (homonym), while 'critical' and 'urgent' may be two different words for the priority of an incident requiring immediate attention (synonym).

Across the entire lifecycle (creation, change, and deletion of business terms) things can go wrong. Very often the reason is a lack of understanding of what constitutes a good definition, and a missing awareness of what the impact is. Likewise, homonyms and synonyms may not be eliminated at an early stage, which is less the task of the individual and more that of (IT) governance instilling appropriate business term reuse. The end of the lifecycle of a term can go unnoticed because no one (especially its owner) cares for it anymore, yet it is still around.

The degree of coverage that a metadata base has of the overall solutions portfolio within the scope of the metamodel is defined as its *completeness*. Deficits are most often caused by inadequate adherence to (binding) processes. For example, an application may find its way into the productive environment without the architects ever having heard of it. Or, a new product is introduced, but it is not registered in the company catalog.

From a lifecycle point of view, creation and change of model elements are the events where completeness must be ensured, but where metadata is sometimes not captured. As in the case of intelligibility, lack of ownership often leads to the problem that the metadata is not updated about model elements whose end of lifecycle has arrived. This leads to an 'over-complete' portfolio, if you wish, which is not terribly worrying but is a cost factor.

Correctness of metadata is achieved when a model element indeed does have the characteristics as reified. For example, if an application is deployed in three different locations, but the metadata claims there are only two, that is an incorrect piece of metadata. Or, a legal entity may own 50 % each of two subsidiaries, but the metadata claims it is a mere 25 %. Note that this only applies to the point in time when a change to the model object occurs. Correctness deficits that occur later because of lost updates are the realm of actuality (see below).

Typical causes of incorrect metadata include manual capture of metadata, specifically when done *ex-post-facto*. However, metadata extraction is also to blame: disambiguation during reification is sometimes not given enough attention, which leads to incorrect assignment of metadata to model elements. All this can happen during creation or change of a model element. Deletion of that element basically eliminates the concern for correctness, and thus is not applicable.

Consistency is defined as the level of adherence of metadata to the rules defined in the metamodel. Consistency deficits are often the consequence of decentralization. Different players may capture different metadata. Ambiguities or, even worse, contradictions can be caused by administrators not coordinating their efforts in the interest of efficiency. For example, some may hold that a model element has reached the end of its lifecycle, while others claim the opposite.

Consistency issues can occur across the entire lifecycle of a model element. More often it is creation and change of such elements that leads to inconsistencies, but deletion can do so as well. For example, if a model element has reached the end of its lifecycle, but the metadata about it claims it is still alive, that is an inconsistency.

Deficits in *actuality* are defined as correctness deficits arising over time due to changes in the model that are not reflected in the metadata. For example, a business term may define an account in the general ledger. Recently the US-GAAP for that account changed, but that change is not (yet) reflected in its definition. Or, an application may once have had three interfaces to other applications, but currently sports four of them, while the metadata still claims it is but three.

Actuality deficits, like their sibling correctness deficits, can sometimes be caused by manual capture of metadata. However, the main cause is often lack of adherence to the processes binding metadata for a model element. More specifically, this often occurs in settings where metadata is captured *ex-post-facto*. People do not remember to update the metadata, or they are permitted to do so unpunished. Actuality deficits occur while the model element is in active use (creation and change), and as with correctness, the extinction of a model element renders its actuality obsolete.

There is one exception to the above rules, namely *granularity*. Deficits in granularity are a design-level concern, and so they are avoided or monitored as part of a different process (metamodeling). Therefore, the lifecycle of the metamodel, not the metadata, is used for that instead.

Summing up, lack of ownership and insufficient awareness and understanding (people risks) as well as lack of process adherence (a process risk) are the biggest causes of quality deficits. Some quality deficits become obsolete with the end of the lifecycle of a model element.

8.2.2 What deficits do: how alignment is impacted

From the point of view of your alignment goals (performance, risk, and compliance), you will be concerned about what metadata quality defects can do. This section concerns itself with that question (see Table 8.2).

Insufficient *intelligibility* leads to wrong decisions. This is mostly of concern in risk management, and even more so in data quality management. Data that is not documented adequately in business terminology leads to ambiguities. In particular, computed measures used as risk indicators may or may not cover a particular case, leaving the risk manager exposed to the possibility of assuming what is not really there. A similar argument applies to impact analysis, where the semantics of (dependency) relationships can be misjudged. Accordingly, the impact is medium to high. On the other hand, compliance management can be only marginally affected (e.g., alignment status) or impacted quite dramatically (e.g., when legal requirements are misinterpreted). Performance improvement does not require too much intelligibility: metadata is most often used for model generation. Hence, the model transformation and mapping machinery, which effectively encode the semantics of the mapping between metamodel and

Table 8.2: Quality deficits as they impact the alignment goals

Goal Deficit	Performance	Risk	Compliance
Granularity	low...high	medium	N/A
Intelligibility	low	medium...high	low...high
Correctness	low...medium	low...medium	medium...high
Consistency	medium...high	low...medium	low...medium
Actuality	low...medium	low...medium	medium...high
Completeness	low	low...medium	high

model(s), lead to more or less immediate validation of assumptions about the metadata. Misunderstandings can thus be cleared quite quickly.

By the same token, performance improvement is usually only mildly affected by *correctness* and *actuality* deficits. If there are mistakes, the forward-engineered solution is exposed to real life, thus validating the metadata. However, note that depending on the granularity and structural complexity of the metamodel, this will become increasingly difficult. Linking effect to causes (tracking model deficits back to metadata deficits) is harder as the techniques become more sophisticated.

As for compliance, the impact of incorrect metadata is slightly higher than that of unintelligible metadata. Since unintelligible metadata usually reveals itself much quicker than incorrect metadata, the likelihood of faulty decisions is higher. As for risk, the impact can have a wide spread. In the typical risk management settings (data quality, dependencies), the effects of incorrect metadata can be diverse. For example, the fact that a dependency exists (yet is factually pointed in the wrong direction) will help get a better understanding of the impact some change may have. Complementary knowledge will always help to put the dependency in perspective. By the same token, a data quality report that is out of date may lead to a significant error of judgement of the data quality, but that will only be indirectly responsible for an error of judgement about the data itself.

Any *completeness* deficit will most decidedly impact your compliance goals. Missing coverage will lead you to overlook some corners in your company, processes, or applications that must be compliant. You will not check them, thus leaving the door open to compliance violations. As for using incomplete metadata in risk management, your impact analysis will perhaps be affected, but (depending on the amount of incomplete coverage) only moderately. In data quality assessments, missing metadata will be noticed and therefore alert the person to that fact, reducing the impact. Finally, performance improvement will be only slightly affected: if certain models cannot be mapped or transformed completely, that incurs a (higher) friction cost due to unstructured change adoption. However, the impact will be limited.

The impact of *inconsistency* is biggest on performance improvement. Model generation requires consistent metadata, since the algorithms used to transform or map models are based on consistency. The consequence of such deficits can be that the model generation process does not complete. Worse even, it may produce inconsistent models, which can go unnoticed for a while and thus cause costly repairs. On the other hand, compliance and risk management will generally not be greatly impaired: inconsistencies affect more than just one model element. Since compliance and risk processes use complementary sources as well (not least of them the human being), deficits are spotted more easily.

For each of the above, a mid- to long-term consequence of quality deficits is that the users of metadata will lose faith in it and defect to other methods. You will not want to let it go that far. Therefore, the next sections discuss ways to detect and handle such deficits before they cause any harm.

8.3 Intelligibility: getting a grip on language

Avoiding intelligibility deficits works most reliably with *ex-ante* quality controls. This means checking for the likes of homonyms, synonyms, or insufficiently defined terms. The controls are enacted before a model element is bound, which is typically when the documentation is published. You will strive to achieve a glossary of business terms that is concise, yet comprehensive in its description of the language to use in modeling. Only homonyms can be automatically detected, all other deficits are visible only to the human eye. Therefore, *ex-ante* quality controls require the eye of a skilled, knowledgeable person who understands the complexity hidden behind names and definitions. This can require a varying amount of work.

Take the following example: in the Linnaean biological classification system, all creatures are organized in a hierarchical taxonomy:

Superregnum → Regnum → Subregnum → Superphylum → Phylum → Subphylum → Infraphylum → Superclassis → Classis → Subclassis → Infraclassis → Ordo . . . and so on.

Companies often organize their hierarchical structures (line management, cost centers, profit centers) in the same way; that is, have business units at the top level, regional divisions below, and somewhere the (bookable) profit centers. Sometimes a profit center cannot be fitted into the existing scheme. Instead of wedging it in somewhere, people 'invent' artificial 'filler' business units or regional divisions, often with the exact same name as the unusual profit center to be inserted. Theoretically this should confuse people because of the many homonyms that creates, but in practice it does not. The reason is that tacit knowledge (e.g., only level $n > m$ profit centers are used for booking) helps users disambiguate rather quickly. As such, these homonyms are no practical problem.

Some recommendations for manual assessment of intelligibility can be given, however. For example, conjunction phrases such as 'Aviation & Space' or 'Property & Casualty,' though seemingly innocent, merit extra scrutiny because they offer the potential for misunderstandings. This is because humans often use logical operators ('and,' 'or,' and others) inconsistently, which can be confusing, and at best ambiguous. This is the reason for classifications of generic and specific terms, as in the following examples:

- 'Property' and 'Casualty,' which belong under the 'Property & Casualty.' From the logical perspective, it should rather be called 'Property or Casualty,' because both are subsumed.
- 'Bar/Discotheque/Dancing,' which describes three terms in one. The three should be hierarchically ordered, but were put together to save time.
- 'Accident War/Political Risks,' which includes war and political risks.

- 'Accounting & Consulting/Professional Services (LCR),' my personal favorite, is a mixture of an 'or' (oddly marked by an '&'), another 'or' (the '/'), and an abbreviation ('LCR' stands for 'large corporate risks').

Filtering out terms that contain symbols like ampersand, slash, braces, or the words 'and' and 'or' are candidates to be subjected to controls. Abbreviations are another area in which intelligibility may be impaired, because they may not be readily understood by the audience. Automated checks can help; that is, detecting groups of capital letters that may be abbreviations. For example, the above 'Accounting & Consulting/Professional Services (LCR)' is a value in the attribute 'Large corporate risk (LCR) economic activity,' which has 38 values, each of which contains the abbreviation '(LCR)' somewhere in its name.

Especially when business terms are maintained decentrally, hard- and fast rules cannot be imposed and do not make sense in each and every case. Idiomatic solutions like style guides, working policies, or naming conventions can help prevent misunderstandings. They can be overridden where required, but should hold up in general.

So much for avoiding intelligibility deficits. Domain-orientation is one method of *controlling* the impact magnitude of intelligibility deficits: the bigger the number of domains, the smaller their scope and, likewise, the smaller the likelihood of misunderstandings. People will understand more with tacit knowledge and misunderstand less – even if the general public will find a term name or its definition tricky to understand. For example, in financial accounting the abbreviation 'DFI on FX' is readily understood to mean 'derivative financial instruments on foreign exchange,' and 'DIC/DIL' is clear to the underwriting community, to which it reads: 'Difference in conditions/difference in limits.' However, note that the smaller the domain, the more inconsistencies you will find to other domains.

Exploiting human tacit knowledge present in a domain is in fact a creative use of *semiotics*, the science of signs. In semiotics, an utterance is understood to use a set of conventions (the *langue*) to express a particular meaning (the *parole*). Using intrinsic uniformity in the parole gives you the opportunity to simplify our model of the langue. Or, less cryptically, by *assuming* that certain things are always named or defined the same way in a domain, you can waive reification of that circumstance in our metamodel. As an effect, your metamodel becomes simpler. I personally recommend you try to use it.

Finally, *monitoring* for intelligibility deficits by means of *ex-post* quality controls will help you to detect and eventually correct them. Here you will normally rely on statistical methods that detect potential deficits. With these methods you will try to find repetitive use of standard phrases in definitions ('to be completed,' 'self-explanatory,' '–,' or '?'). Once definitions of a certain length show up in a statistically significant form, you can follow up on them by grouping alike definitions and start with the entries that occur most often. By the way, monitoring is typically a central activity.

As an example, take again the business terminology management case from Section 3.5. At one point in the past, the glossary contained 6700 terms with a definition length of 1–3768. As you can see in Figure 8.1, seven data points stick out. An explanation could be found for each of these with an extremely high confidence rate. The results have been summarized in Table 8.3. Generally speaking, either the spike turned out to mark a true deficit ('tbd' or 'self-explanatory'), a repetitive use of a phrase that had a reserved meaning in the domain ('subtotal' and 'business unit' for financial accounting), or a technical object ('all values in the attribute [. . .]' auto-generated by the glossary). For this anecdotal piece of evidence at least,

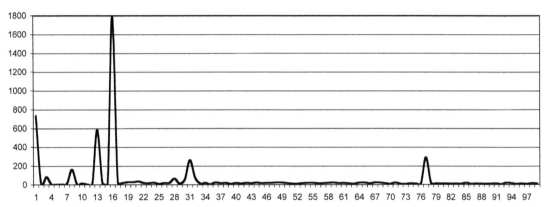

Figure 8.1: Length distribution of definitions in a business term glossary. Spikes hint at the use of standard phrases and clauses. The data are cut off at *length* > 100, since there are no outliers beyond that point

Table 8.3: The worst offenders with respect to bad definitions were mostly true deficits (' – ,' 'tbd,' or 'self-explanatory'), had a reserved meaning in the domain ('subtotal' and 'business unit' for financial accounting), or represented a technical object ('all values in the attribute [. . .]' auto-generated default)

Definition length	Term count	Worst offender	Offender count	Offender contribution (%)
1	733	' – '	733	100
3	83	'tbd'	79	95
8	161	'subtotal'	155	96
13	582	'business unit'	508	87
16	1794	'self-explanatory'	1766	98
31	261	'counter party of otc traded dfi'	245	94
77	290	'all values in the attribute [. . .]'	276	95

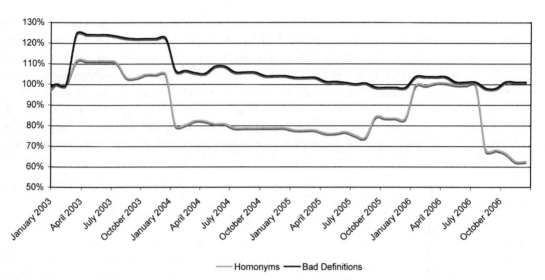

Figure 8.2: Bad definitions (black) versus homonyms (gray) in the glossary over time. The relative number on January 1, 2003 is each 100 % In four years, nothing had changed substantially. The main contributor to drops and surges were mass changes, mostly due to reorganizations

the lesson is that statistical distribution is a very convenient, yet precise, instrument to detect bad (that is, unintelligible) definitions.

For another example, consider the historic development of two quantitative measures in the same glossary as depicted in Figure 8.2: over time, the rate of homonyms as well as the rate of bad definitions relative to glossary volume did not change significantly. The occasional bump here and there is explained by company reorganizations, but generally the line is flat. It tells a story about the limits of quality assurance in this area: the homonym rate lies at around 1 %, which is more or less as good as it gets. However, the rate of bad definitions lies at around 30 %, which is unsatisfactory. For years, quality improvement has been tried in this company, so you can learn yet another lesson from this example: first, homonyms are not such a big concern, but bad definitions are. Second, improving the intelligibility of definitions is a costly, politically charged, and often an ultimately futile exercise *when done ex-post*. Keep this in mind before you take a lenient stance on definitions.

8.4   Completeness: maintaining an overview of things

Completeness is always measured relative to the (assumed, imagined, or real) total extent of a portfolio. Hence, *avoiding* incompleteness is a little bit of a tricky goal. Unless you can ensure at all times that you know the extent of your portfolio, it is futile to prevent deficits *ex-ante*.

The only chance you stand is to find a formal definition for the elements of your portfolio. Each time they change during their lifecycle, they must be checked against that definition to decide whether to take them up or drop them.

For example, in SOX compliance (as discussed in Section 6.6.2) the relative contribution of a legal entity to total assets and/or revenues is used as a proxy to its relevance for the scope of alignment. Likewise, a particular relative contribution of an account to overall profit or loss is taken as the threshold for considering accounts to be in or out of scope.

As another example, consider the data language presented in Section 3.5, where the criterion of relevance for attributes or applications is their contribution to company-wide reports. This can be internal reports (e.g., risk exposure, performance figures) as well as external ones (e.g., financial results, regulatory reporting). Applications that play the role of hubs are considered in scope as well, due to the multiplicator effects they have.

Controlling the magnitude of the effect of completeness deficits is difficult. The biggest effects of such deficits are in compliance, but you will find it hard to limit their impact. Since compliance is often an either/or affair (an element of the portfolio is either in scope or not), there is very little you can do once you have decided to take it out of scope. However, if you do not fear being perceived as bureaucratic, enlarging your scope is a safe bet, as it reduces the risk of false negatives. Or, in the words of this chapter's motivating quote, there will obviously be no more deficiencies.

Your best shot at managing completeness deficits is to *monitor* them. Finding a concise scope definition can prove hard. For metadata about relations (which captures connections between portfolio elements), it is easier to develop a rough idea, use it, and cross-check it against other portfolios. This is known as *gap/overlap analysis*: you chart two portfolios up against each other, filling cells when there is a relationship between the portfolio elements of either type (Table 8.4). Gaps in the form of empty rows or columns in the matrix indicate one of the following:

- completeness deficit: metadata is missing;
- coverage too large: the scope should be reduced.

The completeness of a portfolio (that is, of the list of model elements) is monitored *ex-post* for deficits. This is different from avoiding completeness deficits, which is done *ex-ante* You will use monitoring more intensely if the maturity of your governance processes (which take care of capturing 'relevant' elements) is low as well, *and* the percentage of in-scope to out-of-scope model elements is low. Used this way, you can ensure smooth execution of the core process without letting too many true positives go undetected.

For example, the data language mentioned in Section 3.5 knows about relevant applications and relevant attributes, of which there are an estimated 50 and 300, respectively. The implied message is that for each relevant attribute we can find one relevant application that processes

Table 8.4: A usage matrix is a good way to check for gaps and overlaps. Two groups of elements are charted up against each other, marking where they share a relationship. Empty columns or rows (as for B3) indicate either missing data (completeness deficit) or an obsolete element. Duplicate entries in columns or rows can also be an indication that the granularity is too coarse (Group A may have to be refined to highlight the specific ways B5 is using the other group)

Group B \ Group A	1	2	3	4	5	6
1	X					
2		X				
3						
4		X				
5			X	X	X	
6						X

it, and vice versa. Even more to the point, if a relevant attribute is not processed by at least a handful of applications, that can be taken as a sign that the attribute is in fact not so relevant at all. A simple usage matrix can reveal such gaps and overlaps. In the same vein, the number of interfaces that an application shares with its peers is taken as a proxy to relevance.

As another example, CRUD (create, read, update, delete) matrices are a well-known tool in architecture management. They depict the use of data in processes. Actually, if you prefer, data flow diagrams are an extended form of CRUD matrices that add the time dimension (what happens in which order).

Finally, consider the case study in Section 5.6.4: here it is the mapping of solutions to platforms that is maintained and used to assess the coverage of standards. If, for example, many solutions use very few technical platforms, that may indicate a lack of compliance metadata coverage.

8.5 Correctness and actuality: making sure metadata reflects reality

Correctness and actuality have very similar characteristics when it comes to detecting and handling deficits. Therefore, I present them together here.

For starters, to *avoid* deficits, your best hope is to increase the level of awareness and understanding of the people doing the modeling. This is an important success factor. Setting up a training program or establishing a network of experts is a measure at your disposal that you should consider. However, it is only an indirect factor.

As another organizational measure, the four-eye-principle (one person designs a model, another person publishes or authorizes it) helps reduce the risk of incorrect metadata. But it is not a very sharp knife to cut with. Typically it works just with small numbers of model elements, which can be looked at in one go, such as in parametrization and feature modeling.

Metamodel simplification reduces the risk of a material impact once metadata is indeed incorrect. What you are effectively doing is to lower the level of granularity in exchange for more human intervention and interpretation, thereby *controlling* exposure. This is rarely an option for complex model generation settings, but risk and compliance management may benefit. Obviously, with this technique you are not facing the correctness challenge, but rather avoiding it. If the cost of going there is too high, this might be an option to ponder. It is telling that many of the case studies feature comparatively simple approaches, indicating that companies make better experiences with simpler metamodels. The price to pay for that is more manual effort; that is, cost. Areas with a high rate of change are not ideal for doing this.

One technique that indirectly *monitors* and *avoids* deficits is straight-through processing (STP). This is a measure where you use architectural means to achieve a metadata quality goal. In STP, you use metadata without any manual intervention in the applications supporting your core processes. Any correctness deficit shows up directly, neither watered down nor delayed. This has the effect that incorrect metadata will *have to* be corrected as soon as possible, should it occur. Essentially you are establishing a feedback loop. On the downside, this approach can significantly increase your operational risk. For that reason it should only be pursued if the metamodel, and thus the parts of the core processes that are affected by metadata changes, is comparatively simple. Lacking mature metadata quality assurance or well-trained metadata administration staff, a company performing full-blown meta-programming is at risk of serious disruptive events due to (inevitable) mistakes. STP is not for the faint-of-heart.

Yet another technique of checking quality is the comparison of the 'as is' with the 'to be' state. This is especially helpful in situations where it is possible to (completely) extract the 'as is' state as reified in the metamodel. It enables you to compare the two different states and take corrective action. Typically the 'as is' state is amended, as it is assumed that the 'to be' state represents what has been previously authorized and that the differences in the 'as is' state are the result of imperfections.

Differences between 'as is' and 'to be' states are more likely to occur over time, as the 'to be' metadata ages. This is why another monitoring technique helps: you can use metadata time-stamps as a gauge of how up-to-date it is. With a decent understanding of how often a solution changes or, even better, by knowing exactly when it last did so, you can see when the last update to the metadata occurred and draw your conclusions. Typically humans are quite adept at making the right assumptions about whether the metadata is still up to date.

As an example of straight-through processing, let me again refer to Section 3.5. The company's applications obtain metadata from designated (master) sources and validate incoming data with it. It happens occasionally that data is rejected, because the delivering application did not comply with the valid data standard. However, sometimes the cause is to be found in the metadata source, which leads to a correction.

The case studies on automated derivation of data quality measures (Section 5.6.1), rule-based exception handling (Section 5.6.2), tax-related compliance metadata (Section 6.6.4), and the detection of candidates of money-laundering cases (Sections 6.6.3 and 6.6.5) are all examples of metamodel simplification. Since the real world was too complex, more human intervention was needed to compensate for the fact that rules were sometimes not 100 % correct.

The case study presented in Section 6.6.2 is an example of comparing the 'as is' with the 'to be' state. Here the metadata of installed applications, middleware, hardware, or other infrastructure can be scanned and discovered, which enables comparisons. A quality assurance process has the responsibility to follow up on deficits.

8.6   Consistency: moving towards metadata reuse

Consistency deficits can obviously be *avoided* by defining a fine-granular metamodel. The disadvantage is a corresponding higher cost of metadata capture and, potentially, more bureaucracy. However, that is not your only option. In some cases you do not want to or, possibly, cannot reify a certain concept in the metamodel. In this case your biggest foe is redundancy in the metadata. Administrators who design models will occasionally repeat themselves, thereby risking that, once a change occurs, one instance is changed and the other is not (see Section 6.6.7). If they work on a team, the risk is compounded by the challenges of collaboration.

Either way, you may want to start thinking about organizing metadata reuse. The more you reuse existing metadata, the more you isolate the impact of changes. Managing reuse successfully reduces the risk of inconsistencies by ensuring compliance. Yes, this is where you end up in a meta-metamodel world! This is the point where your efforts have led you back to square one: performance, risk, and compliance. Once you start thinking about establishing reuse mechanisms in your metamodel, the time has come to think about *monitoring* alignment, which is done in the same way as discussed earlier in this book.

Controlling the impact of inconsistencies, should they occur, requires architectural measures. It is expensive. Any machine assumes certain constraints as given that form part of the model on which the computation is based. That is the safety net that types give you in programming languages, for example. If you give up that safety net, all bets are off. Hence, the only thing you can do is to check the consistency rules at all times metadata is used. Once an inconsistency is detected, the algorithm terminates or otherwise gracefully deals with the impasse. The impact on the computation performance should be clear, and terminating computation is an almost pathologically controlled way of going about the issue. Hence, unless you really have to, think twice whether you want to go down this route.

As an example, take the case study from Section 6.6.7: consistency was relatively unharmed as long as one individual administered the rules. However, as the rule base grew and especially as more administrators were added, the number of inconsistencies grew substantially. In this situation, further measures started to become necessary.

Take another example, that of the data language mentioned previously. In Figure 8.3 you can see a histogram of the total number of terms in the glossary charted against the relative number of values in an attribute. Both climb in union as the size of the glossaries increases and more business terms are standardized. However, starting in 2004 and increasingly after 2005, the number of values per attribute drops in comparison. This can be explained as follows: until about the end of 2005, more terms were included in the glossary, but very little consolidation (that is, reduction of redundancy) took place. Starting in 2006, however, the relative size of attributes drops visibly, and yet their number increases. This means that we may not really have started consolidating either. But, and that is the point of the diagram, there are quantitative measures that can guide your decision where to do so. In this particular case it turns out that the important attributes (e.g., line of business) have in fact grown in size, the opposite of what we want.

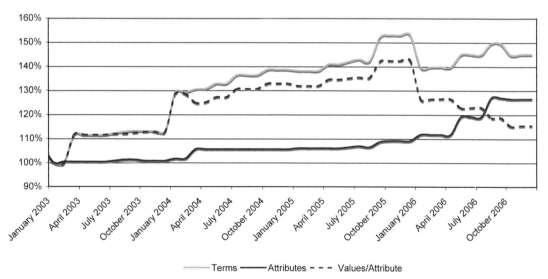

Figure 8.3: Term volume (black) versus terms per attribute (gray) versus attribute count (dashed) in the glossary over time. The relative number on January 1, 2003 is each 100%. The relative drop of the number of terms per attribute may suggest that a consolidation has taken place, but that effect is mostly due to a higher number of attributes

8.7 Granularity: model and metadata working together

Finally, granularity deficits can be *avoided* by putting good people on the modeling problem. It is a matter of the right level of knowledge, awareness, and understanding. As such, people are the best investment you can make. But that does not mean that all is lost on the process side. Since metadata determines the characteristic properties of all models within its reach, interesting comparisons can be drawn to *monitor* the granularity of metadata, at least in certain cases.

Take a look at Figure 8.4, which is based on data taken from a data warehouse. You see charted the relative contribution of categories (metadata) offered to employees of an insurer who enters bookings (data) to categorize transactions. For reasons yet unknown, 12.5 % of 'loss reasons' are sufficient to describe the context in 95 % of transactions categorized, while for the 'lines of business' the curve is much flatter. When you consider Figure 8.5 as well, you see that the categories at the top of the 'loss reasons' tree are used disproportionately often. (You also see that quite a few transactions have not been classified.) For the 'line of business' it is just the opposite.

What has happened here? Well, in the first approximation the demand does not quite match the supply. Categories are used in a way that does not correspond to their number. Or, put differently, there are quite a few categories that are statistically *obsolete*. They are superfluous, excess baggage. They do not add value. In this particular setting, the categories offer too high

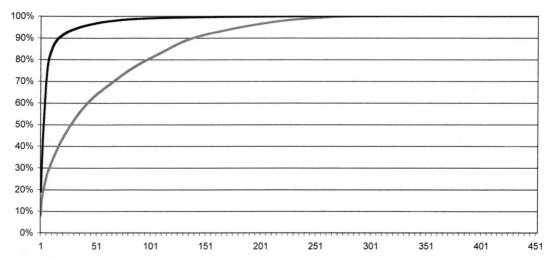

Figure 8.4: In this graph, values in two attributes, 'loss reason' (black) and 'line of business' (gray) are ordered by intensity of use. After that, their relative contribution to the total number of uses across all transactions is plotted. As can be seen, very few 'loss reasons' are sufficient to cover almost all such bookings. You can use a graph like this to detect potential inconsistencies

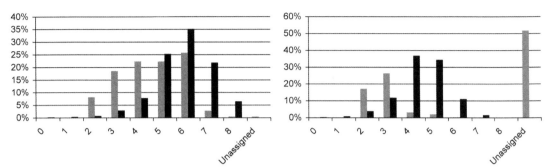

Figure 8.5: Offered categories (black) versus density of bookings (gray) of the 'lines of business' (left) and 'loss reasons' (right) in a large data warehouse. About 35 % of values are offered at level 6 of the "line of business" tree (the root being level 0), but only 25 % of the transactions use it. The disparities between the number of offered and used categories is a hint at potential granularity deficits. For example, the values on level 7–8 of the 'line of business' are practically superfluous and can be eliminated

a granularity that is not justified by their actual use. They can be eliminated without much damage.

Comparing the use (referencing) of metadata in models is a good way to find out whether the offering stands up to the reality test. This applies to granularity whose level is too small or too big. In the particular case presented here it was made easier because the concepts are hierarchically structured, thus aligning granularity with position in the hierarchy. As a matter of fact, there are many more forces at play here. Regulatory requirements are partially to blame for the distribution of 'loss reasons.' Intelligibility is also a factor. The principal issue persists, and it becomes visible in the usage. This is the wedge you can use to monitor granularity.

Last but not least, consider again the case study in Section 5.6.4: the mapping of solutions to platforms helps assess the granularity of architectural standards. If, for example, many solutions indicate that a specific platform is 'not applicable' to them, it may be time to reconsider that platform's design. Maybe the building blocks it offers are too coarse-grained? Likewise, the occurrence of too many non-compliant solutions may hint at possible granularity deficits. However, it may just as well hint at compliance process deficits, but that is another matter.

Wrapping up, we can say that the important ingredients to the successful achievement and maintenance of high-quality metadata are awareness and understanding, as well as ownership. How to obtain them will be the subject of the next chapter, which also concerns itself with another ingredient to success: the mastership of politics.

9

Sustainability: Ownership, Awareness, Understanding, and Politics

The strongest is never strong enough always to be master unless he transforms strength into right and obedience into duty.

Jean Jacques Rousseau

9.1 Overview

- The three main responsibilities of an owner are to act as a keeper of metadata content, to answer questions related to that content, and to take decisions on change requests. A custodian may take over parts or all of these responsibilities.
- It is important that the owner is not a bureaucrat, but identifies with the topic and carries it forward, looking after metadata in the name of the company rather than regarding it as their property.
- Individuals, committees, and line organizations may act as owners. The latter are the best achievable option, but also the most difficult to arrive at.
- To convince owners to commit to the task, appeal to their ambitions, promise them control, or play to their desire for recognition as an expert.
- There are different types of owners, torchbearers, willing collaborators, fundamentalists, high-brows, and competent allys. Each can be helpful at certain times and a hindrance at others, but high-brows rarely play a supportive role.

- In order to create buy-in and alleviate the fears of owners, offer consulting services, prepare an owner's cookbook, explain the scope with examples, and allow for complexity comparisons.
- Scaling change management almost always means decentralization of decisions. Ensuring good, widespread communication and allowing for escalation can alleviate some of the ensuing problems.
- As a general rule, 0.1 % of your total workforce should concern themselves with managing metadata per metamodel.
- To plan and execute a campaign to raise awareness and understanding, target it to the different roles in the company, such as solution designers, power users, intermediaries, and the general employee public.
- Metadata management suffers so much from politics because it tries to raise transparency and consistency by means of objectification. Political goals, such as maintaining ambiguity and using power to exert control, counteract metadata management goals.
- In order to lock in on previous achievements, create barriers to exit. Your main goal should be to make metadata management an integral part of the core process it supports. Credibility and trust can only complement it.
- In order to increase the reach of metadata management, sideline detractors, decentralize responsibility, and use a legitimatory framework where possible to frame the debate.
- Using force and pressure, rewards, negotiation, or appealing to rational thinking is usually not an effective tactic on the offense.

9.2   The soft side of success

When I attend conferences or ask colleagues about their opinion of what determines the success (or failure, for that matter) of metadata management, one thought comes up with people almost immediately: 'management support.' It seems many are convinced that the only thing that really matters is to have the buy-in of an executive high up the corporate food chain who gets stuff going. Otherwise your ambitions are doomed to evaporate.

I do not think this sentiment is generally wrong, and high-level management support *can* play a decisive role in making metadata management a success. However, I do contend that this is an overly rosy picture verging on the idyllic. One single person can perhaps make or break a project in a particular instance, but it is not true that anyone (given the right rank) can do so on each and every project.

The reasons for success are often complex, multi-faceted, and sometimes elusive, as are the reasons for failure. I remember how I took over a tool for managing business terminology under the banner of 'metadata management.' The idea at the time was to evolve and extend the existing tool to accommodate more requirements, such as the ability to integrate directly with applications, and store data about reports, data models, etc. From the technical perspective this seemed like a straightforward job: extend the repository model, beef up configuration management abilities, and iron out some 'look-and-feel' quirks.

Yet, it did not turn out quite so. While we were planning for the all-new solution, our management changed. Our group was transferred to another department, which featured two more groups concerned with data management. The project changed course (and scope) drastically, and started to focus exclusively on business terminology, which I personally regarded as a mistake. New colleagues joined the team, bringing in their own ideas and methods which I did not like very much either.

The weird thing that happened, though, was that our project's exposure grew dramatically and, to my dismay, all of a sudden became part of another project's planning. There was this non-life data warehouse project which, you could say, banked on the solution we planned to deliver. Even more, that project explicitly bought into our idea of a repository-based platform for managing (simple) data types throughout the company.

That alleviated my concerns a little, because this was an opportunity as much as a challenge. However, another (large) group in financial accounting had been using the previous repository version, and regarded it as almost its own property. Suggestions to simplify, consolidate, or otherwise change the way the solution was working were generally met with resistance, if not outright disdain. Since that group had so far made up the biggest user community, and may I say, also the most successful and comprehensive, there was little to complain about. Obviously, you do not meddle with success. On the other hand, the existing solution had grown pretty baroque, with numerous features that made little sense when taken together, or had been developed with a single, consistent metaphor in mind. Lifecycle management for business terms was almost absent (there was an arcane, idiomatic way you could mimic it with, but you did not have to). In a word, from a conceptual point of view the situation was a fair bit rotten.

Then there was the political situation. The people in financial accounting had successfully established a comprehensive, global, and stable change process. We saw in 2002 that their way of seeing the world was in and by itself consistent, but that other parts of the company had to be taken into account as well (such as the people from the non-life business). Attempts to convince them to agree to some form of organized data reuse based on the repository were knocked down rather swiftly and decisively.

So, at that point we were in a weak situation. What I realized, however, was that the data warehouse project offered a unique opportunity to shift the balance of power. The thing was to get them on board and use them as an ally in our ambition to establish one single way of managing data in the company. They had high-level management backing, ambitious goals themselves, and their project staff were generally positive towards our ideas. In fact, to an extent I think they shared our feelings about the financial accounting guys. Yet, they did not have the means (and, may I add, interest) to establish a data management solution, processes and so on by themselves. In a sense, they depended on us in return – a classic win-win situation. We teamed up.

The new repository was delivered, and system interfaces allowed the warehouse to obtain the official lines of business, types of business, and so forth from there. However, hidden in the design of the interfaces was a flytrap: the lifecycle management mechanisms only worked if you used the business term identifiers that were unique to the repository. If you used the codes of other applications (e.g., 'CHF' for 'Swiss Franc' or 'USD' for 'United States Dollar'), you got no support. Because the data warehouse loaded the business terms automatically on a regular basis, it had to use 'our' identifiers, essentially locking them in with the repository as a technology. Not only that, it also locked them in with the organization that maintained it. I deliberately designed the repository and the interfaces that way, knowing what effect that would have.

Now, this is not to say that we short-changed those colleagues. We did deliver a powerful solution nonetheless. It enabled them to handle change in a whole new way, more reliably and consistently. The point is that we used the win-win situation as an opportunity to create buy-in, yet tied it to a specific technological solution, thus locking in on our achievement. The hope was also that the data warehouse, which had a hub function in the application architecture, would 'transmit' the business term identifiers to downstream applications, thus 'infecting' them as well. (It had been their express intention to establish these identifiers as a company standard.)

The project concluded successfully around mid-2003, and the size of the repository content has grown ever since. More applications began obtaining their business terms from there. As expected, the hold that the financial accounting team had on the content and the design of the repository, weakened substantially and continues to do so. However, at the time the repository only served (business terms describing) data used for classification. Requests were made to us to come up with a more comprehensive framework for managing (what came to be named) master data throughout the company. We took up the task, and the effort moved along at moderate pace for a while.

In 2004, however, about a year after completion of the project, in the wake of the Enron, WorldCom, and Parmalat scandals, the word 'governance' was all the rage. Everyone ran around the company, labeling their effort by that latest hype word. So did we. This was the time when we truly started pushing on a global framework for managing data in our firm. And, interestingly, ideas from years ago came up again. The embedding into the IT governance processes (e.g., project management, architectural sign-off) was something we tried to achieve in order to get a hand on reviewing projects that delivered solutions with respect to data. Our team (and a second, complementary one) had the mandate to perform such reviews, only the conceptual basis for it was missing. What we needed was an idea of what 'compliance' would really mean, and what a solution should be 'aligned' against. We started out with a rough notion of compliance, which was practiced de-facto already by one team, and embedded into the overall IT governance framework. As can be expected, this raised yet more difficulties and produced resistance, leading to various compromises. At the end of 2005, after 18 months of political haggling, however, we established a global IT standard that established for the first time a comprehensive, unified approach to managing data at the company. One of the central pieces of that standard was the conceptualization of a phrase that was first brought up at the end of 2002. From inception to implementation, three years passed.

Today, governance is not as hip as it used to, but the business term repository is an established fact in the company. The data management standard is being applied, and more and more content is being brought under its umbrella. Slowly, but progressively, the company is maturing in its handling of data. There are now various, distributed groups in the firm who take care of this task, and a gremium for handling data management topics of global concern to the firm is slowly emerging.

This chapter is about the soft side of success: politics, ownership, awareness and understanding. It is a story wholly different from architectural and design issues, and processes and models. As I mentioned earlier, you are in the business of organizing other people's work when you establish metadata management. Such changes give rise to a variety of reactions, most of which are neither technical nor rational. I strongly believe these reactions must be considered as part of your basic approach to metadata management, because, they come up regularly.

You are changing the way people work and collaborate. This changes the social fabric of the company and alters collaboration structures that give rise to human interaction. You create potential for resistance to change because, to an extent, you challenge the existing (sometimes cultural) foundations of the firm. This is why the following issues are worth your attention:

- *Ownership:* in any change process, someone must decide whether, and how, a requested change should be adopted. This implies some form of ownership role, but it also raises the question of how other stakeholders, who may make an equally viable claim on decisions, can be taken on board as well.
- *Awareness and understanding:* designing models, even simple ones, can be a challenging task. Unless all work is left to specialists, people with limited knowledge must understand the impact of their decisions when administering metadata. But not only them; even those who are mere consumers of that data must be aware of the sometimes complex workings within the company.
- *Politics:* metadata management has unique potential for trouble. People can block your efforts, try to sideline you, or just refuse to cooperate. You must understand the reasons behind such actions, the mechanisms to defend yourself against them, and be able to launch an offensive on your own.

As can be seen from the story above and others below, these three challenges are normal. They almost always occur in one form or another. It took years until we reached the point where we are today, and there were years before that where other people tried. In my experience the glacial pace of progress is the rule, not the exception. In fact, I considered us (and continue to do so) very successful in comparison to other companies. But it also shows that it is often not the technical problems that cause metadata management to fall, but the limitations and fallibility of corporate human nature.

9.3   Establishing ownership

In an earlier assignment I was responsible for the metadata management platform for the corporate data warehouse. One part consisted of an environment in which business users could administer the business terminology describing the semantics of the data stored in the warehouse. The idea was that privileged users would maintain the terminology itself as well as link it to the data model elements (e.g., tables, columns).

The platform we had developed was part of a bigger program to transform the company's approach to analytical applications, so we relied upon others to take care of coming up with the list of (the most important) business terms. We only provided the administration platform. This was understandable, since the program had started as an IT effort. Its main goal was to provide a technical platform to develop and operate analytical applications. Therefore, the establishment of a business terminology catalog, though not forgotten, was a side-issue.

The list of terms never came about. There were several attempts to jump-start a steering committee of business people interested enough in the overall topic, but nothing came to fruition. Given this debacle, we took things into our own hands and started to enter the business terms ourselves. However, given the delicate nature of this effort, we still wanted to obtain some kind of sign-off from someone close to business – if only to validate our assumptions. It so happened that we had good connections with the data mining team, who not only critically depended on understanding data in the (marketing part of the) warehouse, but also expressed an interest in working with us.

We started with the core component of the data warehouse and identified about 100 business terms to be defined. When we sat together with our colleagues the question came up of how much work this would be. We told them that, based on our own experience, they should calculate two, maybe three, hours per term, including all discussions we would jointly have. They kindly refused, pointing out that none of their team members would consent to, let alone be capable of, being relieved of their operational duties for almost two months in a row.

We were still undeterred and continued to try. But eventually our effort turned out to be a complete failure. No one provided any terminology to the platform, and to our knowledge, none of the few business terms we entered were used by anyone. We had produced an empty shell without life in it. Upon closure of the overall warehouse program we invited our customers to a retrospective in order to understand why things had turned out this way. The sobering answer was: it was too much work for our customers to collect and maintain the business terms, and as for the ones we had provided ourselves it was unclear how authoritative (read: trustworthy) their definition was.

In hindsight, our problem was (lack of) *ownership*: no one felt responsible enough for the business terms, their administration, and their maintenance, or for caring to help other people use them. As result, a crucial piece in our vision for a comprehensive metadata management platform was missing.

Establishing ownership is one of the hardest, yet one of the most effective ways of achieving metadata quality. In and by itself, metadata does not do much. I sometimes joke that we are the people who support the people who support the people who do real work. Metadata management is a support process to a support process. As long as it is not actively taken care of, it can and indeed does fall by the wayside and get forgotten. To make it live and prosper, someone needs to take care of it. If no one does, it withers away or is doomed to an existence in life-support as long as some enthusiast carries it. This is also what happened to me: it took about half a year after I left that company for the platform to die, despite the technical prowess we had put into it. I learned something from the experience (and fared *much* better on my next assignment), and so I want to share it with you here.

9.3.1 Who should take up the task?

Your first question around ownership should be: Who is to take up this task? In order to bring metadata to life you not only need a repository but also owners who care for its contents, the metadata. The main responsibilities of the role are:

- *Acting as a keeper* of content: the owner takes care of metadata quality. This typically applies to factual correctness and actuality, but in a broader sense means looking after the well-being of the content in general.
- *Taking decisions* on change requests: the owner is ultimately responsible for accepting and rejecting changes in his or her capacity as a keeper of the content.
- *Answering questions* related to content: when consumers of metadata need explanation, must verify their assumptions, or require expert advice on the content in another form, the owner should be available for comment.

These responsibilities can be (partially or wholly) delegated to a *custodian* who looks after the metadata on behalf of the owner. This is often done in cases where the owner is a high-level manager who does not have the time to spend on the day-to-day topics, but still has the desire to exert control over the fate of the metadata.

Joint ownership does occur but should be an exception, not the rule. As has been pointed out in Chapter 7, there are different ways of deciding what to change (e.g., producer-consumer, peer collaboration). This should not extend to ownership, however. The owner role is really designed to identify a spot in the organization for people to point to and say: 'Go there for counsel.' Ownership thus implies more than just authority. It implies a deep and direct involvement with the content in question, because *an owner is not a bureaucrat, but identifies with the topic and carries it forward.* Mere administrators are therefore not enough. So, who should be considered a candidate for ownership, and what are the consequences?

- *Individuals:* people are the first choice when identifying an owner. One individual is named the owner and becomes personally accountable.
- *Committees:* particularly for topics of bigger importance, committees sometimes take ownership of a topic. Decisions are taken by some form of consensus, and the responsibility is carried by all its members.
- *Organizations:* when a topic has gained a certain size, a dedicated team may act as owner, with the team head being the outside 'face.' Decisions can be taken in many different ways, with the team head often having a casting vote or veto power.

From top to bottom, the ability of the owner to live up to his or her responsibility normally increases. First, a topic is picked up by individuals interested enough to concern themselves with it. Then, as the scope spreads, an ad-hoc group is formed to coordinate efforts, often piggybacking on existing committees somehow commissioned to deal with similar topics. However, committees sometimes disband. Finally therefore, for those cases where the handling of a topic becomes thoroughly understood, a dedicated unit in the organization may be named to take things forward, thereby ensuring prolonged support.

Individuals are the first choice when identifying an owner. They are personally accessible and able to carry a topic forward by their own will. However, the clout they exert often corresponds to their position in the corporate hierarchy, and high-level managers do not often expend the time to deal with such topics, irrespective of how important you may find it. Therefore, individuals typically act as transitory owners.

Committees can be elusive owners. Because they sometimes come and go, they may not carry authority or guarantee sustained operation. For this reason, you should be looking for groups that have a certain track record. Otherwise you risk being embarrassed by a deserting force. On the other hand, committees normally attract managers of a certain clout. This can be a helpful factor in bringing your own interests forward and sustaining the continued care for content.

Last but not least organizations are your best choice from a sustainability perspective, but they are also the hardest to chase up. One often-heard complaint by units is that they 'have enough to do' already. Getting them to commit to more responsibilities can be tricky. It is wise to pick organizations that have some proximity to the content at hand. On the other hand, once you get them to commit, they offer a decent guarantee of considerate and sustained care for the content they now own.

After you have identified a candidate, you must obtain their commitment to becoming an owner. Commitment is an implicit, long-term social contract between you and the owner in which the latter promises to do something. When you first approach a prospect, therefore, how can you motivate them to take on the task? Here are some good arguments:

- First and foremost, you can *appeal to their ambitions*. When they are motivated to improve the way the company is working, try to suggest they are the best to bring it about. Appeal to their sense of pride.
- *Promise them control* over content. As an owner, they exert some degree of authority. This works best in areas that need a jump-start, but are not highly political (yet).
- Play to their desire for *recognition as an expert*. Many people feel charmed when described as a competent person. This, coupled with your intermediate support, will perhaps get them to commit.

In rare cases, trying to chase up owners will prove futile. In that case, before giving up you may want to take things temporarily into your own hand. This is not an ideal solution, but it can keep an initiative alive for a certain time until an appropriate owner is found. I have seen this work in one case where a single, central organization took care of content on behalf of yet unnamed owners. Make no mistake, though: such an approach is subject to political scrutiny and often wears out the people taking on the task, since it is a thankless job to take care of things others should really be worried about.

9.3.2   *How to identify and keep candidates*

Unless you are completely out of luck, you will start with a decent idea of where candidates might be found. As you go on your search for suitable candidates, some of them may already be known to you, or perhaps colleagues have told you about this and that. In a word, you will have some candidates available but must decide which of them best suits your purposes. You should be mindful of their different (personal) traits, which can influence the way they practice their newfound role:

- *Torchbearers* are typically outspoken individuals with considerable enthusiasm for the topic and willing to take on difficult challenges. They have some history in the area and often bring with them solid expertise and a deep network of like-minded colleagues.
- *Willing collaborators* are mostly passive observers who, when asked, will participate in the process but otherwise expend little energy on this otherwise unloved task.
- *Fundamentalists* are often already known for their (strongly held) opinions, and expend enormous amounts of energy to mold the world for the better. They display substantial willingness to annoy their peers while still feeling righteous.

- *High-brows* are the type of breed who think they have been there, seen it all, and now cannot be bothered to consider your request or, worse even, know they know better. They tend to be unapproachable.
- The competent ally is perhaps the ideal owner: knowledgeable, accessible, progressive, and balanced in their views. Consider yourself happy to have them.

These are obviously stereotypes, and such traits are expressed by people, not organizations or committees. On the other hand, the *esprit de corps* of the latter can indeed sometimes resemble such stereotypes as well. The culture and characters inside these groups can, to the outside observer, be reflected by a representative just as well.

Most of the above characters can be helpful at certain times and a hindrance at others. Some are rarely ever helpful, because they want to maintain the status quo you are trying to overcome (especially the high-brows). Also, not all of them occur equally often. This depends on the culture of the company for which you work, the originating culture of your colleagues, and the history of metadata management there (for example, whether there were major failures before). For the average large western financial service company it is possibly safe to say that willing collaborators and high-brows make up the biggest group, whereas the rest can often be counted on the fingers of a few hands.

Mix and match characters to achieve your goals. But understand that they alone are not making a commitment when agreeing to act as owners – you are as well. Assigning ownership is not easily undone. It is a matter of careful consideration, if you have the luxury of choice: you are not likely to have it very often, I am afraid. Also, keep in mind that reorganizations sometimes dissolve groups owning content. This will cause you frequent pain if you choose owners from an environment in which changes in line management structure are likely. Committees are typically a bit more stable, but very few companies (I know of none) have such a thing as a gremium inventory, which would enable you to at least know when one of them disbands. You cannot properly track their lifecycle, leading to vacant ownerships. Company-wide inventories for people and organizational units, on the other hand, are typically available and well-groomed, giving you a chance, for example, to track internal transfers of individuals.

When no owner can be found in business, it sometimes helps to ask owners of IT solutions to volunteer. They often have a good-enough understanding and are usually respected by business. If you do so, keep in mind that owners of operational solutions, which support core business processes, normally have a slightly more focused viewpoint. Owners of analytical solutions, which support the steering processes, often have a much wider view, but they also sometimes lack the clout to really move matters.

One final word about picking the owner: you must instill in the owner a sense of custodianship of the content, especially if it is an individual. As stated above, ownership requires more than just bossing-about the others. An owner looks after metadata in the name of the company and carries responsibility more than authority. People who have a tendency to perceive content as their personal property are perhaps not the type of owner you would like to choose.

9.3.3 How to create buy-in and alleviate fears

When you first approach prospective owners, two typical questions from them will be: What's in it for me? and What do I commit to? Your inability to address these questions will limit your ability to recruit owners. It is important to know how to obtain their buy-in while alleviating their fears.

Help owners understand their responsibilities. Make sure they are not overwhelmed. Make sure they feel in control. Committing to ownership of metadata is to take on responsibility for an occasionally quite complex area. At the very least you should assume that the topic is pretty new to them, and requires a fair amount of preparatory work.

Convincing prospective owners that they gain from this newfound task is sometimes difficult. Since metadata is used to reify properties of a *portfolio* of solutions, the task of taking over responsibility for it is a cross-cutting endeavor. Quite often you will see individual solution owners (such as the business sponsor of an individual application or a single process) turn down your request, since they do not stand to gain from it. On the other hand, people and groups in the corporate center are usually more likely to have an open ear. They often suffer from integration problems, which are the natural habitat of metadata.

Obtaining owner commitment is usually a process that takes weeks if not months to conclude. From first contact to final agreement, the owner must get used to the idea of taking on the additional responsibility and embedding it in his or her existing day-to-day duties. There are several techniques to alleviate their fears along the way:

- Offer *consulting services*: hold the hands of the owner for a while, guaranteeing ensured access in case of questions. Regular meetings to reassure owners they are doing everything right are a good alternative.
- Prepare an *owner's cookbook*: explain in an accessible form what steps an owner typically has to take. Use examples (a lot). Provide phone numbers of other owners with whom to network.
- Provide a *scope overview*: the extent of the responsibility taken on is understood better when you provide three elements in your description: formal definition, (example) model elements in scope, and (example) elements out of scope.
- Permit *complexity comparisons*: position the profile of an area of responsibility against others to help compare complexity, risk, political potential, and other measures (see Figure 9.1). Owners often learn more from such comparisons than precise scope definitions.

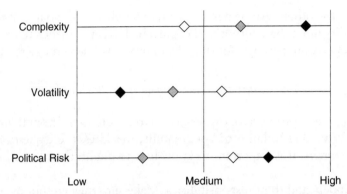

Figure 9.1: Positioning an area of responsibility relative to others is a quick and simple way of giving a prospective owner an idea of how challenging the task might be. In the above diagram, three areas of responsibility are classified along three categories (complexity, political risk, volatility). The 'black' area would probably best be taken on by an experienced, politically-skilled owner, while the 'gray' area may be a task for someone less ambitious

By the way, a welcome side-effect of the scope overview is that it can be used to engage in discussions. This gives owners an opportunity to include or exclude explicitly certain elements they definitely want to own, or with which they feel uncomfortable.

Over time as your owner base grows you should establish a community network. This network will become more and more self-sustaining as it grows. Organize get-togethers in early phases of development, or arrange lunches with owners who have not previously met. They are likely to appreciate your effort, and you will be relieved of support tasks. However, do not expect miracles to happen. For any reasonably large company the timeline of events from kickoff to maturity is more in the order of years, not months. The social order in a company changes much slower than any official structure, so you should be ready to live with being rejected time and again.

For example, I once talked to colleagues about feature modeling and configuration management. They were originally financial accountants but had since taken over the responsibility of managing the change process for business terminology in that area. What I observed was that they kept repeating certain modeling tasks over and over again. To me it seemed like a clear-cut case: you establish a baseline model (based on business terms and their relationships) and then model variants by adding *and* removing detail. At that point, in 2003, the team modeled variants *only* by removing detail. Furthermore, changes to variants were not grouped in the best conceivable way. To me this seemed like a waste of resources, a risk, and just generally way behind the current state of the art. However, when I approached them with my ideas, the answer was a clear: No, too risky. It may have been because the step that they (imagined they) had to take was too big. What I definitely missed pointing out to them, though, was that the new modeling feature would be purely optional. They feared the risk of changing their way of working completely, which kept them from considering what I believed to be a very reasonable proposal.

9.3.4 Scaling to global scope

Unless you (and your team) are the sole owner of the metadata, you need to establish a sense of community for things to work without your intervention. This also reduces the likelihood of bottlenecks and bureaucracy. Centralizing ownership can become detrimental. On the other hand, the bigger an area owned, the bigger the potential overlaps with other areas, or other quality deficits. How do you balance scale and quality?

There are structural and communication answers to this question. Structural approaches tie owners together in some form and institutionalizes their interaction. Communication tries to improve the flux of information between owners without mandating any official structure at all. In this section I talk about structural approaches to scaling ownership to global scope, for communication, see Section 9.4.

In any large organization, responsibility can (perhaps should) be decentralized. Each owner has an area of responsibility, be it an individual model element or groups thereof. The universe of all model elements (of a certain type) is divided into roughly equally-sized groups, which may be subdivided again, and so on. At each level, an owner is assigned such that you can find an owner for an individual model element up to the owner of the entire company's model elements. The idea is obviously to delegate responsibility for smaller-scale problems to specialists (ownership of a few or one individual element) while escalating points of contention up the hierarchy when issues of larger scale need be addressed. It works best when such issues arise only very rarely at the upper levels of the hierarchy, thus giving owners at the lower levels maximum freedom without compromising overall quality too much.

Typically you see two to four levels. Anything bigger than that is impractical. You may also see a multi-level hierarchy with the topmost owner's post deliberately left vacant. The latter model is one of collaborating peers (albeit very important ones) rather than of team members. This model is often chosen when political interests (or lack of management guidance) prevent agreement on whom should have the last word.

For example, in the case study described in Section 6.6.2, three different levels of owners sign off on changes to components: component owners, unit owners, and the CIO. Many changes are local to one component without affecting the inbound or outbound interfaces (thereby triggering changes to other components) at all. As part of the change process, component owners can decide freely which changes to agree to, as long as no other components are affected. (This is established as part of impact analysis.) If other components are affected, however, their owners must be involved as well. When any conflicts arise, the matter is escalated to the unit owner (who is responsible for, say, all components concerned with financial accounting).

Conflicts of company-wide concern are eventually discussed at the highest IT management level and then trickle down after resolution.

The owners of domains as mentioned in Section 7.3.1 are peers. They (currently) coordinate on a voluntary basis. If they disagree, there is nowhere to escalate a matter to, which sometimes happens. The collaboration style between the domain owners edges more toward 'peer-collaboration' instead of 'provider-consumer.' On the other hand, this very point can be used as an argument to lure prospective owners into signing up.

9.3.5 No stakeholder left behind

Owners are only one side of the equation; for each owner there is a number of other parties in the company who can be affected by changes to metadata. For example, in an analysis I once did at one of my employers, each application was found to have an average of six interfaces with other applications (maximum was 39, median was 3).

In order to ensure constructive collaboration between the owner and other *stakeholders*, it is critical to establish a sense of fairness: even if your peers are not in charge, they can make your life miserable – be you the owner, the change process manager, or the architect of the metadata management solution itself. Bickering over details, haunting others with formalisms, or blowing up miniscule issues is unwelcome behavior. This is why fundamentalists and high-brows are often a very bad choice as owners when there is a high number of participants, or when at least a few of them are equally influential. Keeping bureaucracy in check increases the perception of fairness as well. But how do you do that?

First off, helping people *solve real problems* also spreads the good news and ensures that stuff is being done in the right way. As an organizer of a metadata management process, you should consider offering consulting services to outside parties, especially owners and stakeholders. They will definitely appreciate, and perhaps also reciprocate. The proverbial ivory tower phenomenon does damage to the perception of fairness.

Second, you should arrange for adequate resources. According to my own observations, *at least 0.1 % of the total workforce* is the absolute minimum you should assign to:

- metamodeling;
- running the change process;
- supporting owners and stakeholders.

Note that this assumes that the 0.1 % allocate 100 % of their available time, and also note that *this is for a single metamodel* only. If, for example, you plan to manage metadata for the corporate processes and data, that would run up to 0.2 % and so on. Beyond a certain scale it is practical to have full-time staff allotted to such tasks, and the percentage drops again because of synergies. Part-timers are possible, but this carries the known risks of multitasking:

very often such employees postpone work on the (seemingly) uncritical topic of metadata, and quality suffers as a consequence.

It is important to give newbies a good first experience as a head start. In the long run, you will benefit from establishing *rituals* in your community. Rituals provide the unofficial structural glue that holds players together and lets them conform by rules even if they are unwritten. In a way this is like developing an ecosystem in the mold of open-source projects. There will be participants with different levels of expertise, to which you should try to delegate responsibility as they mature: novices, regulars, leaders, and last but not least, elders.

Finally, if you can, be careful to design the metadata management solution in a way that makes it easy to solve simple tasks, yet possible to solve complex tasks. Try to avoid adding too many features that only appeal to a small group of stakeholders. They will lock you in, both by establishing exclusive knowledge (exerting control over you) and by making the solution difficult to get used to (erecting a barrier of entry for others).

9.4 Raising awareness and understanding

Bringing owners and stakeholders on board is one thing. The other aspect is to inform not only them about the current goings-on, but also the many other employees affected by changes. Imagine that you have, and this is really pushing the envelope here, 1 % of your workforce working on organizing and executing systematic change management. That leaves potentially 99 % of the workforce affected, yet so far uninvolved. These people may be surprised, if not confused, by sudden changes. In reality the number confused will be much smaller than 99 %, but one problem remains: how to reduce friction when changes are propagated throughout the enterprise.

This is not a theoretical problem: I have seen several exercises affecting almost the whole of a company, each of which brought its own set of challenges. In one case, the list of profit centers was completely overhauled. Due to the profound impact of this change the planning took months, but the rollout was performed on a single weekend. The potential impact of wrong planning or incomplete information could have impaired operations quite a bit. Work went as planned, but it illustrates that many different roles must work together to make a change happen, while ensuring a smooth operational transition.

Newsletters, road shows, and training are the best way to raise the level of *awareness and understanding*, that is the knowledge employees possess about the motivations behind, composition, and consequences of changes to metadata. The key to this is thorough information. The two main questions you should ask yourself in this context is: Who must be informed? and: What should you inform about?

First, there are the *designers*, who create models and, therewith, metadata. These are typically skilled employees who have in-depth knowledge. Consequently, they do not usually need to be informed about their own area of expertise. What I have seen to be helpful, however, is to inform them about what goes on in other areas. Especially when reponsibilities overlap, it is beneficial to know what goes on elsewhere. A low-frequency newsfeed (once a month should be enough) that informs about current project activities, topics of potentially high impact, or long-term strategy will suffice. Experts are typically . . . er, experts at picking out the relevant pieces of information they need to know. Flooding them with detail will only serve to obfuscate.

Second, you will need to inform *power users*, who often act as *intermediaries*. These folks are also typically well-informed, but take a less active role in the change process itself. They understand the importance and effects of metadata changes, and have strong ties with business. Furthermore, they are often more involved in operational tasks, less so in project-type work. For this reason, you should inform them predominantly about the immediate effects they are about to experience. For example, circulating a newsletter that explains the most important changes about to be propagated alongside their likely impact will prepare power users to act in their capacity as intermediaries: expecting that things will mostly work as planned, such a newsletter enables them to prepare for the reaction of other employees. For example, the newsletter may point out known pitfalls or effects on existing working policies. Or it may outline the history of a change, its strategic importance, or the regulatory requirement it aims to fulfill.

Finally, there is the *general public*, which makes up the largest part of your audience. These employees will take changes just like the weather: all they want is to concentrate on their task and otherwise not be bothered too much. Sometimes, however, especially with fundamental changes, you should make an extra effort to point out to them what they need to know, perhaps in the form of a road show that reaches the biggest possible audience. Stick to the most important problems. Use as many examples as possible. This audience cannot expend much time understanding the subtleties of a change. Your primary aim should be to avoid overload for the power users. If you can, invite them along so that they can take questions on specific topics.

If you want to train your colleagues to climb the knowledge ladder, it is helpful to embed your own program into that of others that are more established. I know of one example, where the people responsible for the company data language managed to embed one module of their training course in the overall business analysis training program. This ensures that everyone who becomes a business analyst knows at least something about the topic. And, as an aside, this also builds a foundation for grass-roots support: according to their experience, fresh business analysts typically buy into the idea of consistent data management rather quickly. Although this still wears off to an extent when they are exposed to real life, a certain residual enthusiasm remains.

9.5   Playing politics

The field of tension between structured and unstructured change adoption evolves constantly. In any large company you will settle for less than a comprehensive solution, but where you settle is itself subject to change. Not everything can be regulated, so ambiguities will remain. Depending where you look you will see the use of metadata management located somewhere between required bureaucracy and anarchy (hopefully somewhere in the middle). The gap between bureaucracy and anarchy is filled by *politics*. It is inevitable that this happens. Any organization of humans is prone to exhibit political activity, and I would like to explain why. In fact, many people complain about politics having ruined their metadata management effort. But can you do anything against it?

9.5.1 On the nature of political activity

I contend that political activity is likely, if not inevitable, to occur during any attempt to establish metadata management processes. When humans organize themselves, when they agree to collaborate in a particular way, some degree of ambiguity is likely as to how *exactly* that collaboration will work, what rules it is subject to, and which players will play what part, in other words: their precise interactions cannot be completely settled. For practical purposes therefore, or even by design, some things are left unsaid. This is where political activity sneaks in.

Such activity is not in and by itself beneficial or damaging. I would in fact posit that political activity is necessary; it is the results of that activity that matter. When people work together, personal interests and company interests merge, collide, or reconcile. Along the way, the balance as to how individuals and the corporation at large determine the course of action shifts. This is the first important characteristic of political activity: *subjects are the main actors, whose personal interests influence their activities.* The positivist ideal of a clockwork institution where everything is subject to objective assessment, rational processing, and balanced judgement is a hoax. In any real institution, there are, indeed must be, people who make a gain by exploiting opportunities for their own personal advantage. Obviously I mean legal behavior that is permitted under the unwritten rules of engagement of social interaction in organizations.

In a way, a company is like a soccer game: there are written and unwritten rules; there are strategies and tactics; there are defenders and attackers; players play on a team against another; there is the referee. The goal is to win and, at least for professionals, to make a buck and become famous. In politics, this is pretty much the same, only that you do not play by passing balls and doing moves on the pitch, but by *exerting power over other actors*. A political player is skillful at managing the mutual interdependencies present in any social group. Power is used to influence the behavior of other actors, be they people or groups. Here is how:

- Politicians refer to established *legitimatory frameworks*, to justify their activities, which allegedly claim exactly what the politicians have just done or proposed.
- *Change, instability, and opportunity are exploited* to further personal interests. While other players are still asleep, turf is claimed, resources acquired, or existing rules redefined. Until the next move they provide a stable basis from which to operate.

- *Ambiguity is used to further own goals.* Creative reinterpretation of the rules set out in existing frameworks (call it 'spin' if you want) gets the politician away with doing what he or she wants and needs.

For example, company-internal standards can provide a legitimatory framework. Established cultural rules provide another frame of reference. The apt politician will appeal to whichever framework is convenient at the moment, kindly remaining mute about all the others. Or, more subtly, the priorities between the frameworks are set differently depending on what suits the politician's bill at the time. Company reorganizations are typical events where political activity gets into full swing, as well as the occasional land-grab when an opponent has failed to deliver.

In all this, you will not be acting like someone alone in the desert. Politics is above all a social game. In any organized form of work, people depend on each other. To the extent that people exert control over each other, they also yield power. Power can be brought to bear to change conditions. However, power is also not unlimited. Individuals can resist power; they may have a different attitude vis-a-vis some topic, or they may simply not like to change their ways of working. Groups can resist change by hiding information, collectively standing up against power, or by dragging out decisions, thereby stalling an effort. Even the powerful require a certain degree of collaboration and goodwill from others in order to succeed. In politics, as in many other places, the motto is: 'No man is an island.'

There are two different sources of power: first, there are *individual* sources like charisma, authority, trust, or competency. Second, there are *structural* sources, which mean control over all forms of resources, financial, people, or information. The individually powerful will typically bring their power to bear in direct human interactions, whereas the structurally powerful have more techniques at their disposal that can act in the background without being detected.

How much should you be worried about politics? Does it really matter? Indeed it does, and quite a lot. The central goals of metadata management run counter to all the interests of the politician. In fact, I would go so far as to say that metadata and politics are arch-enemies. Metamodels try to reify common characteristics of solutions, helping to enforce solid alignment with (for example, architectural or regulatory) rules. In a word, metadata management tries to raise transparency and consistency by means of objectification that is reification in the metamodel. And worse, especially when you think about model generation, it tries to do so by exerting control over how people work. Political goals thus counteract metadata management goals (arbitrariness versus transparency, power versus control, objective versus subjective). This conflict between political activity and metadata management cannot be avoided. It can only be creatively resolved and, to the extent possible, used for your own advantage.

The topic of politics comes up for another reason as well: power is associated with control over resources. Since metadata management normally starts out on a small scale, you are typically fighting giants. In any typical financial services company there will be a number of core banking or insurance applications that run the day-to-day operation. Their owners will be powerful, look back on a long career in the organization, and, correspondingly exert substantial influence. One day sooner or later you will have to take them on, and then you will have to play politics. Furthermore, as was already argued in Part II, the value creation of metadata management is limited to specific areas. Outside these areas, your chances of mustering any level of support, let alone power, are pretty slim.

So, playing politics is the call. To me, there are two basic such moves: offensive and defensive. On the offense, you try to expand your reach and increase your level of control elsewhere. On the defense, you try to fight back when attacked, holding on to your achievements from earlier so that, over time, you will be able to have expanded metadata management to the whole company.

9.5.2 Defense: locking in on previous achievements

A few years ago there was a project that approached us for a service. They needed metadata for access control. In this particular case it was about two attributes, the lines of business and the profit centers. At the time we had already established our repository as the official source for lines of business. There was a change process in place, owners were assigned, and interfaces made the metadata readily available to applications. Some of our staff had already established closer ties with people in the financial accounting department, so we thought it a good idea to suggest to them that we maintain the profit center list in our repository as well. This way, so went our assumption, we would be able to offer a valuable service to our customers. In fact, we had an argument in our favor: at the time there was another official source for the profit centers, which could have been chosen instead. However, for organizational reasons that source was missing metadata from the Americas region, something that we were able to offer. Furthermore, the top three levels of the profit center hierarchy were already maintained by another group in our repository. Since there existed a certain time pressure on the part of the project, we were able to exploit the timing issue to our advantage.

We offered the project to maintain both attributes in our repository and, as a service, take care of the liaison with financial accounting. In addition to that, we thought that we had a unique selling proposition: our repository was able to provide a historized view of the data plus the lifecycle status of the attribute values, something quite critical to manage transitory phases. This also appealed to the project, and so they agreed to attach their applications to our repository.

However, the story has a caveat: since many (if not all) applications used the technical codes of the 'official' source to represent profit centers, the profit center identifiers used in our repository were regarded as mere surrogates. We tried to convince our colleagues from the project to use 'our' identification mechanism, for the obvious reason that they would get much better change management support. However, we were not convincing enough. Still, we went forward with providing the service.

Time passed, and a year or so later there was a major shakeup in the company. The entire firm was reorganized globally; a big deal. This is the proverbial pudding in which the proof was thought to lie: huge change, complex dependencies, and all very important to the company. If we proved ourselves during this change, another milestone would have been taken. Above all, we had the (faint) hope that the technological superiority of our repository would come to shine brightly. Alas, it did not come so.

The reorganization was announced in late summer, and it took the best part of autumn and winter for the company to come to grips with how the new corporate structure should look. It was supposed to become effective during the first quarter of the next year. So understandably, time was running out for IT to get prepared for the switch. We were in close contact with our customers to make it happen, to make it a smooth ride. Yet, the effort was jeopardized by events that were wholly unexpected: the profit centers were still maintained in two sources, and changed as part of two different change processes: one each for the top three layers, another for the remaining bottom layers. It so happened that the two groups that stood behind all this (loosely to be described as the corporate versus the divisional perspective on profit centers) would not agree until the very last moment how their two viewpoints would fit together. This caused quite some chagrin for our own customers: since we acted as liaison to financial accounting, all the communications reached them even later than they did reach us. Hence, we could not even provide a consistent set of test data to our customers. What is more, inconsistent statements were made, people started getting nervous, and the whole situation just went downhill. In the end it was a personal act of professional heroism on the part of one of my colleagues (read: working long hours) that brought about the required structures, but deadlines could not be held by our customers unless huge risks were taken (read: not testing the applications).

Something was lost during that period. A task force was set up to investigate the reasons for all the hassle and to make suggestions as to the way forward. In the end it was decided to bypass our repository and obtain the profit centers directly from the original, albeit (in our opinion) deficient, source. The battle had been lost.

This story should tell you one thing: *all the good you have done in the past is worth little to nothing unless you can lock in on it.* If others do not depend on you strongly, they will cut loose as soon as something goes seriously wrong. And, chances are someone will mess up one day. In the above, I am convinced, it was not anybody's personal fault that things turned south. The design failed. It was too complex, with too many elements in the chain that could and did fail. Whatever the reasons, our customers cut loose because they could. If, on the other hand, the customers depend on you a lot, they will go the extra mile and wait for you to improve your service, because the alternatives are just too bad to even consider.

In order to prevent your customers from cutting loose, use a technique known in other realms as *lock-in*. Lock-in creates barriers to exit. Try to create a solution that has unique advantages of great appeal to customers, for example in the following areas:

- Technology: platform accessibility, ease of use, or development tool integration.
- Data: scope, granularity, actuality, or consistency.
- Process: tight integration, one-stop-shop, or higher service level.

Finding that sweet spot is sometimes not easy. In the above case it was serendipity. We had created a repository with very advanced configuration management features, something no one else in the company could offer. In any event, once you have found that spot, closely tie its use to the use of another feature of your offering that drastically increases their *switching costs*. If they have a hard time changing service providers, they will be much more likely to stick with you.

In the above case, our customers did not agree to use our repository identifiers in their applications. Consequently they had little difficulty switching to the other source. Similarly, the process integration was weak, for which reason they could also bypass us in that respect. When the crunch came, the ties were too loose to hold.

This may sound a little like metadata Machiavelli, and to an extent it is. Your ability to control critical resources will play an important role in your defensive strategy. Ideally you should try to move into a *hub* position in your company's dependency structure. This structure has many dimensions (like processes, data, or technologies), and it is likely that you will not be the center of attention in all of them. But be the hub in one or two areas, and you will have obtained the power to defend yourself pretty well. When it comes to metadata management, therefore, aim to achieve some of the following:

- *Make your technology an integral part of a model generation process.* This creates very strong lock-in. Knowledge of the technology's internal workings like the algorithm is a strong source of power, and the switching costs can be further increased by using specific modeling techniques.
- *Become the change process manager.* This is a little weaker than the above, but you exert control over some crucial resources like the change log or the stakeholder list.
- *Provide mapping services.* Mappings integrate models, and your knowledge will give you a knowledge advantage over other players. This technique is even weaker than both of the above, because it requires you to obtain a substantial amount of knowledge, which takes a lot of time. Furthermore, that knowledge is in the heads of people, which you can only control to an extent.

These steps are designed to gain *hard power*, that is control over resources. However, you can also try to influence decisions of other people with *soft power*: credibility and trust. Because social routines and loyalties migrate slowly, hard power is attained only over a long period of time. Also, the operational risk incurred by using metadata management techniques is difficult for some people to assess in the beginning. Trust is gained when you demonstrate to your counterparts that you (and the proposed approach) are a reliable partner who works together with them to achieve common goals. More than that, trust implies that they assume you know some things better than them, that you can do certain things better than they can. Because of that, they entrust you with the task, even though they are not required to.

Obviously this requires a substantial amount of credibility. The best way to gain credibility is to stick to your promises and deliver value. Offering services to (early) adopters of a metadata-based solution is a good way to demonstrate that. It is absolutely crucial that you do not prove yourself to be a fundamentalist insisting on orthodoxy. Picking fights is generally not a good way of establishing trust. You are not sitting on the central committee, after all. 'Transparency comes before consistency,' I always say.

As a case in point, consider again the project from the beginning of this chapter in Section 9.2. There were two different groups of people in charge of managing the content. Both had fundamentally different philosophies with respect to the treatment of (in my mind a miniscule aspect of) terminology. Because both sides would not budge an inch, emotions began flying high. The atmosphere became so poisoned over this detail that collaboration almost ceased, despite the fact that the two groups had to work together.

In this context, let me give you one more tiny piece of advice: spacial proximity builds trust, distance undermines it. I know not one company that had no problems establishing trust across continents without making an extra effort. If you have to live blocks or even countries apart from each other, arrange for people to meet on a regular basis. If you can, schedule for them to meet before they start collaborating. In my experience, one single eye-to-eye contact can lower defenses drastically.

Finally, if all else fails, you can also take a piggyback ride: attaching oneself to an existing, established organization that is reasonably close to your own interests can give your effort shelter. For better or worse, metadata management is often located within an architecture or portfolio management group. This approach has the advantage that you can exert a certain clout right from the start. However, be advised that this can run counter to your goal of establishing trust. Quite easily you will be associated with the overall goals of that unit, or worse even, come to be 'known' as an ivory-tower group. Hence, take this step with great care, and try to catch the right moment to disassociate yourself with an organization that has a tainted reputation.

9.5.3   Offense: expanding reach and influence

Defensive activities are designed to secure the turf you previously obtained, and the offense is there to grab land. Someone told me once in this context that 'harmonization is the end of all harmony.' When you try to establish metadata management across the company, you are setting off people, one way or another. As was stated before, achieving transparency, consistency, and the like is not appreciated by many. And, you are often dealing with powerful opponents.

For starters, surprise attack or frontal assault should not be your strategy. This barely ever pans out well, unless you have the support of a very high-up sponsor who is willing to shake the company. Furthermore, these successes are typically short-lived. As soon as the support subsides, you will be on your own again. In my experience, the following approaches usually do not work:

- *Force and pressure:* you will often be in a position of limited influence, and in some cultures it is even off-limits to use pressure in the workplace.
- *Reward:* you have limited incentives to offer, so why would people listen?
- *Appealing to rational thinking:* it is difficult or impossible to identify a single 'right' way to do things. Hence, it will be tricky to prove by rational argument that you are right.
- *Negotiation:* this is related to rewards, since you most often have a one-sided dependency to others, not vice versa. Therefore, it will be difficult for you to offer much in negotiations.

Your wisest first step therefore will be to forge alliances with or against someone else, and to obtain commitment from actors. One way of doing that is to identify synergies between yourself and your alliance partner that make the extra effort more palatable. Try to find the unique service or functionality that you can offer your colleagues. Or, along the lines of the case study in Section 6.6.5, look to assuage fears by offering a 'no worries' package to partners too busy to take care of it themselves. Establish yourself as a one-stop-shop for certain services.

Sometimes, appellation (or escalation) to higher authorities can help as well. This provides official legitimation and effectively clears any ambiguities there may have been. You do this at the risk of losing, however. Pick your fights wisely.

An important thing to get right in this context is to *frame the debate* correctly. The interpretation of the rationality, value, and legitimation of the activities going on in the company is central to how discussions are led. For example, just because you say you will bring order to the company's way of changing does not mean that your opponents will fold. They will happily claim that everything is indeed already in order in their area of responsibility, and that there is no work for you to do there. How will you answer?

I remember one (particularly funny, yet instructive) incident in this context: we had built strong allies in the people behind an application in the non-life area. They were promoting (and benefiting from) the use of terminology metadata. In one meeting one of us was trying to convince another stakeholder from the risk management department to publish the formulas and measures they were using to calculate risk capital. When that did not work, the colleague from the non-life team cornered him so well that the now infamous statement was made that it was not necessary to publish those descriptions, because the risk management function was 'an information sink.' This is really a fantastic example of framing a debate: the argument 'you must be transparent, because we need to work together consistently' was countered by the argument 'we do not have to be transparent, because we are not answerable to you.' That stakeholder had just shifted the frame of legitimation away from where our ally had positioned it.

Framing is about interpreting rules in a way that benefits you, or at least does not benefit your opponent. From your own perspective as someone who wants to establish metadata management, you should look out for key phrases currently *en vogue* and use them for your own purposes.

On the other hand, obviously your opponents will try to frame the debate as well. You should therefore prepare yourself for some arguments you are likely to hear. Most try to delay or muzzle an effort, such as:

- *Questioning the value:* 'We don't have time for this.'
- *Belittling the effort:* 'We're fine. We've already solved that problem.'
- *Obfuscation:* 'You don't understand our business enough to tell us what to do.'
- *Procrastination:* 'We'll get back to you.'
- *Grabbing the headlines:* 'We've done that all along.'
- *Questioning practicality:* 'It won't work.'

Your best defense against such statements is twofold: questioning the value, procrastination, and questioning the practicality are aimed at delaying your efforts. Unless you have a legitimatory framework to appeal to (such as the backing of someone powerful), you should try not to push the issue further at this point, but work towards sidelining these parties and get them on board later (see next). Belittling the effort, obfuscation, and grabbing the headlines are best answered by decentralization: you delegate responsibility for playing on the field to the parties opposed to your ideas, while (seemingly) just setting the rules governing the game. This way you obtain some level of commitment, and you can strengthen your hold of the rules later.

Once you have gained some critical mass, you can start sidelining opponents by placing them outside the mainstream, thus embarrassing them: 'Everyone is doing it this way, so why is it so difficult for you to do it as well?' But note that the gains fought over are immaterial and often difficult to measure. It is difficult to declare victory, which must be used in some way or another to isolate resistant groups.

Finally, the incremental nature of your effort will exploit the *contrast* effect: people compare requested changes to what they currently know and have. Over a long time, you will be able to move people slowly out of a corner (or into it, for that matter), without them realizing it. For example, starting with metadata extraction and, once a reasonable level of maturity has been reached, to switch to model generation is a practical approach.

In closing, let me spare a few words on organization. When setting out to establish metadata management in your company you have the choice between two main forms of making that happen. One is a dedicated project, the other is operational activity in some line unit. Both have their pro's and con's. A project is typically characterized by well-defined deliverables, a clear timeline, and a properly delineated scope. Line activity normally offers a higher degree of longevity, continued support for affected parties, and the possibility of establishing a network of people working together on the topic. In this area as well you should mix and match your approach to ensure the long-term sustainability of your effort to establish metadata management.

10

Parting Words: Institutionalizing Change Management

Love as a principle and order as the basis; progress as the goal.

Auguste Comte

10.1 Converging change, risk, and compliance management

With an increasing complexity in financial services, new methods for managing change, risk, and compliance are needed. Metadata management is uniquely positioned to address this challenge, even more so when it comes to IT. Looking back on this book, I would like to outline a vision for the way forward. This is based on my own observations in various banks and insurance companies over the years.

Central to this vision is a two-pronged approach: managing architecture and managing metadata in union so that, taken together, you are able to address the challenges of change. Architecture and metadata belong together, and they must be considered inseparable when it comes to managing the structured transformation that is of increasing importance to financial services corporations.

10.1.1 The role of enterprise architecture

It may not surprise you that I am thinking mostly about *enterprise architecture* when I talk about architecture. Enterprise architecture comprises all layers of abstraction, describing building blocks and their relationships from the operational, technical, up to the strategic, business

Aligning Business and IT with Metadata   Hans Wegener
© 2007 John Wiley & Sons, Ltd.

level. These building blocks are needed to lay the foundation for a constructive handling of the endemic complexity in large corporations.

In order to align the business with IT, architecture is the first step to be made: building blocks almost enshrine alignment in that they offer a guarantee that, once you use them in the way they are supposed to be used, you are certain to be in alignment with the rules of the respective architectural layer. By extension, if you use the building blocks of all layers, you can be certain to align with the business at large.

It is the governance processes that ensure your solution is in fact playing by the architectural rules, and it is the task of architecture processes to ensure that the building blocks do in fact align with the business. By the same token, the governance processes are there to establish what residual operational risk your particular solution incurs, whereas the architecture processes need to lead to an understanding of the residual generic operational risk incurred. It is the promise of enterprise architecture that, by simplifying the alignment of business and IT with these measures, performance improves as well.

Hence, enterprise architecture serves two purposes: first, *it is used to assign responsibilities*. Once it has been defined, it is clear where and how alignment (with what) is ensured or (and this is an option as well) it is clear that alignment is not ensured. Second, *it is used to control scope*. Some alignment problems are not solved explicitly by the architecture, because they are too difficult, occur too rarely, or are just otherwise not worthy of attention. Responsibility for alignment is thus handed back to the solution designer, who must play by the architectural rules to achieve it. This is the entry point for metadata.

10.1.2   The role of metadata management

Building on a thoroughly-defined enterprise architecture, its scope, and its building blocks, metadata management acts as the glue that greases the wheels of change. The composition of building blocks is reified in metadata, thereby providing useful insight into the risks and compliance issues associated with change and supporting their systematic management. It also opens the door to model generation, improving performance by automating the production process.

Metadata management is also an entry point for systematic consolidation, reuse, and maturation of the enterprise architecture. It sheds light on the identification of reuse potential, highlights gaps and overlaps, and guides the establishment of new, higher-level building blocks. In this, metadata is the cornerstone of an enterprise architect's systematic approach to managing the solutions portfolio, and aligning the architecture with business needs.

As a general rule, the enterprise architect focuses on the topics common to many solutions, whereas the metadata manager focuses on the aspects varying between them. Architectural building blocks are designed to be relatively stable, since they will be integrated more tightly with solutions. Metadata, on the other hand, is there to deal with the more rapidly evolving facets of solutions, since it is loosely coupled with solutions and their models.

Therefore, metadata management serves a third purpose: *it complements enterprise architecture in managing change*. The architect seeks to isolate the impact of changes to building blocks, whereas the metadata manager picks up the remainder and reifies what is worth being reified. What is left is subject to unstructured change adoption.

10.1.3   The model-centric convergence of change, risk, and compliance management

The question of where to align business and IT under changing conditions, that is whether building blocks or metadata are chosen as the conduit of alignment, must be answered in union. That gives rise to an organizational convergence of managing change: architecture is managed competently in many corporations, metadata is managed competently in some. However, the two are almost always dealt with separately, making it difficult to look at change from a single perspective.

The transition required for making this single perspective possible is the organization of change management around models. At the center of alignment activity lies the model, not the building block. Changes drive all activity, leading to model evolution, transformation, or integration. Occasionally, the boundaries between architecture layers evolve, the building blocks change composition or granularity, and correspondingly they are complemented by changes to metadata (and, occasionally, metamodels). This process can be described as a continuous crystallization, melting, and reorganization of models and metamodels.

This way of organizing change management is undoubtedly more complex. But it is also more powerful, consistent, controllable, and ultimately, more effective at improving performance, managing risk, and ensuring compliance. The key to mastery of this delicate balancing process between fluidity and firmness is an integration of perspectives. This integration must find its expression in a comprehensive discipline that incorporates the practices of enterprise architecture and metadata management, and it must be handled consistently across the entire company where necessary.

10.2   Elements of a corporate change function

Systematic, model-centric management of change across the company calls for a corporate function. Risk management as a function seeks to limit the company's exposure to risk to a tolerable level. Compliance management as a function seeks to control corporate activity in a manner that ensures behavior is compliant with regulations. Risk management deals with risks, and compliance management deals with regulations. What is the subject that change management deals with?

Organizing change management means to organize the way the company handles its reaction to change. This means not just establishing some technology, architecture, or metamodel. It means to look at the corporation at large and make sure that all the relevant pieces are in place to manage change holistically:

- *processes* to organize the way participants work together;
- *metadata* to support change adoption in processes;
- *architectures* to support execution of processes;
- *roles* and their responsibilities to assign to participants;
- *key performance and risk indicators* to steer the execution of processes.

The goal of a corporate change function is to attain, foster, and sustain the ability of the company to react to change. In this, it uses the techniques common to the practices of enterprise architecture and metadata management. But not only that, it unites them both under an umbrella that optimizes the benefits. It focuses on the challenges arising from a unified perspective:

- choosing where to express commonality versus variability;
- balancing simplicity versus expressiveness;
- managing quality and maturity;
- managing ownership, awareness, and understanding.

Choosing where to express commonality and where to enable variability tries to find the optimal distribution of responsibilities between architecture-based and metadata-based approaches. Once such a distribution has been found, the change function ensures the establishment of an architectural governance process, as well as roles responsible for driving it. Furthermore, it assigns ownership for the metadata based upon which change is managed. That also drives the management of quality, which is based on key performance and risk indicators to be identified. In all this, the change function seeks to strive for as simple a solution as possible, while maximizing its expressiveness so that complex changes can be managed successfully as well. Educating the general public within the company is yet another responsibility. Finally, tracking ownership should be taken up, which most likely will remain a central responsibility due to its company-wide nature.

The corporate change function manages the way the company works together to optimize its ability to change. To achieve that end, it needs to develop metrics which measure that ability, track figures, and steer the company accordingly. The figures will also be of crucial interest to the people implementing the business strategy, and the ensuing optimization problems of highest importance to executive management. The more changing (or, for that matter, being able to change) becomes the lifeblood of your company, the more you need this function to help you achieve that goal.

10.3   Dos and don'ts

10.3.1   Success factors

The most important success factor in bringing metadata management to work is *simplicity*. Handing over responsibility for metadata to business people requires them to understand the motivation behind, concept, and implications of such an approach. For the uninitiated, *simple configuration* and perhaps *feature modeling* tasks are all they can take. Remember, they usually have other things to do. A simple metamodel is also easier to convey: its benefits and risks become clearer, and it is also more likely that someone will feel comfortable to commit to owning the content.

The second success factor is *balancing automated and manual adoption of changes wisely*. The case of trade automation with business rules did not come without a mechanism to handle situations for which rules would be too complex. Hitting the proverbial 80:20 % division is really important. Besides the issue of value creation, it is hard to find out where the 80 % and where the 20 % really are. It is wise to start carefully, slowly increasing the amount of automation.

Try all you can to *use metadata in a generative manner*. Metadata extraction, for all that it does to save you from political harm, and for all that it helps to phase in metadata management smoothly, does very little to sustain itself. Model generation educates people; it requires the organization to mature and become disciplined in the execution of its processes. Hence, although you may not enter the game with model generation, you should certainly aim to exit it that way.

Another way to achieve this goal is to *use metadata in governance processes*. In this case, alignment is assessed using metadata, but the metadata may not be used in the further (change adoption) process. However, the corrective power of passing through a compliance check should not be underestimated. It offers a strong incentive to work with metadata from the start. Note, however, that this approach depends on *a metamodel that offers a precise understanding of what constitutes compliance*.

Good tool support can carry you a long way as well, and in roundtrip-engineering scenarios it is a must. As the asset management example has demonstrated clearly, using a powerful tool that allows model generation and metadata extraction decouples two viewpoints to the maximum extent possible, while still ensuring mutual alignment and consistency. I would still posit that tool support is second to a good metamodel and organizational embedding, but you are able to compensate for a fair bit of imperfection with a good tool.

Obviously, *getting the value proposition right* is the 'sine qua non' condition of success. I hope this book has given you a fair share of advice on the topic. However, if I would have to reiterate only one piece of advice, it would be this: *aim for a company-specific approach to metadata management*. I believe the most potential lies in exploiting the peculiarities of your company, wherever you are in financial services. People who tell you about the great value of unified, comprehensive metadata management approaches are merely trying to sell you something.

Organizationally, *decentralized responsibility for metadata maintenance*, coupled with its use in governance processes, can do metadata quality a lot of good. Put the metadata where the knowledge is, but make sure that there is a central place in the organization to which it flows back so that the management of a portfolio for compliance takes root. Also, providing a *support structure* that people can turn to in case of questions further strengthens the foundation of a company-wide implementation of metadata management.

And yes, *high-level management support* can make things happen and get people moving. But please, believe me when I say: this is so unbelievably difficult to obtain and so rarely achieved that you could just as well work without it. Take it as a stroke of luck or serendipity if you happen to come across it and say thanks. Honestly.

10.3.2   Common mistakes

In a mirror-image kind of way, *aiming too high with metadata* is a common mistake. Full-blown meta-programming, as aesthetically appealing as it may be, is too complex for the average financial services guy and cannot be sustained unless specialists take care of it. Once they are moved to other places the effort usually dies off rather quickly. Business people particularly have neither the skills nor the nerve, and they cannot see the point of committing to such, as they see it, 'academic' exercises.

Another mistake is *not taking other people's rightful concerns seriously*. Automation incurs its own set of operational risks. Metadata management's leverage effects can have very unwelcome effects, and brushing over the worries of people responsible for operations does not win their hearts and minds. They will do their best to thwart your effort.

In like mind, *not taking your time* and trying to grow too quickly is a mistake you should not make. Remember, you are in the business of changing the way other people work. They will need time to accustom themselves with the new ways, they will have questions, and they will make mistakes. Trust and commitment need time to grow. Whatever you may think about them, they are ultimately the colleagues you have to deal with. This is as good as it gets, and if fate has blessed you with a slow group, then there is no point in rushing things. You will receive resistance and fail.

Especially with respect to business terminology, *underestimating the effort required to define business concepts precisely* happens all too easily. Apart from the challenge of agreeing what a term actually stands for, boiling that meaning down to a text that is readily understood by a wide range of people is hard – really hard. The corresponding expenses are rarely made, and you should not bank on this happening.

What you should be wary of as well is *underestimating the power of collaboration patterns*. People can compensate for a lot with their network of colleagues. At first sight you will be making their life more difficult by forcing them into the straightjacket of metadata management; at least this is how they are likely to see it. Embrace this factor rather than playing against it. If people have a way of compensating, then that is perhaps not a place where you should begin to change things. Instead, build on top of these people's tacit knowledge and allow them to perform their tasks even more effectively. The case studies on data quality management highlight the power of tacit knowledge, and yet they also illustrate that metadata can play a constructive role.

Another common trap to fall into is to *start reuse efforts too late*. As soon as more than one person administers metadata like business rules, you must seriously prepare for metadata quality management. One mechanism to do that is to increase the number of building blocks, and that means reuse. As you have seen in the case of relationship opening, 10 000 rules are really hard to keep consistent. And, as the business terminology management case has demonstrated, when the whole company is beginning to work with metadata, it becomes the lifeblood of the whole effort.

Finally, and this is my own summary of this list of success factors and common mistakes, I guess that *domain-orientation is key*. Many of the insights found in this book could not have been made from a purely technological or, for that matter, purely generic point of view. Factors such as the following have a profound effect on which solutions work:

- the financial service industry's value chain;
- the strong influence of legacy;
- the limiting effects of division of labor;
- metadata quality;
- politics, awareness, and understanding.

Yet, they often do not show up on the radar of people that do not take the utility for the domain into account. And as a last remark, I cannot really say that it matters whether you start bottom-up or top-down. The dos and don'ts listed above have such a strong influence on your success that you need not worry about this problem.

10.4 Wrap-up

10.4.1 What has been said

In summary, this book has looked at the subject of managing change in large international banks and insurance companies. The main motivation for taking up this topic is the increasing need for systematic, structured management of change in an environment that is marked by a bigger emphasis on sound risk and compliance management, while the pressure with respect to performance improvement persists.

Chapter 2 outlined the role of metadata management in supporting change. The gist of metadata management is to achieve a systematic adoption of change by separating structured from unstructured changes (and their respective impact), and automating the adoption of the structured part. Metadata is used in a supporting fashion to manage (structured) change adoption. As such, data becomes metadata only if it is used in this particular way. The key to this 'meta-ness' is the coupling of core and support process(es) based on reified data about models used in the core process.

Chapter 3 discussed the relation between models, metadata, and architecture in aligning business and IT. Models help you look at the real world in a structured way. In this, they formalize decisions about how business processes, data, organizations, etc. should be represented and run by IT. Architectural building blocks simplify alignment in that they offer a guarantee for it. IT solutions use these building blocks in particular ways, thus aligning themselves with business in part. Metadata reifies and describes how exactly that happens, giving rise to systematic support for compliance measurement and management. The process of alignment thus can be established alongside the lifecycle of models, supported by metadata.

Chapter 4 picked up the question of value creation from a cost and speed perspective. A cost-benefit analysis reveals that there are only limited opportunities for metadata management to create value. The bottomline is that a company should aim at achieving performance improvements in the company-specific adoption of technology for its own business domain.

Chapter 5 outlined the process of risk management and looked at the drivers (investors, analysts, regulators) in this area. When it comes to risk management in general, data quality metadata (semantics, lineage, correctness, consistency, etc.) was identified as a prime candidate for metadata management support. When it comes to operational risk management in particular, change management, and more specifically, impact analysis is the area where metadata can create a lot of value as well.

Chapter 6 took up the topic of compliance and governance. The regulatory landscape at this point in time is dominated by efforts to curb crime (e.g., money-laundering, terrorism) as well as to ensure proper financial reporting (e.g., SOX). A challenge that continues to persist in financial services companies is controlling access to data. Compliance management with metadata entails reification of the ways in which alignment can take shape, and then capturing that alignment metadata after solution models are bound, or generating those models from metadata.

Chapter 7 highlighted the main practical problems to master when managing evolution: scoping, metamodeling, deciding what to change, impact analysis, and change propagation. The bottomline is that it is crucial to get the utility of the metadata right, since you are in the business of organizing other people's work. From there, various techniques have been presented that address situations often met in financial services firms, such as the need to retain and regain consistency, optimizing risk versus return, handling legacy, or organizing impact analysis.

Chapter 8 focused exclusively on the topic of metadata quality. The main lesson is that you must expect and prepare for quality deficits (intelligibility, correctness, consistency, actuality, or completeness) to occur. The different ways of detecting and handling such deficits are discussed, as is their impact on metadata utility for the processes using them.

Chapter 9 addressed metadata management from a sustainability perspective: its socio-technical nature (changing both technology/architecture and process/organization) makes it susceptible and sensitive to political activity and problems of ownership, awareness and understanding. Typical situations, ways of establishing trust, commitment, raising the level of organizational maturity, as well as advancing and securing the reach of metadata management, were all discussed.

Therefore, successfully establishing metadata management encompasses more than just building and operating a repository. It leads to a profound transformation in the way your company works. This step is not easily made, and the achievements are not easily locked in, but the benefits to be reaped from a successful transformation are indeed profound as well. And, even better, the organizational maturation that accompanies you along the way will yield a harvest well beyond what mere process integration could achieve.

10.4.2 Keep an eye on what is reasonable

Metadata management will not solve all your problems; it cannot cure all ills. As I have pointed out repeatedly in this book, my firm belief is that not all change problems are best handled in a structured fashion. Sometimes it is better to leave things in the hands of skilled employees. Learning the craft of metadata management, if you can call it that, is about developing an eye for the reasonable. It is about striking a balance between bureaucracy and anarchy. Granularity is of the essence. Of course, none of this is really new. These challenges occur almost equally prominently in architecture circles. The difference is the aesthetic appeal of a solution humming like clockwork, the drive for seamless organization. As anyone in industrial manufacturing will tell you, the clockwork notion is a dangerous hoax.

Coupling processes via metadata can be a really messy business, with constraints galore. For that reason, you should consider your steps carefully. I have not talked much about methodology in this book, but I am convinced you will already know that I think that an incremental approach is best suited to achieving good results. I have also come to believe that there is very little chance you will succeed with a straight, waterfall approach. Whether you start off bottom-up or top-down is a matter of current conditions and personal taste. I have seen both work and would feel comfortable starting with either. Yet, be sure to take your time. You are not going to win the war overnight.

If I can give you one last recommendation, read books on industrial manufacturing and usability engineering. Both take a look at a messy problem: getting humans and machines to work together. In industrial manufacturing, one of the central concerns is the (automated) production process, while in usability engineering it is tailoring processes to the abilities and limitations of human beings. Books on these subjects shine a light on the tricky conditions under which processes creating complex products must be made to work, and they offer insightful advice as to the nature of good design.

In closing, this book has highlighted the many boundary conditions under which metadata has to be put to use in aligning business and IT in the financial services industry, but it also outlined the unique abilities that metadata offers you in achieving it. Engaging in metadata management should be well thought through, but the advantages to be gained from it are, in my personal view, unachievable with any other way of organizing change. For your own endeavors I therefore wish you all the luck you need!

Bibliography

Yakov Amihud and Geoffrey Miller (Eds.). Bank Mergers and Acquisitions. Kluwer Academic Publishers, 1998

Gunnar Auth. Process-Oriented Organization of Metadata Management for Data Warehouse Systems (in German). Ph.D. thesis, University of St. Gallen, 2003

Bank for International Settlements. International Convergence of Capital Measurement and Capital Standards: a Revised Framework. June 2004, available from http://www.bis.org

Pedro Pita Barros, Erik Berglöf, Paolo Fulghieri, Jordi Gual, Colin Mayer, and Xavier Vives. Integration of European Banking: the Way Forward. Monitoring European Deregulation 3. Fundaciòn BBVA, 2002

Len Bass, Paul Clements, and Rick Kazman. Software Architecture in Practice. Addison-Wesley, 2nd edition, 2003

Peter Bernstein. Against the Gods: the Remarkable Story of Risk. John Wiley & Sons, Inc., 1996

Joël Bessis. Risk Management in Banking. John Wiley & Sons, Inc., 1998

Jan Bosch. Software Product Lines: Organizational Alternatives. In Proceedings of the 23rd International Conference on Software Engineering 2001, Toronto, Ontorio, Canada, published by the IEEE Computer Society. pages 91–101

Jonathan Charkham and Helène Ploix. Keeping Better Company: Corporate Governance Ten Years On. Oxford University Press, 2005

Paul Clements and Linda Northrop. Software Product Lines: Practices and Patterns. Addison-Wesley, 2002

Alan Cruse. Meaning in Language: an Introduction to Semantics and Pragmatics. Oxford University Press, 2000

Marcelo Cruz. Modeling, Measuring and Hedging Operational Risk. John Wiley & Sons, Ltd, 2002

Christopher Culp. The Risk Management Process. John Wiley & Sons, Inc., 2001

Krzysztof Czarnecki and Ulrich Eisenecker. Generative Programming: Methods, Tools, and Applications. Addison-Wesley, 2000

George Dallas. Governance and Risk. McGraw-Hill, 2004

William Emmons and Stuart Greenbaum. Twin Information Revolutions and the Future of Financial Intermediation. In Amihud, Yakov, and Miller, Geoffrey (Eds.). Bank Mergers and Acquisitions. Kluwer Academic Publishers, 1998, pages 36–57

European Central Bank. The New Basel Capital Framework and its Implementation in the European Union. December 2005, available from http://www.ecb.int

Eric Evans. Domain-Driven Design: Tackling Complexity in the Heart of Software. Addison-Wesley, 2004

David Frankel. Model-Driven Architecture: Applying MDA to Enterprise Computing. John Wiley & Sons, Inc., 2003

General Insurance Association of Japan. Japanese Insurance Regulation. Available from http://www.sonpo.or.jp

Ron Goldman and Richard Gabriel. Innovation Happens Elsewhere: Open Source as Business Strategy. Morgan Kaufmann, 2005

Jack Greenfield, Keith Short, Steve Cook, and Stuart Kent. Software Factories. John Wiley & Sons, Inc., 2004

Rainer Grote and Thilo Marauhn. The Regulation of International Financial Markets: Perspectives for Reform. Cambridge University Press, 2006

Richard Herring and Til Schuermann. Capital Regulation for Position Risk in Banks, Securities Firms, and Insurance Companies. In Scott, Hal (Ed.). Capital Adequacy Beyond Basel: Banking, Securities, and Insurance. Oxford University Press, 2005

Luke Hohmann. Beyond Software Architecture: Creating and Sustaining Winning Solutions. Addison-Wesley, 2003

Information Systems Audit and Control Association. Control Objectives for Information and Related Technology. Version 4, December 2005, available from http://www.isaca.org

William Kent. Data and Reality. 1st Books, 1998

Gary Klein. Sources of Power: How People Make Decisions. MIT Press, 1998

Roderick Kramer and Margaret Neale. Power and Influence in Organizations. Sage Publications, 1998

Ruben Lee. What is an Exchange? The Automation, Management, and Regulation of Financial Markets. Oxford University Press, 2002

Robert E. Litan and Anthony M. Santomero (Eds.). Brookings-Wharton Papers on Financial Services: 1999. Brookings Institution Press, 1999

Kecheng Liu. Semiotics in Information Systems. Cambridge University Press, 2000

Thomas Malone, Joanne Yates, and Robert Benjamin: Electronic Markets and Electronic Hierarchies. Communications of the ACM, 30(6): 484–497, 1987

David Marco. Building the Metadata Repository. John Wiley & Sons, Inc., 2000

David Marco and Michael Jennings. Universal Meta Data Models. John Wiley & Sons, Inc., 2004

Adam Mathes. Folksonomies: Cooperative Classification and Communication Through Shared Metadata. December 2004, available from http://www.adammathes.com

Frederic Mishkin and Philip Strahan. What will Technology do to Financial Structure? In Litan, Robert E. and Santomero, Anthony M. (Eds.). Brookings-Wharton Papers on Financial Services: 1999. Brookings Institution Press, 1999, pages 36–57

Robert Moeller. Sarbanes-Oxley and the New Internal Auditing Rules. John Wiley & Sons, Inc., 2004

Oswald Neuberger. Micropolitics (in German). Enke, 1995

Office of Government Commerce. IT Infrastructure Library. Available from http://www.itil.co.uk

Hubert Österle. Business in the Information Age. Heading for New Processes. Springer, 1998

Jeffrey Pfeffer. Managing with Power: Politics and Influence in Organizations. Harvard Business School Press, 1992

John Poole, Dan Chang, Douglas Tolbert, and David Mellor. Common Warehouse Metamodel. John Wiley & Sons, Inc., 2002

Susan Randall. Insurance Regulation in the United States: Regulatory Federalism and the National Association of Insurance Commissioners. Florida State University Law Review, 26(3): 625–699, 1999

George Rejda. Principles of Risk Management and Insurance. Addison-Wesley, 6th edition, 1998

Lori Richards. Current Examination and Enforcement Issues. October 2003, available from http://www.sec.gov

Jeanne Ross, Peter Weill, and David Robertson. Enterprise Architecture as Strategy. Harvard Business School Press, 2006

Gerhard Schroeck. Risk Management and Value Creation in Financial Institutions. John Wiley & Sons, Inc., 2002

Hal Scott (Ed.). Capital Adequacy Beyond Basel: Banking, Securities, and Insurance. Oxford University Press, 2005

Frank Seifert and Andreas Wimmer. Towards Networked Banking – the Impact of IT on the Financial Industry's Value Chain. In Proceedings of the 9th European Conference on Information Systems, June 27–29 2001, Bled, Slovenia, pages 474–484

Carl Shapiro and Hal Varian. Information Rules: a Strategic Guide to the Network Economy. Harvard Business School Press, 1999

Mary Shaw and David Garlan. Software Architecture: Perspectives on an Emerging Discipline. Prentice-Hall, 1996

Kaja Silverman. The Subject of Semiotics. Oxford University Press, 1983

Sol Steinmetz and Barbara Kipfer. The Life of Language: the Fascinating Ways Words are Born, Live and Die. Random House, 2006

Adrienne Tannenbaum. Metadata Solutions: Using Metamodels, Repositories, XML, and Enterprise Portals to Generate Information on Demand. Addison-Wesley, 2002

Arlene Taylor. The Organization of Information. Libraries Unlimited, 2004

Guy Tozer. Metadata Management for Information Control and Business Success. Artech House, 1999

Peter Weill and Jeanne Ross. IT Governance: How Top Performers Manage IT Decision Rights for Superior Results. Harvard Business School Press, 2000

John Zachman. A Framework for Information Systems Architecture. IBM Systems Journal, 26(3): 276–292, 1987.

Index